When Did The Mahabharata War Happen?

The Mystery of Arundhati

Nilesh Nilkanth Oak

Danphe, USA

ISBN-13: 978-0983034407
ISBN-10: 0983034400

Printed in the United States of America

To,

Rupa

Acknowledgements

To Mangesh Murdeshwar, for discussions on wide ranging subjects and for introducing me to works of P V Vartak; Shashikant B Potdar for introducing me to celestial couple, Arundhati and Vasistha; Narahari Achar, for his paper 'On the identification of the Vedic *nakshatras*' and for introducing me to works of P V Kane; K. Chandra Hari, for providing multiple papers on '*Rohini*-Shakat *Bheda*', which in turn removed one of the many roadblocks in my work; and Aravind Kanho Kulkarni, for his help in procuring books of P V Vartak.

To Dave Rich, for exciting and all encompassing discussions on philosophy, science, astronomy and finance, and for indirectly rejuvenating my interest in Mahabharata astronomy and works of Karl Popper; Jeremiah Smedra, for introducing me to Idea mapping, which was so critical in keeping my thoughts together while writing this book; Deepa Pawate, for suggesting a title for this book 'The stars were aligned', which is preserved in a modified form as title for one of the chapters - 'The planets were aligned'; Eugene Milone (and his graduate students), for educating me on basics of astronomy measurements; Tim DeBenedictis of Carina Software, for his professional assistance and helpful suggestions; Pranisha Shrestha for her assistance with Figures 1 and 2.

I am indebted to all past and current Mahabharata researchers (Table 1) for their works. Their theories and proposals provided me opportunities to test their proposed year(s) of the Mahabharata War and to analyze their theories. Their works provided me numerous insights and made my job easier.

The views represented in this book are my own and not necessarily of those who have been kind to me, directly and indirectly in this endeavor. Paramatma inspired me and sustained my faith in the words of Vyasa. Popper's specific approach to falsification and corroboration of a theory allowed me to interpret words of Vyasa. There is very little of mine in it.

Contents

Introduction

Introduction

If you cannot – in the long run – tell everyone what you have been doing, your doing has been worthless.

– Erwin Schrodinger

Fifteen years ago, I stumbled on '*Arundhati*'[1] observation, recorded in Bhishma *Parva* of Mahabharata. I liked this observation for two reasons. The observation had very high improbability associated with it. The only rational I could imagine on the part of Mahabharata author, to include such an improbable observation, was due to this being a factual observation at the time of Mahabharata War. If I could somehow test it, the observation held the key to falsification of 'astronomical' observations within the Mahabharata text. I could comprehend this observation, unlike numerous other astronomical observations within Mahabharata. I wanted to convince myself of the authenticity (or absurdity) of astronomical observations from the Mahabharata text, and '*Arundhati*' observation was the most suitable for my purpose and abilities.

Around this time, I also stumbled on the writings of Vinoba Bhave, Joseph Campbell and Karl Popper. While Vinoba Bhave and Joseph Campbell influenced me most with their lives and their writings, this book has benefited immensely from works of Karl Popper. All three of them, through their writings, offered me the experience of '*Tesham swaira kathalapa upadeshani bhavanti*'. I had read books of Karl Popper as early as 1993 A.D. and enjoyed them thoroughly. Even then, I did not appreciate the efficacy of his methods until I began testing statements, astronomical or otherwise, from the ancient literature.

It was not until 1997 A. D. when I began testing '*Arundhati*' observation and it was not until 2009 A. D. when I succeeded in solving the mystery of *Arundhati*. My tests of '*Arundhati*' observation not only resisted my falsification attempts, but also provided higher and lower bounds for plausible year of the Mahabharata War. The discovery of mine, as far as I am aware, is the first instance of such a precise prediction, albeit an interval bounded by higher and lower

limits, for the plausible year of an ancient event, based on astronomical observations.

Predicting the Year of Mahabharata War

Once I established the Epoch of *Arundhati* (Chapter 6) as the
plausible interval for the timing of Mahabharata War, I was eager to
search this interval for the specific year of Mahabharata War. As a
first step, I began searching for the works of other researchers. I collected 20+ works within a span of six months, thanks to the Internet,
by those many different researchers. Nearly 125 dates, ranging from
6th millennium B.C. to 1st millennium B.C., have been suggested by
researchers for the year of Mahabharata War. I could not access all
of these works in the original and therefore my introduction to works
of some of these researchers is based on works of others. Only 4 of
these researchers had proposed years for the Mahabharata War that
fell within the Epoch of *Arundhati*. On further inspection, I realized
that 2 of these 4 works had suggested only an approximate time interval rather than a specific year for the Mahabharata War. I began
my work by testing specific years proposed by remaining 2 researchers.

I was determined, unlike other researchers, to employ only
internal astronomical observations, i.e. internal to Mahabharata. My
decision is not due to any artificial sense of 'pure' evidence. Rather
my rationale is simple. Mahabharata had tremendous impact on later
generations of Indian writers, astronomers, historians and purana
writers and many of them have tried to estimate the timing of Mahabharata War. Their efforts in determining the year of Mahabharata
War are valuable nonetheless they should be treated as conjectures
which must undergo testing, as opposed to being treated as proven
hypotheses.

Many researchers in last two centuries working on Mahabharata have precisely made this mistake. Some have used commonly
accepted norms of astrology (and not astronomy), e.g. 'Astrological
drishti' in describing Mahabharata references of a specific planet afflicting specific *nakshatra*. The problem with this approach is that
once one starts using astrological interpretations, there is no stopping
and thus anything anywhere can be explained!

Many others have employed theories of VarahaMihir and those of others to explain Mahabharata observations; and worst part of these efforts is that these researchers have explained *away,* rather than *explain* Mahabharata observations. It would be reasonable, although conjectural, to rather assume that many interpretations in current Indian astronomy (or for that matter astrology) as well as works of VarahaMihir, Ganesh Daivajna, Aryabhatta, Nilkanth and others are based on astronomical data of the Mahabharata text, and trying to make sense of it.

I have endeavored to be rational and scientific in researching this problem. These words, of course, mean little since even the approach of science and rationality is misunderstood. I have seen both glorification and denigration of science, due to a mistaken theory of science and rationality– a theory, which speaks of science and rationality in terms of specializations, experts and authorities. Writes Karl Popper,

> Science and rationality have very little to do with specialization and the appeal to expert authority. It is critical to realize how little we know and how much that little is due to people who have worked in many fields at the same time. Orthodoxy produced by specialization and the appeal to authorities is the death of knowledge. Method of science is the method of critical discussion, and of critical examination of competing conjectures or hypotheses.

Mahabharata Story

The Mahabharata is the national epic of India, in very much the same sense that the Iliad is the national epic of Classical Greece. Mahabharata is the story of Great Indian War written in Sanskrit verses some 100,000+ couplets long and 4 times the length of India's first epic Ramayana. The Mahabharata text with about 2 million words is roughly 8-10 times the length of Iliad and Odyssey combined.

I request the reader to explore Wikipedia and other Internet based resources, which provide additional details of Mahabharata and the Mahabharata War. My objective is to state bare minimum details of Mahabharata, sufficient to enable the reader to understand the context of Mahabharata War.

Mahabharata recounts the story of paternal first cousins, between the five sons of King Pandu and the one hundred sons of King

Dhritarashtra. They became bitter rivals and fought the war at Kuruk-shetra in northern India, known as Mahabharata War (The Great Indian War) or Kurukshetra War, for the possession of their ancestral kingdom. Dhritarashtra and his sons behaved viciously towards the Pandavas. They humiliated the Pandavas in a game of dice, and forced the Pandavas into wilderness for twelve years. The preset condition also required the Pandavas to live somewhere in disguise, without being discovered for a year following this twelve year period. The Pandavas fulfilled their part of the bargain but Duryodhana, the eldest son of Dhritarashtra, was unwilling to restore the Pandavas to their kingdom even after the thirteen years had expired.

Krishna, friend, relative and advisor to the Pandava camp attempted a peaceful resolution without success, and both sides called upon their allies. Two armies arrayed themselves at Kurukshetra in northern India. The War lasted for 18 days, resulted in horrendous bloodshed and victory to the Pandavas. Bhishma, Drona, Karna, Shalya, Duryodhana, Kripa, Ashwatthama, Jayadratha were some of the key warriors on the side of Dhritarashtra (The Kauravas). Krishna, Dhristadyumna, Satyaki, Abhimanyu, Virata, Drupada were some of the key warriors on the side of the Pandavas.

The Mahabharata text is divided in 18 *Parva*s. Adi and Sabha *Parva*s discuss incidents leading to the twelve years exile of the Pandavas. Vana *Parva* describes incidents of their time in exile while Virata *Parva* narrates incidents of the year in incognito, spent at the court of King Virata. Udyoga *Parva* describes Krishna's peace efforts and preparation for the war by both parties. Bhishma, Drona, Karna and Shalya *Parva*s describe incidents of the 18-day War. Sauptic, Stri, Shanti and Anushasan *Parva*s describe post-war activities, instructions of Bhishma and *Bhishma Nirvana*. Ashwamedhic, Ashramvasic, Mausal, Mahaprastanik and Swargarohan *Parva*s describe post-war instances after *Bhishma Nirvana and those* leading to the death of the Pandavas.

I employed two versions of Mahabharata editions, edition published by Gita Press, Gorakhpur (GP) and Critical edition (CE) published by Bhandarkar Oriental Research Institute, Pune. I extracted Mahabharata observations from both editions, with astronomical flavors, and have listed them at the end of the book. I have also stated alternate readings from CE, when appropriate. I also referred to two additional translations of Mahabharata in English.

Organization of the book

I have three specific aims in writing this book,

1. The Primary aim is to make a case for my work, presented in this book, as a better theory for the prediction of the timing of Mahabharata War. The theory proposed is tested using astronomical observations from the Mahabharata text. The book is primarily a scientific study of how astronomy observations within Mahabharata assist us in not only determining the timing of Mahabharata War but also shading light on ancient tradition of astronomy observations in India.

2. The second aim is to make such knowledge easily accessible and enjoyable to a layperson. I meet many individuals who find the subject of Mahabharata or astronomy exciting and fascinating, however feel, incorrectly I think, incapable of comprehending the details. Only prerequisite I think the reader need is intense interest in the subject of Mahabharata, willingness to learn visual astronomy by going few levels deeper, and perseverance. Visual astronomy is one of the few areas within the Mahabharata text that is not quite trivial and deserves to be known and understood by every lover of Mahabharata. It can be easily explained to those who do not dislike numbers and visualization, but even those who dislike numbers and visualization should understand the matter easily if they are not too impatient and prepared to re-read relevant portions (from Chapter 3 & 4) when required.

3. My third aim is to illustrate a method to test an observation and subsequent falsification and/or corroboration of a theory. A further aim is to establish baseline for comparison of numerous theories, those already proposed and those that will be proposed in the future, for the prediction of the year of Mahabharata War and similar ancient events.

Chapter 1 states the problem and lists specific objectives. I provide brief review of Mahabharata research, specifically focused on the dating of Mahabharata War. I describe my method, details of the Mahabharata texts and other tools employed in my research. Chapter 2 lists background assumptions behind my theory, and emphasizes the importance of stating background assumptions as well as tentative nature of background assumptions. My theory is stated next and then the procedure to test my theory.

Chapter 3 provides basics of astronomy required to understand astronomy observations and their explanations. This chapter describes motions of the Earth, phenomenon of the precession of equinoxes, movement of North Pole due to the precession of equinoxes, solar and lunar eclipses, Gregorian and Julian calendars, and coordinate system for positions of stars and planets. Chapter 4 explains uniquely Indian and/or Mahabharata concepts of astronomy and calendar. These concepts include luni-solar nature of Mahabharata/Indian calendar, which in turn necessitates understanding of five year *Yuga*, lunar months, *Paksha*, *Tithi* and *nakshatra*. Astronomical concept of nodes of planets and nodes of the moon as well as retrograde and oblique motions of planets are also explained.

Chapter 5 deals with one of the many Mahabharata astronomy observations and makes a case for an ancient tradition of astronomy observations in India. This Mahabharata observation, although not directly relevant for dating of the Mahabharata War, was instrumental in my designing of new experiments to test the key observation of *Arundhati*. Chapter 6 discusses the problem of *Arundhati* observation and my solution to the problem. The solution resulted in well-defined time interval for the plausible year of Mahabharata War. My solution of the *Arundhati* problem also falsifies all but 4 (4 out of 125+) proposals for the year of Mahabharata War. Chapter 7 explores the time interval defined by *Arundhati* observation, with the help of Mahabharata observations of planets and comets, searching for the year of Mahabharata War and succeeds in establishing the year for Mahabharata War. Chapter 8 employs Mahabharata observations, specifically phases and positions of the moon during the 18 days of Mahabharata War, to predict the first day as well as the lunar month of Mahabharata War.

Chapter 9 deals with Mahabharata observations, which appear to conflict with my theory and its predictions, and provides alternate explanations. I stumbled in corroborating an observation related to passing away of Bhishma. This observation contradicted my proposed year of the Mahabharata War. This forced me to re-read the Mahabharata text, and by luck, I could propose a solution to the problem. My solution not only resolved the apparent contradiction but also falsified all other known proposals for the year of Mahabharata War.

Chapter 10 outlines theory of P V Vartak, points out impressive aspects of his work, but mostly focuses on contradictory, irrefutable and tautological aspects of his theory, and compares it with my theory. Chapter 11 re-states my theory and my proposed timeline of the Mahabharata War, highlights key contributions based on severe tests of certain Mahabharata observations and then analyzes my theory against criteria of 'a better theory'. This chapter also analyzes impact and/or usefulness of specific Mahabharata observation(s), by testing each observation against criteria of 'degree of falsifiability'.

Chapter 12 touches briefly on implications of my work, predictions inferred from my timeline of the Mahabharata War, and new problems resulting from my solution of old problem. The issues discussed in this chapter are actively being discussed in academic and public discourses. The critical discussion of even a better theory always leads to new problems, multiple problems of increasing complexity and my objective is to only highlight few of them. Therefore the list is short.

Skeleton Key to 'When did the Mahabharata War Happen'

Exciting part of the book begins with Chapter 5 however first 4 chapters are equally important to understand what distinguishes this book from all previous efforts, on the subject of the dating of Mahabharata War.

This book is a research document and an easy read for anyone who is already familiar with the works of other Mahabharata researchers, specifically those researchers who have employed astronomical evidence to predict the year of Mahabharata War.

The reader not familiar with visual astronomy will benefit from Chapters 3 and 4 while readers familiar with Indian and modern astronomy may skip these chapters, and return to them only if, and when, required. The word of caution though. If you are not familiar with astronomy and/or works on scientific investigations, you may not understand everything the first time you read it. However if you have not stopped reading the book yet, I can assure you that re-reading of it will be highly rewarding. I won't disappoint you.

Numerous Mahabharata observations are understood best when illustrated using dynamic visual astronomy (DVA™), a technique I developed while testing Mahabharata observations. I have included few schematic figures & tables to explain these Mahabharata observations at the end of this book.

Figures would assist the reader to visualize journey of various planets during the time interval of Mahabharata War and to appreciate beauty behind astronomy phenomenon such as 'Fall of Abhijit' or 'The Epoch of *Arundhati*'.

Figure 1 illustrates various motions of the Earth and Figure 2 depicts Right Ascension (RA) and Declination (Dec), astral coordinate system of measurement. Figure 3 documents movement of *Abhijit* (Vega) through one complete cycle of precession of equinoxes (~26000 years) and illustrates the phenomena of *Abhijit* becoming Pole Star. Figure 4 documents Right Ascension Delta (RAD) between *Arundhati* and *Vasistha* over a period of ~42000 years and defines 'the Epoch of *Arundhati* (11000 B.C. – 4500 B.C.). Figure 5 provides visual illustration of why *Arundhati* would have been seen as walking ahead of *Vasistha* during 5561 B.C., my proposed year for the Mahabharata War. Figures 6 through 10 provide visual descriptions of Mahabharata observations of planets. These visual descriptions will assist the reader in understanding Mahabharata descriptions of planets and their multiple positions. And for a more critical and astute reader, there are tables documenting these same visual illustrations.

Table 1 summarizes timing proposed by other researchers while Table 2 lists days of equinoxes and solstices as well as time intervals of seasons for my proposed year of the Mahabharata War. Table 3 lists *nakshatras*, their respective *YogaTara* and Deity. Table 3 also states positions of *nakshatras* (Right Ascension- RA and Declination – Dec) along with their rank(s) per Sayan and Nirayan methods of measurements. Right Ascension (RA) and Declination (Dec) coordinates are stated in 'arc-sec' in all tables except Table 12.

Table 4 documents positions of Arundhati & Vasistha and difference between their Right Ascension coordinates in the context of the Epoch of Arundhati. Table 5 documents positions of Jupiter & Saturn leading to the first day of Mahabharata War. Table 6 documents positions of Mars over a period of two years during the

Mahabharata War and Table 7 documents positions of Jupiter, while crossing the ecliptic, near *Shravana*. Table 8 documents positions of Venus near *Purva Bhadrapada*. Table 9 lists positions of astral bodies along with their relevant Mahabharata references through 18 days of the War and Table 10 does the same for positions, phases and illumination of the moon. Lunar and Solar eclipses around the proposed timing of Mahabharata War are listed in Table 11. Table 12 provides the details of plausible scenario proposed by me for *Bhishma Nirvana* (Error Elimination – Experiment 67), in the light of interpretation suggested by P V Kane.

Figure 11 makes a case for simplicity (and thus testability) of an observation being directly proportional to the relevance of that observation for the dating of Mahabharata War. Higher the testability of an observation, higher is its relevance for the dating of Mahabharata War and thus higher is the worth of such an observation! Of course, this is not a new realization but rather a validation of Popper's emphasis on falsifiability, simplicity and testability. Figure 12 illustrates rationale for compact time interval of 2000 years (6500 B.C. - 4500 B.C.) for the plausible year of Mahabharata War.

My claim is modest – better approximation to the timing of Mahabharata War and better tested theory for predicting the year of Mahabharata War, i.e. better than proposals and theories of all current and past Mahabharata researchers. While I encourage readers, familiar with the works of other researchers, to compare my work with the works of these researchers, I request readers not to make a dogma of my findings as 'the truth'. I claim my work – theory and predictions – as better approximation to the truth and nothing more. Einstonian revolution taught us that scientific theories are essentially hypothetical or conjectural, and that we can never be sure that even the best established theory may not be overthrown and replaced by a better approximation.

Somerset Maugham said that while author's aim is perfection, they are wretchedly aware that they have not attained it. I would appreciate reader's feedback. I request readers to write their questions or comments, share criticism or their original research. My email address is NileshOak@gmail.com

1

The Problem

Though we are small men, we can stand on the shoulders of giants and perhaps see a little farther.

– *Vinoba Bhave*

I had conjectured, the first time I read it, *Arundhati* observation as the factual visual observation at the time of Mahabharata War. When I finally corroborated this observation, after 15 years, I wanted to bring this discovery to the attention of people in general and Mahabharata researchers in particular. A white paper would have been sufficient to illustrate my efforts, which is what I had in mind. On the other hand, my small success made me eager to explore works of other researchers and I was rewarded in my efforts when I found numerous works on the dating of Mahabharata War. I was curious to know how others solved the problem that bothered me for many years. As I read these works, I realized that no past researchers had solved the mystery of Arundhati, and that many had simply ignored the observation. I also realized, against this background, how spectacular my solution of *'Arundhati'* observation was!

1

I was happy to see many researchers interested in dating of the Mahabharata War, the subject I was also researching for a long time, however I was disappointed by their style of research. Each researcher felt cocksure about his proposed timeline. This in itself did not bother me. After all what is the point of putting forward one's theory if one does not believe in it. Many of them, with the exception of one or two, selectively included only those Mahabharata observations that supported their proposed timeline, with scant regard for numerous other Mahabharata observations, which in fact contradicted their theories and predictions. Some of them introduced contradictions in their theories by explaining away numerous observations that would have falsified their proposed timeline. To top it off, they appeared to be unaware of these glaring blunders. Barring one or two exceptions, these researchers did not bother to criticize their own work and for most part showed convenient ignorance towards the works of others. Some of them did explore inaccuracies and flaws in logical reasoning of others however failed to apply the same standard to their own works.

I began with a goal to test the single Mahabharata observation of *Arundhati*. Now I was sitting on an ambitious plan to address multiple issues. I made a list of objectives and referenced it while writing this book. The reader can decide how far I succeeded in my endeavor.

Objectives

1. Propose a theory for the interpretation of astronomy observations within the Mahabharata text
2. State the background assumptions and assertions for my proposed theory
3. Discuss alternate interpretations, when relevant, of Mahabharata astronomy observations by other researchers.
4. Test my theory against all astronomy observations within the Mahabharata text.
5. Predict the broader time frame and if possible (i.e. if lucky) predict specific year, day & month of the Mahabharata War.
6. List all Mahabharata observations, those corroborated as well as NOT corroborated by my theory

7. State new problems generated by my theory (and my proposed year) of the Mahabharata War
8. Suggest implications of my proposed Mahabharata timeline for the growth of knowledge

The Problem - When did the Mahabharata War happen?

The Mahabharata War was the center point around which entire Mahabharata text is written and thus determining the timing of Mahabharata War is synonymous with determining the timing of Mahabharata itself. One can also ask the question this way – When did Mahabharata or the Mahabharata War took place and when was Mahabharata written? I inferred based on the Mahabharata text that details of the War as well as rest of Mahabharata instances were recorded during Mahabharata times and were used while compiling the Mahabharata text.

What methods could I employ to determine the timeline of Mahabharata? The correct answer is rather trivial: whatever I have at my disposal and whatever can be employed to accomplish the task. Archeology, Astronomy, Historical records- Genealogies of the Kings, Geology and Genetics are some of the methods one may use in solving the problem of the timeline of Mahabharata War. I grant that there are additional methods that can also be utilized.

The methods I listed are capable of providing information that is independent of the other, and thus in principle may provide good corroborative evidence. I loosely used the word 'corroborative evidence', however by evidence, I mean critical evidence that will allow us to test any conjecture critically and derive objective outcome. One should consider critical tests that would make any proposal for the year of Mahabharata War falsifiable as the most desired, however, when one is not so lucky, corroborative evidence may be one's unpleasant but acceptable choice, as long as one does not give up one's desire to develop critical experiments and tests.

While many researchers began with the assumed beginning of *Kali Yuga* or time interval based on genealogies of kings, I began my search by testing astronomy observation of Arundhati and have deliberately restricted myself to observations, astronomy or otherwise, within the Mahabharata text. I have also insisted on corroboration of all Mahabharata observations.

3

Very brief review of Mahabharata research

Mighty river Saraswati is assumed to have existed during the time of Mahabharata War. Some researchers have employed geological evidence for the drying of Saraswati to estimate the timing of Mahabharata War. Multiple references in Purana literature refer to Krishna's passing away at the beginning of *Kali Yuga*. Many researchers have made efforts to estimate the beginning of Kali *Yuga* and in turn employed the beginning of *Kali Yuga* to estimate the year of Mahabharata War. I call this method *'KaliYuga-Mahabharata Nyaya'*, analogous to *'Shakha-Chandra Nyaya'*. Travel records of foreign visitors to India as well as records from Puranas have documented genealogies of kings of various Indian royalties. Some researchers have used these genealogies to estimate the year of Mahabharata War. These lists do not begin with Mahabharata but rather go back into further antiquity; they are not perfect and only prominent kings have been mentioned. In addition, years documented for the rule of these kings are at best approximate. This documentary evidence is indeed useful, however it can only provide higher and lower bounds on the estimation of the year of Mahabharata War and even then one must acknowledge fuzziness of these boundary estimates. Archeologists have unearthed pottery, which is assumed to be from the time of Mahabharata era, and along with other references, have made estimates for the year of Mahabharata War. It is important to recognize that archeology has to depend on external (external to archeology) conjectures in order to interpret the data as belonging to a certain epic period.

Finally, I want to mention the method of using astronomical evidence from the Mahabharata text to estimate the year of Mahabharata War. Many researchers have employed astronomical evidence along with other evidence to estimate the year of Mahabharata War. This book focuses exclusively on astronomical evidence and only that evidence which is internal to the Mahabharata text.

Numerous dates (more than 125) have been suggested, ranging from 6th to 1st Millennium B.C., for the Mahabharata War, out of which ~60 fall around 3300 B.C.- 3000 B.C., traditional date for the beginning of *KaliYuga*, while ~40 of them fall after 1500 B.C. and the remaining dates fall elsewhere within the specified range (between 6th & 1st Millennium B.C.).

4

My Method

My approach is piecemeal. I state a problem I am trying to solve and then provide summary of attempts by other researchers aimed at solving the problem. Next, I state the conjecture I put forward to solve the problem. I describe the critical tests I designed to test my conjecture and then summarize the outcome. The development of critical tests is a trial and error process, not to be confused with random process. Creativity played a significant role in the development of critical experiments however availability of technologies, i.e. availability of accurate astronomical data or availability of sophisticated software to simulate Mahabharata astronomical observations were keys to my success.

I considered a test successful if it could decisively falsify the Mahabharata observation. I also considered it a success if it could not falsify Mahabharata observations in spite of my strenuous effort to do so. On the other hand I considered it a failure if the outcome led to subjective interpretations of my theory. I either eliminated the conjecture or re-stated it in a modified form and repeated the tests for the modified conjecture. When I was not so lucky to come up with critical test(s) for a given astronomical observation, I did my best to provide criticism of my theory based on alternate possibilities. When my conjectures withstood the critical tests, I have discussed their implications for the timing of Mahabharata War. I have also discussed tests or observations, which failed to uphold my conjecture and their significance for the dating of Mahabharata War.

I documented Mahabharata observations, which did not pass critical tests, for the benefit of future researchers. My toolset included Mahabharata manuscript(s), multiple translations of Mahabharata in English, Hindi and Marathi, books or articles specifically attempting prediction of the timing of Mahabharata War, Sanskrit dictionaries (Sanskrit-English, Sanskrit-Marathi), Astronomy software Voyager 4.5™ and Star atlases.

The method I have employed is the hypothetico-deductive method. One starts with a problem and proposes a tentative solution. This tentative solution (theory) is tested by developing critical experiments and the outcome of the test results in either acceptance (albeit tentative) of the theory or rejection of it. The development of critical experiments and testing is the process of error elimination. A theory that survives these critical tests is accepted as a better theory. One cannot overemphasize the tentative nature of even the most successful theory. Newly successful theory in turn leads to new and more challenging problems than the ones it solved. The process continues in iterative fashion. This may be said to be the method of physical sciences.

Physical vs. Historical Sciences

I also want to point out differences, albeit minor, between physical and historical sciences. Unlike physical sciences, which are interested in finding and testing universal laws, history (in this case Mahabharata) is characterized by its interest in actual, singular or specific events.

In case of Mahabharata, astronomical observations from the time of Mahabharata War already exist. This makes the task doubly challenging, i.e. decoding twice – first the interpretation of astronomical observations of Mahabharata author and second the interpretation of the Mahabharata text in the light of our current knowledge of astronomy. The task is challenging indeed, however not necessarily a disadvantage. This complexity, I believe, has an added advantage of corroborative weight if, by luck, one succeeds in explaining these observations.

When I say 'current knowledge of astronomy', I am referring to the fact that I would be taking all kinds of knowledge for granted – validity of Newton's laws, sophistication of Voyager 4.5™ software or accuracy of astronomy data used by Voyager 4.5™, which in turn is collected by NASA.

Another difference between the current problem I am trying to solve and problems of physical sciences is that newer observations are possible for the latter, while the number of observations to be tested for my problem are limited, i.e. limited by the manuscript of Mahabharata.

Future theories of physical sciences will lead to new tests and in turn new experiments and subsequent new observations based on these tests. Future theories of Mahabharata will also lead to new tests however will result in re-searching of Mahabharata manuscripts for previously un-noticed observations. Thus, new theories of Mahabharata and their corresponding critical tests will identify yet

6

unnoticed (but interesting in the light of new theory) observations, but these observations are limited by what is recorded in Mahabharata manuscripts. Of course I cannot deny the possibility of someone discovering an expanded manuscript of Mahabharata, in which case such expanded Mahabharata manuscript would add to the database of current Mahabharata manuscripts.

The method I have in mind is the same irrespective of the subject it is applied to and thus would amount to deductive causal explanation, prediction or testing. The reader may visualize this method as an equilateral triangle with 'explaining', 'predicting' and 'testing' as three corners. In solving the problem at hand, I will assume the two out of three in order to explain, test or predict the third. What is assumed depends on what I consider to be my problem with respect to the specific Mahabharata observation. I will in turn also criticize and defend my assumptions, the remaining two corners of this metaphorical triangle. The method employed can be visualized as interplay between these three corner points and that there is no distinct difference between explanation, prediction or testing. The difference exists, but it is rather of emphasis. Writes Karl Popper,

> If it is not our problem to find a prognosis, while we take it our problem to find the initial conditions or some of the universal laws (or both) from which we may deduce a given prognosis, then we are looking for an explanation (and the given prognosis becomes our explicandum). If we consider the laws and initial conditions as given (rather than as to be found) and use them merely for deducing the prognosis, in order to get thereby some new information, then we are trying to make a prediction. (This is the case in which we apply our scientific results.) And if we consider one of the premises, i.e. either a universal law or an initial condition, as problematic, and the prognosis as something to be compared with the results of experience, then we speak of a test of the problematic premise. The result of tests is the selection of hypotheses, which have stood up to tests, or the elimination of those hypotheses which have not stood up to them, and which are therefore rejected.

All discoveries made in this book can be understood using this framework of 'Explanation', 'Prediction' and 'Tests'. This is the method of science. I encourage readers to apply this method as they

7

become familiar with these discoveries. I am confident that the reader will find this approach fascinating.

The Mahabharata Text

I referenced two editions of Mahabharata; first with Hindi translation published by Gita Press (GP), and second, the critical edition (CE) without any translation, published by Bhandarkar Oriental Research Institute (BORI). I provide Mahabharata references, employed in writing of this book, at the end along with references to their corresponding location within GP and/or CE editions.

Records of astronomical observations made around the time of Mahabharata War begin in Udyoga *Parva* and end in Anushasan *Parva*. Udyoga *Parva* has records of pre-war astronomical observations. Bhishma *Parva* is full of astronomical observations; it records pre-war observations going back up to a year or longer before the War, observations through the first ten days of the War, and post-war observations. Drona *Parva* and Karna *Parva* are rich in observations related to five days and two days of the War, respectively. Shalya *Parva* contains observations of the last few days of the War. Shalya *Parva* also records astronomical observations related to Krishna's visiting Hastinapur on peace mission as well as Balarama's *Tirthayatra*. Sauptic *Parva* and Stri *Parva* are devoid of specific astronomical observations however contain references useful for building chronology of post-war events. Shanti *Parva* and Anushasan *Parva* contain few astronomical observations and numerous references useful in building chronological narrative leading to the death of Bhishma. These observations from Shanti and Anushasan became critical, shockingly and surprisingly, and to my delight, not only for corroborating my timeline but also for falsifying proposals of all other researchers.

I have been thorough, thorough as I could be in identifying Mahabharata observations with astronomical flavor. My search for such observations has been exhaustive; however it will be only foolish on my part to claim my search as accurate and complete. Each observation, newly identified from the pages of Mahabharata, will serve as an additional critical test of my theory; if the test fails, it will falsify my theory and/or offer me an opportunity to refine my theory. If the test resists falsification of my theory, the observation would serve as additional corroborative evidence in support of my theory.

8

Whenever a Mahabharata reference, either from Gita Press edition or from BORI critical edition, did not make sense, I researched through alternate verses (for the same Mahabharata reference couplet) from other manuscripts of Mahabharata, as presented in the BORI critical edition. I accepted alternate reading whenever such an exercise resulted in additional clarity or led to logically meaningful interpretation. I have mentioned all such specific changes and have documented them in the book.

Any scientific experiment assumes a lot in conducting an experiment and in interpreting the outcome of the experiment. Next chapter lists my background assumptions and assertions employed while interpreting and testing observations of Mahabharata.

2

Theories, Conjectures
&
Background Knowledge

A fact is a simple statement that everyone believes. It is innocent, unless found guilty. A hypothesis is a novel suggestion that no one wants to believe. It is guilty, until found effective.

- Edward Teller

Background Knowledge: Assumptions & Assertions

Testing, explanation or interpretation of an observation assumes (or asserts) significant amount of background knowledge. While in everyday life we take this background knowledge for granted, I believe it is critical to state such background knowledge in an endeavor such as my present effort. My objective is to be as clear as I can in stating my assumptions and assertions. My goal is to be as complete as possible in stating the background knowledge assumed in my research however by definition the goal would be incomplete as background knowledge assumed remains infinite.

10

Assertion always carries with it a burden of proof. Assertion implies significant commitment to the proposition asserted. On the other hand, assumption requires only the agreement of the respondent (or the reader in my case) and carries with it no burden of proof on either side. Presumption is halfway between assertion and assumption. Presumption means that the proponent of the proposition does not have a burden of proof, only a burden to disprove contrary evidence. All I said about assertion, assumption and presumption remains my assumption!

Why state assumptions and assertions?

I would like to think of myself as a rationalist, but I also know that I am a human being and I do not assert that human beings are rational. What I am trying to emphasize is the importance of rationality for a human being. By rationality, I mean a critical attitude towards a problem, the readiness to learn from one's mistakes, attitude of consciously searching for one's mistakes and for one's prejudices.

I feel passionate about my interests and am aware of the risk of losing rational mind-set and not realizing it. To keep oneself rational, one should work on only one problem at a time. This means dealing with criticism in a piecemeal fashion, irrespective of whether one is providing criticism or receiving it, i.e. criticism can only be criticism of some tentative theory, which one has formulated and thus is an object to be investigated and criticized. But to investigate a single theory, huge amount of knowledge of all kinds and of all levels of importance is used, and mostly unconsciously. This is 'background knowledge' and is difficult to identify (since most of its use could be at an unconscious level). This background knowledge is used in investigation and thus it is taken for granted. My objectives behind stating my assumptions and assertions are,

1. To state key aspects of background knowledge in testing my theory, while recognizing that background knowledge assumed is infinite
2. To allow criticism of my assumptions and assertions
3. To allow others to study, understand and critique not only my theory but also key assumptions and assertions behind it

11

4. To allow and to insist on piecemeal criticism of either the assertion of a theory or assumption of background knowledge.

I group assertions and assumptions together, since calling them by one name or the other does not change one's ability to provide criticism. Writes Karl Popper,

> While our criticism cannot tackle more than one or two problems or theories at a time – and should try to tackle, preferably, only one – there is no problem or theory or prejudice or element of our background knowledge that is immune to being made the object of our critical consideration.

Experts, Authorities, University Chairs, Degrees & Titles

Experts and authorities do have a role to play if they strive hard to explain their work in a language everyone can understand so that anyone interested in such subject, but without specific educational background, would able to understand what is being said. I prefer argument doing its own talking rather than the title of the arguer behind it. I paraphrase statement of Vinoba Bhave,

> If one considers oneself ideal celibate or *Sanyasi*, let the quality be seen by others through one's behavior and actions rather than through the color of the robe, or via the number of followers.

The point Vinoba made and I am trying to make is generic, and is extended to include academia and social institutions where robes and followers might be replaced by titles, degrees, accolades, certificates, number of graduate students, memberships in organizations or number of honorary doctorates awarded.

I noticed the tendency on part of many Mahabharata researchers to quote experts and their titles and to offer glowing praise whenever a researcher wanted to quote 'the expert' in defense of researcher's own proposal. This type of evidence is untenable in support of any proposal and is no different than support claimed on the basis of speculations, opinions of experts, published books, peer-reviewed journal articles, specific academic communities, authorities, gurus, traditions or scriptures. All these sources could be valuable, but not without critically analyzing their content and even then recognizing their vulnerability and possible overthrow of their corroborative weight.

Key Assumptions and Assertions

1. Astronomy simulations provided by Voyager 4.5™ (which in turn are based on cosmological formulae and astronomy data from NASA database) are assumed to be accurate and precise enough for the problem under consideration.

2. Mahabharata War was a factual event that took place in ancient times in northern India.

3. *Nakshatra* system of time reckoning was well established at the time of Mahabharata War.

4. The Mahabharata text, as available, speaks of three (or even four) recensions. Vyasa wrote it after the War and taught it to five of his disciples. Vaishampayan, one of the disciples of Vyasa, recited Mahabharata to King Janmejaya (great grandson of Arjuna) during latter's 'Snake Sacrifice'. Sauti, one of the listeners of Vaishampayan recension, retold Mahabharata to group of sages assembled for twelve-year sacrifice in Naimisharanya. The Mahabharata text available to us is documentation of above recensions.

5. The Mahabharata text tells us story of the Kuru dynasty. The main story is interrupted by digressions of *'upa-akhyana'* (other stories).

6. State of Mahabharata astronomy is as described in the Mahabharata text.

7. Mahabharata was written, per statements within the Mahabharata text, some 18 years after the Mahabharata War and writing of it took 3 years. The descriptions of the deaths of Krishna and the Pandavas were added during later recensions.

8. Vyasa wanted to write Mahabharata to preserve history of the Kuru dynasty. He used the occasion to preserve knowledge of Dharma, Artha, Kama and Moksha, as understood during Mahabharata times.

9. Vyasa wrote Mahabharata. The Mahabharata text is not detailed and specific enough for me to speculate if

13

Mahabharata is work of multiple authors. It is not unreasonable to assume that Vyasa could have used assistance of his disciples in composing grand work such as Mahabharata however this remains my pure speculation with no corroborative evidence whatsoever. The Mahabharata text available today is documentation of multiple recensions and, in that sense current Mahabharata text is work of multiple authors.

10. Vyasa wrote Mahabharata, in a secluded cave in Himalaya, per statements of the Mahabharata text.

11. It is reasonable to assume existence of transcription and transmission errors in the Mahabharata text. Critical edition along with footnotes, prepared by BORI, provides corroborative evidence in support of this assumption. The second assumption commonly stated is that of insertion of obscurities, exaggerations and contradictions pertaining to religious, cultural and sociological themes into the Mahabharata text due to vested interests. This is a serious charge, and anyone claiming 'specific text' of Mahabharata to be so has an obligation to provide his rationale for such claim along with corroborative evidence in support of his claim. The third assumption is insertion of later names (places, countries, people, etc.). All such specific claims must be backed by rationale for such insertions and by corroborative evidence.

My Theory

My theory has three main theses,

1. All astronomy observations in the Mahabharata text are 'visual observations' of the sky.

2. Mahabharata astronomers were meticulous and patient empirical astronomers. They were inheritors of even farther ancient tradition of astronomy observations. Mahabharata astronomers had means to observe objects in the sky, which would not be otherwise visible to a naked eye.

3. Mahabharata author's motivation for noting down specific astronomy observations during and around the time of Mahabharata War was to create records of the timing of Mahabharata War. These observations were embedded in

14

the Mahabharata text. Mahabharata author embedded these observations as is and also in the form of similes signifying bad omens, engagement of key warriors on the battlefield or death of principal warriors.

I believe that it is possible to identify additional descriptions of planets, positions of the Moon and the Sun or other astronomy observations in the Mahabharata text, in addition to what have been already identified by previous researchers. Although I cannot be certain of my prognosis, what I feel confident is that these additional observations, if found would (should) fit the descriptions of my Mahabharata War timeline. Current and future researchers have responsibility to test newfound astronomical observations, if and when they are found within the Mahabharata text.

Critical Tests

I proposed critical tests for each Mahabharata observation (and for group of Mahabharata observations when relevant). The reader would able to repeat these critical tests independently and verify my claims. The reader or another researcher would then able to provide criticism of my work. It goes without saying that by 'criticism', I mean rational criticism.

I have used the format of stating the problem by referring to specific Mahabharata observation and my English translation of it. I briefly discuss attempts of other researchers and then describe critical tests I undertook, with the help of Voyager 4.5™, to solve the problem. When I felt that I did solve the problem, I state my preferred solution and provide critical discussion in defense of my solution. When appropriate, I have presented the outcome of my solution with the help of figures and tables, depicting positions of planets in the sky, visually and in terms of celestial coordinates of Declination and Right Ascension.

I also discuss the consequences of my 'ad hoc' modifications and whether these modifications result in expansion of knowledge, i.e. growth of knowledge content or if these modifications lead to explaining away the problem. In case of latter outcome, I have preferred to record the observation as contradicting my timeline, rather than to eliminate the observation from discussion as if it did not exist.

15

Critique of Mahabharata Researches

I could sense that all researchers, whose work I evaluated, were convinced that the timing of Mahabharata War is much farther in the past than the careless opinions thrown around for 500 B.C. or 1000 B.C. The dates proposed by these researchers are as early as 7300 B.C. and as late as 1400 B.C.

While critique has its place in research work of the kind presented in this book, I have avoided the temptation. My rationale for this decision is driven by the conviction that if I am successful in stating my proposal in a sufficiently definite form, a form in which it can be critically discussed; there would be no need to prove weaknesses in the works of other Mahabharata researchers. When I began writing critique of Mahabharata work of others, I could fill multiple pages and I wondered whether my emphasis was to present my theory and propose a date for the Mahabharata War, or to provide critique of other proposals. Falsifying proposals of others is a necessary step however is not to be construed as assertion or justification of one's own position. As such stating one's own proposal and critiquing those of others are not two different things. It is indeed an illusion to think that lighting a candle and eradicating surrounding darkness are two independent things! I have limited my critique of other's work to a minimum and only when I felt necessary to describe previous attempts to solve a specific problem, before describing my solution.

Next two chapters introduce basic concepts of astronomy.

3

Astronomy Basics

It is through the medium of astronomy alone that a few rays from those distant objects can be conveyed in safety to the eye of a modern observer, so as to afford him a light, which, though it be scanty, is pure and unbroken, and free from the false colorings of vanity and superstition.

- John Playfair

In this chapter, I introduce the concepts required to understand basic visual astronomy, necessary for the reader to understand the problems, experiments, results and inferences discussed in this book. The reader familiar with the basics of astronomy can safely skip this chapter. I request the perseverance of the reader, new to astronomy, to go through this chapter and the next, in order to understand, appreciate and enjoy discoveries made in this book.

I have deliberately restricted the scope to bare minimum basics of astronomy, sufficient for a layperson to understand the experiments, arguments and explanations presented in this book. I have provided basic definitions and have avoided relatively complex astronomical explanations of causes for the described phenomenon.

Astronomy basics described are with respect to the Northern hemisphere. This is worth remembering during the discussion of seasons, solstices or equinoxes. The Indian astronomy has northern bias. This is also true of the western astronomy.

Although visual astronomy may include lot more, the content of book can be well understood by focusing on specific aspects of visual astronomy viz., the motions of stars, the planets, the Moon, the Sun, Mahabharata *nakshatra* system, orbit of the Sun as the reference plane for all planetary motions, astronomical events such as solstices and equinoxes, the North celestial pole and cardinal directions (east, west, north and south).

Motions of the Earth

Any motion is relative in nature and must be specified with respect to another object. One can describe the motions of the Earth with respect to the Sun and the background stars of the sky. Figure 1 shows schematic diagram of the Earth's motions. The circle, with solid line, at the bottom of the picture represents the Earth. Imagine a horizontal line drawn through this circle. This imaginary line would be 'ecliptic of the Earth', i.e. the plane of the earth's orbit around the Sun! This ecliptic is our plane of reference. The solid line at an angle, connecting the Earth and the zigzag circle at the top, represents the celestial axis around which the Earth rotates around itself. The celestial axis, in the northern hemisphere, points towards the northern pole star. The vertical dotted line is the ecliptic axis of the Earth and is perpendicular to the ecliptic. The Earth rotates around the Sun in a circle (actually in an elliptical path) but also at an angle to the ecliptic. This angle is the angle between the celestial and the ecliptic axis of the Earth.

The Earth rotates (R) around itself at an angle with respect to the plane of the ecliptic and completes one rotation in approximately 24 hours. This is the diurnal motion of the earth. This angle, with respect to the plane of the ecliptic, oscillates slowly across a range of 3^0 with mean around 23.5^0 and a full cycle of this oscillatory motion takes approximately 41,000 years. This oscillatory motion can be termed as 'nod' of the Earth and is not shown in the Figure 1. Earth's axis experiences the wobble, known as the precession of equinoxes (P) and completes one cycle in approximately 26000 years. The zigzag motion of this wobble is known as nutation (N). The Earth rotates around the Sun along the ecliptic and completes one cycle in approximately 365 days. Earth's rotating around itself is the cause of days and nights at any given location on the Earth. Earth's rotation, at an angle (with respect to the plane of the ecliptic) around the Sun, is the cause of different seasons as well as days and nights of varying duration. The Earth wobbles, nods, and spins as it travels through its orbital path around the Sun. The Earth spins around itself in a day, orbits around the Sun in a year, completes a wobbling cycle in 26000 years and finishes nodding in 41000 years.

Earth's precession was historically called 'the precession of the equinoxes' because the equinoxes moved westward along the ecliptic relative to the fixed stars, opposite to the motion of the Sun along the ecliptic. The precession of the Earth's axis has a number of observable effects. First, the positions of the south and north celestial poles appear to move in circles against the space-fixed backdrop of stars, completing one circuit in approximately 26000 years. Thus, while today the star Polaris lies approximately at the north celestial pole, this will change over time, and other stars will become the "north celestial stars" in succession.

As the celestial poles shift, there is a corresponding gradual shift in the apparent orientation of the whole star field, as viewed from a particular position on the Earth. Secondly, the position of the Earth (with respect to background star field) in its orbit around the Sun, at the solstices and equinoxes, relative to the seasons, slowly changes. For example, suppose that the Earth's orbital position is marked at the summer solstice, when the Earth's axial tilt is pointing directly towards the Sun. One full orbit later, when the Sun has returned to the same apparent position relative to the background stars, the Earth's axial tilt is now directly towards the Sun: because of the effects of precession, it is a little way "beyond" this. In other words, the solstice occurred a little earlier in the orbit. Thus, the tropical year, measuring the cycle of seasons (for example, the time from solstice to solstice, or equinox to equinox), is about 20 minutes shorter than the sidereal year, which is measured by the Sun's apparent position relative to the stars. Note that 20 minutes per year is approximately equivalent to one year per 26000 years, so after one full cycle of approximately 26000 years, the positions of the seasons relative to the orbit are "back where they started".

In actuality, other effects also slowly change the shape and orientation of the Earth's orbit, and these, in combination with precession, create various cycles of differing periods. For identical reasons, the apparent position of the Sun relative to the backdrop of the stars at some seasonally fixed time, say the vernal equinox, slowly regresses a full 360° through all reference points in the sky (*nakshatra* or constellations of the zodiac), at the rate of about 50.3 arc-sec per year (approximately 360^0 divided by 26000), or 1^0 every 72 years.

We know that Sun does not rotate around the Earth, rather the opposite, however still thinking of Sun's orbit around the Earth might be helpful in understanding visual astronomy in general and specific visual astronomical references from Mahabharata in particular. The reader is expected to have similar understanding with respect to motions of planets, the moon and other stars. The reader is also requested to keep in mind that seasons are described, as they would appear in the Northern hemisphere. The Southern hemisphere would experience equivalent opposite seasons. In fact it is not a bad idea to forget all about what is happening in the southern hemisphere. This deliberate forgetfulness will not be a disadvantage. On the other hand it can simplify things a little.

Equinoxes and Solstices

A solstice is an astronomical event that occurs twice each year, when the tilt of the Earth's axis is most inclined toward or away from the Sun, causing the Sun's apparent position in the sky to reach its northernmost (Summer solstice – *Dakshinayan bindu*) or southernmost extreme (Winter Solstice – *Uttara*yan *bindu*). Solstice means 'Sun stands still', because at the solstices, the Sun stands still in declination; that is, the apparent movement of the Sun's path north or south comes to a stop before reversing direction. The term solstice can also be used in a wider sense, as the date (day) when this occurs and we are precisely interested in this latter meaning, for both solstices and equinoxes.

An equinox occurs twice a year, when the tilt of the Earth's axis is inclined neither away from nor towards the Sun, the Sun being vertically above a point on the Equator. The term equinox can also be used in a broader sense, meaning the date (day) when such a passage happens. The term equinox denotes equal length, because around the equinox, the night and day are approximately equally long. At an equinox, the Sun is at one of two opposite points on the celestial sphere where the celestial equator (i.e. Declination = 0) and ecliptic intersect. These points of intersection are called equinoctial points: the vernal point (*Vasant Sampat*) and the autumnal point (*Sharad Sampat*). By extension, the term equinox may denote an equinoctial point.

North Pole Star

Celestial North Pole is the point in the sky, in the northern hemisphere, along the celestial axis of the earth. If a distinct object such as a star or asterism exists in the vicinity of this point, such object can be designated as Northern Pole star. A pole star, thus, is a visible star (or asterism), especially a prominent one, that is approximately aligned with the Earth's celestial axis (same as Earth's axis of rotation). While other star's positions change throughout (and are visible during the night), the pole star's position in the sky essentially does not. All circumpolar stars make one complete circle around the Pole Star in approximately 24 hours. This is the daily (diurnal) motion.

Whether there is a North Pole star at any given time depends on the current orientation of the Earth's axis, which moves due to the precession of the equinoxes. Polaris is the current North Pole star. Polaris is very close to North celestial pole in our times. Polaris will cease to be a northern pole star in the next few hundred years, to be replaced by Errai (Gamma Cephei) around 4000 A.D.

Pole stars do change over time, primarily due to the precession of the earth's rotational axis that causes its orientation to change over time. If the stars were fixed in space, precession causes the celestial North Pole to trace out imaginary circle on the celestial sphere approximately once every 26000 years, passing close to different stars at different times.

Some of the key stars along this path of north celestial pole include Polaris, Kochab, Kappa Draconis, Thuban, Edasich, Tau Herculis, Deneb and Vega. However the stars themselves exhibit motions relative to each other and this motion is known as proper motion. This proper motion combined with precession of equinoxes and nutation results in apparent drift of a pole star.

Circumpolar Stars

A circumpolar star is a star that, when viewed from a given latitude on the Earth, never sets (that is, never disappears below the horizon), due to its proximity to celestial Pole. Circumpolar stars are therefore visible (from said location) for the entire night on every night of the year (and would be continuously visible throughout the day too, were they not overwhelmed by the Sun's glare).

Sidereal and Synodic Period

The sidereal period is the time that it takes the object to make one full orbit around the Sun, relative to the stars. This is considered to be an object's true orbital period. The Synodic period is the time that it takes for the object to reappear at the same point in the sky, relative to the Sun, as observed from Earth; i.e. returns to the same elongation (and planetary phase). This is the time that elapses between two successive conjunctions with the Sun and is the object's Earth-apparent orbital period. The Synodic period differs from the sidereal period since Earth itself revolves around the Sun.

Celestial Equator

Celestial equator is a great circle (albeit imaginary) that is a projection of the Earth's equator onto the sky. It intercepts horizon at exact East and exact West point. Half of this great circle is visible to us at any given time.

Declination & Right Ascension: Coordinate System for the Sky

Declination (Dec) is one of the two coordinates of the equatorial coordinate system (Figure 2). Declination is comparable to latitude, projected onto the celestial sphere, and is measured in degrees north and south of the celestial equator. Points north of the celestial equator have positive declinations, while those to the south have negative declinations. The sign is customarily included even if it is positive. Beginning at ecliptic going towards the North Pole, then traveling to other side of the ecliptic onto the South Pole and then back to original point on ecliptic would complete 360 degrees. One

22

degree consists of 60 arc-mins and one arc-min consists of 60 arc-secs. Any unit of angle can be used for declination, but it is often expressed in degrees, minutes, and seconds of arc.

- An object on the celestial equator has a Dec of 0°.
- An object at the celestial North Pole has a Dec of +90°.
- An object at the celestial South Pole has a Dec of -90°.

A celestial object that passes over zenith has a declination equal to the observer's latitude, with northern latitudes yielding positive declinations. A northern pole star therefore has the declination close to +90°. At present Polaris is the pole star in the northern direction. Its mean position, taking into account precession and proper motion, will reach a maximum declination of +89°32'23", i.e. 0.4603° from the celestial North Pole, in February 2102 A. D. Its maximum apparent declination, taking into account nutation and aberration, will be +89°32'50.62", i.e. 0.4526° from the celestial North Pole, on 24 March 2100 A. D.

Right ascension (RA) is the other coordinate of the equatorial coordinate system. RA is the celestial equivalent of terrestrial longitude. Both RA and longitude measure an east-west angle along the equator; and both measure from a zero point on the equator. For longitude, the zero point is the Prime Meridian (Royal observatory, Greenwich, UK); for RA, the zero point is the point of Vernal equinox, which is the place in the sky where the Sun crosses the celestial equator at the Vernal Equinox.

RA is measured eastward from the Vernal equinox. Any units of angular measure can be used for RA, but it is customarily measured in hours, minutes, and seconds, with 24 hours being equivalent to a full circle. The reason for this choice is that the earth rotates at an approximately constant rate. Since a complete circle has 360 degrees, an hour of right ascension is equal to 1/24 of complete circle, or 15 degrees of arc, a single minute of right ascension equal to 15 minutes of arc, and a second of right ascension equal to 15 seconds of arc. RA can be used to determine a star's location and to determine how long it will take for a star to reach a certain point in the sky.

Because a star lies in a nearly constant direction as viewed from the Earth, its declination is approximately constant from year to year. However, both the right ascension and declination do change gradually due to the effects of the precession of the equinoxes and proper motions of stars. Since 'RA' and 'Dec' of stars are constantly changing due to the precession, astronomers always specify these with reference to a particular epoch.

Eclipses

An eclipse is an astronomical event when one celestial body moves into the shadow of another, partially or fully obscuring it from view. The two primary types of eclipses relevant to the subject matter, seen from the Earth, are the solar eclipse and the lunar eclipse. The solar eclipse occurs when the Moon travels between the Sun and the Earth, blocking sun's light from the Earth in the middle of the day, and generally giving the appearance of a ring of light in the darkened sky. The lunar eclipse occurs when the Moon moves into the shadow of the Earth during night hours, gradually blocking the view of the Moon from the Earth. Eclipses, be they solar or lunar, occur when the Earth, Sun and Moon are in a line. If the Moon is in-between the Earth and the Sun, it blocks the view of the Sun from some parts of the Earth, and this produces a solar eclipse. If, on the contrary, it is the Earth that is in-between the Sun and the Moon, then the Earth will block the light from the Sun before it can get to the Moon. Since moonlight is just the light the Moon reflects from the Sun, this will darken the Moon, and we get a lunar eclipse.

Since the Moon goes around the Earth every 28 days, shouldn't we expect a solar eclipse about every 28 days (when the Moon is new), and a lunar eclipse in the same period, (when the Moon is full)? Well, this would be so if the orbit of the Moon were in the same plane as the orbit of the Earth around the Sun. But we know eclipses are rarer than that; and the Moon's orbit is not in the same plane. Instead, it is tilted with respect to it, and the Moon does not in general pass directly on the Earth-Sun line. Moreover, the tilt of the moon's orbit tilt varies slowly. To have an eclipse, then, it is not enough that the three bodies be in the right order; the moon's orbit should also be at the right tilt.

The match between the apparent sizes of the Sun and the Moon during a total eclipse is a coincidence. The Sun's distance from the Earth is about 400 times the Moon's distance, and the Sun's

24

diameter is about 400 times the Moon's diameter. Because these ratios are approximately the same, the sizes of the Sun and the Moon as seen from Earth appear to be approximately the same: about 0.5^0 of arc in angular measure.

Whether it is the Moon between the Earth and the Sun, or the other way around, the phenomenon is basically the same: the body in the middle casts a cone of shadow, and if the outer body happens to move into this cone, we have an eclipse. It is important to notice that the shadow is more complicated than just a cone: it actually consists of a darker cone, or *umbra*, where no sunlight reaches, and a lighter region, the *penumbra*, where only some of the sunlight is blocked. Whether you will be able to observe a total or partial eclipse will depend on which of the two regions you are located in.

Solar Eclipse

A solar eclipse occurs when the Moon is directly between the Earth and the Sun. These are not as frequent as one might expect, but there are still at least two each year. That we get total solar eclipses at all is a bit of good luck. The Moon and the Sun appear to have the same size when viewed from the Earth. The Moon is about 400 times smaller than the Sun, but at the same time the Sun is about 400 times farther away from the Earth than the Moon. Because of this, when there is a solar eclipse, the Moon is about the right size to completely cover the disk of the Sun. If the Moon is close enough to the Earth, it will cover it completely, and we get a *total* solar eclipse. This is the most spectacular kind, where the day changes into darkness and one can see the stars in plain day. If the Moon is further away from the Earth, then moon's disk will not be big enough to cover the Sun completely, and we get an *annular* eclipse, where most of the Sun is covered, but an annulus remains, surrounding the dark disk of the Moon. Were the Moon to be smaller, or the Sun closer to the Earth, there would be no total solar eclipses. On the other hand, if the Moon were a bit bigger, the shadow it casts on the Earth during solar eclipses would be larger, and it would be easier to be in the right place to observe them. The dark part of the Moon's shadow is, on the surface of the Earth, a circle of only about 160 miles in diameter. As the Earth moves, this circle traces a path on its surface, called the *path of totality*. To see a total solar eclipse you have to be inside this rather small region. It is estimated that, on the average, a given spot on the Earth will be on the path of an eclipse only about once every 370 years, so it is better to move to an eclipse than to wait for one to come to you.

There are four types of solar eclipses,

- A total eclipse occurs when the Sun is completely obscured by the Moon. The intensely bright disk of the Sun is replaced by the dark silhouette of the Moon, and the much fainter corona is visible. During any one eclipse, totality is visible only from at most a narrow track on the surface of the Earth.
- An annular eclipse occurs when the Sun and the Moon are exactly in line, but the apparent size of the Moon is smaller than that of the Sun. Hence the Sun appears as a very bright ring, or annulus, surrounding the outline of the Moon.
- A hybrid eclipse (also called annular/total eclipse) transitions between a total and annular eclipse. At some points on the surface of the Earth it is visible as a total eclipse, whereas at others it is annular. Hybrid eclipses are comparatively rare.
- A partial eclipse occurs when the Sun and the Moon are not exactly in line and the Moon only partially obscures the Sun. This phenomenon can usually be seen from a large part of the Earth outside of the track of an annular or total eclipse. However, some eclipses can only be seen as a partial eclipse, because the umbra never intersects the Earth's surface.

Lunar Eclipse

Lunar eclipses do not occur every month because of the inclination of the moon's orbit. They do happen at least twice a year and one is far more likely to be able to observe lunar eclipse than a solar one. The reason is that when the moon gets dark, it is because it does not receive the sunlight, and it then is dark for anyone who can see it. So, instead of having to be in a rather narrow path, as happens for solar eclipses, you only have to be in a part of the world from which the moon is visible at the time of the eclipse. Pretty much half the world qualifies! As with solar eclipses, there are partial and total lunar eclipses. If the Moon does not enter into the umbra, the darkest part of the Earth's shadow, then it does not darken completely, and we get a partial eclipse. These are hard to notice; the moon just darkens a bit, but does not disappear completely into the night. The shadow of the Earth can be divided into two distinctive parts: the umbra and penumbra. Within the umbra, there is no direct solar radiation. However, as a result of the Sun's large angular size, solar illumination is only partially blocked in the outer portion of the Earth's shadow, which is given the name penumbra.

A penumbral eclipse occurs when the Moon passes through the Earth's penumbra. The penumbra causes a subtle darkening of the moon's surface. A special type of penumbral eclipse is a total penumbral eclipse, during which the Moon lies exclusively within the Earth's penumbra. Total penumbral eclipses are rare, and when these occur, that portion of the moon which is closest to the umbra can appear somewhat darker than the rest of the moon. A partial lunar eclipse occurs when only a portion of the moon enters the umbra. When the Moon travels completely into the Earth's umbra, one observes a total lunar eclipse. The moon's speed through the shadow is about one kilometer per second, and totality may last up to nearly 107 minutes. Nevertheless, the total time between the moon's first and last contact with the shadow is much longer, and could last up to 3.8 hours. The relative distance of the Moon from the Earth at the time of an eclipse can affect the eclipse's duration. In particular, when the Moon is near its apogee, the farthest point from the Earth in its orbit, its orbital speed is the slowest. The diameter of the umbra does not decrease much with distance. Thus, a totally-eclipsed moon occurring near apogee will lengthen the duration of totality.

A selenelion or selenehelion occurs when both the Sun and the eclipsed Moon can be observed at the same time. This can only happen just before sunset or just after sunrise, and both bodies will appear just above the horizon at nearly opposite points in the sky. This arrangement has led to the phenomenon being referred to as a horizontal eclipse. It happens during every lunar eclipse at all those places on the Earth where it is sunrise or sunset at the time. Indeed, the reddened light that reaches the Moon comes from all the simultaneous sunrises and sunsets on the Earth. Although the Moon is in the Earth's geometrical shadow, the Sun and the eclipsed Moon can appear in the sky at the same time because the refraction of light through the Earth's atmosphere causes objects near the horizon to appear higher in the sky than their true geometric position.

The Moon does not completely disappear as it passes through the umbra because of the refraction of sunlight by the Earth's atmosphere into the shadow cone; if the Earth had no atmosphere, the Moon would be completely dark during an eclipse. The red coloring arises because sunlight reaching the Moon must pass through a long and dense layer of the Earth's atmosphere, where it is scattered. Shorter wavelengths are more likely to be scattered by the small particles, and so by the time the light has passed through the atmosphere, the longer wavelengths dominate. This resulting light we perceive as red. This is the same effect that causes sunsets and sunrises to turn the sky a reddish color; an alternative way of considering the problem is to realize that, as viewed from the Moon, the Sun would appear to be setting (or rising) behind the Earth. The amount of refracted light depends on the amount of dust or clouds in the atmosphere; this also controls how much light is scattered. In general, the dustier the atmosphere, the more that other wavelengths of light will be removed (compared to red light), leaving the resulting light a deeper red color. This causes the resulting coppery-red hue of the moon to vary from one eclipse to the next.

Volcanoes are notable for expelling large quantities of dust into the atmosphere, and a large eruption shortly before an eclipse can have a large effect on the resulting color. War activities are notable for expelling large quantities of dust into the atmosphere.

Julian & Gregorian Calendars

The Julian calendar, a reform of Roman calendar, was introduced by Julius Caesar in 46 B.C., and came into force in 45 B.C. It was designed to approximate the tropical year. It has a regular year of 365 days divided into 12 months, and a leap day added to February, every 4 years which makes average Julian year 365.25 days long. The Julian calendar overestimates the length of the year by ~0.0078 days and this discrepancy results in shifting of equinox or solstice days over a long period of time.

The Gregorian calendar was introduced in 1582 A. D. The Gregorian calendar modified the Julian calendar's regular cycle of leap years, years exactly divisible by four, by introducing a caveat – every year that is exactly divisible by four is a leap year, except for year that are exactly divisible by 100; the centurial years that are exactly divisible by 400 are still leap years. Thus the year 1900 is not a leap year, but the year 2000 is a leap year. This modification changed the mean length of the calendar year from 365.25 days to 365.2425 days. The Gregorian calendar also dealt with the past-accumulated difference between these lengths. Roman Catholic Church thought that the first council of Nicaea had fixed the vernal equinox on 21 March and by the time of Gregory's edict for modification of calendar in 1582, the vernal equinox had moved backwards in the calendar and was occurring on about 11 March, 10 days earlier. The Gregory calendar therefore began by dropping 10 calendar days (5-14 October in 1582 A. D.), to revert to the previous date of the vernal equinox. The marginal difference of 0.000125 days between the Gregorian calendar average year and the actual year means that, in around 8000 years, the calendar will be about one day behind where it is now. It is important to remember that the earth's rotation also experiences some variation and thus the change in the length of the vernal equinox year cannot be accurately predicted.

Historical research uses the Gregorian calendar for the events after 16th century and uses the Julian calendar for the events before 16th century.

4

Mahabharata Astronomy

While the West was still thinking, perhaps, of 6,000 years old universe – India was already envisioning ages and eons and galaxies as numerous as the sands of the Ganges. The Universe so vast that modern astronomy slips into its folds without a ripple.

- Houston Smith

When you gaze at the sky, you might appreciate a single star twinkling more than others around it, a collection of stars forming a well-known constellation, an apparent planet, or a streaking flash of light. Your efforts to observe the vast universe that surrounds you and make sense of what you see, whether novice or advanced, is your participation in the field of *astronomy*.

Since ancient times, people have relied on the sky to serve as a guiding light helping them navigate across land or water or measure the passage of time. The celestial events they observed in the sky further served as a backdrop against which to explain their own fate and fortune – both past and present. The Mahabharata text describes well established *nakshatra* system, Lunar and Solar years including methods for periodic corrections to synchronize these two systems.

30

Mahabharata Calendar

I am using the term 'Mahabharata Calendar' in a broader context. Context I have in mind includes Indian notions of day, month, year, seasons, epochs as well as techniques used to measure them and rules laid down to make necessary corrections. This development continues to this day, however my goal is to restrict myself in describing the calendar system prevalent during the days of Mahabharata. This is a challenging task. My approach is to address the challenge by relying on evidence internal to Mahabharata.

Samvatsara or Varsha (Year)

Mahabharata definition of a year is decidedly Luni-Solar. 'Varsha', 'Satra' and 'Samvatsara' are interchangeably employed to mean 'year' in the Mahabharata text. I conjecture that the Vedic practice of performing 'Yajna' or 'Satra' with clear aim of keeping track of time and to make necessary corrections was well established by the time of Mahabharata. The Mahabharata text does refer to the Pandavas performing 'Satra' during their time in the forest and it may be driven by their objective, if not the sole objective, to keep track of their time in the forest.

Usage of 'Varsha' for a year also suggests the beginning of a year with the rainy season, and in the Indian context that meant on summer solstice. At least one of the many beginnings of a year can be said to begin with summer solstice during Mahabharata time, unless of course the term continued its use from Vedic times when 'Varsha (rain)' and summer solstice were used as beginning of a new year and thus coincided with beginning and end of 'Satra' or 'Yajna' or 'Samvatsara'. Mahabharata is thus not explicit regarding the beginning of a new year. Mahabharata is clear about daily calendar being lunar in origin and also about the fact that approximately two additional months were added every five years in order to synchronize lunar calendar with the solar calendar[2].

Mahabharata calendar employed lunar months in daily practice and this is apparent throughout the text. On the other hand, Mahabharata society was aware of both lunar and solar years, and choice of lunar vs. solar year was responsible for Duyrodhana's confusion regarding the total duration spent by the Pandavas in exile.

31

Luni- Solar year & Yuga

The word 'yuga' has multiple meanings however I want to emphasize one of the many contexts in which it is used in the Mahabharata. *Yuga* I am referring to is the *Yuga* of 5 years. Incorporation of additional two lunar months every five lunar years brought lunar calendar in accord with the solar calendar. Bhishma refers to insertion of two *Adhika masa* (extra months) during each five-year period[2].

Seasons (Rutu)

Six seasons were recognized with each season made up of approximately two lunar months. The seasons (Rutu) were designated as *Vasant* (spring), *Grishma* (summer), *Varsha* (rain), *Sharad* (early autumn), *Hemant*a (late autumn) and *Shishir* (winter).

Lunar Month

The Moon makes a complete orbit around the Earth every 27.3 days (sidereal period). However, since the Earth is moving in its orbit about the Sun at the same time, it takes slightly longer for the Moon to show its same phase to the Earth, which is about 29.5 days. The periodic variations in the geometry of the Earth-Moon-Sun system are responsible for the phases of the moon, which repeat every 29.5 days (Synodic period). This is a lunar month.

Lunar Month: *Amanta* or *Purnamanta*?

Lunar month, per *Amanta* reckoning, begins with new moon (*Amawasya*) day and end with next new moon day. There is no clear reference in Mahabharata, referring to starting point of the lunar month. We have to infer the beginning of the lunar month from available evidence. Available evidence, per P V Kane, suggests two beginnings for the month, one starting with new moon day (*Amanta*), as is the case at present and another starting with full moon day (*Purnamanta*). Mahabharata calendar had twelve lunar months, including one extra month, which was inserted every two and half years[3]. The twelve months were *Chaitra, Vaishakha, Jyeshtha,*

Ashadha, Shravana, Proshtapada (Bhadrapada), Ashwin, Kartika, Margashirsha, Pausha, Magha and *Phalguna*.

Proximity of *nakshatra* to the full moon determined the lunar month and its designation. For example, if full moon appeared near Krittika, then the month was designated as *Kartika* and the full moon day was the midpoint of that month, per Amanta reckoning. *Purnamanta* system recognized full moon day (*Purnima*) as beginning and end of the lunar month with new moon day (*Amawasya*) as the center point of the month.

I have assumed *Amanta* reckoning for lunar months throughout the book.

Paksha (Bright half and Dark Half of the Lunar Month)

Paksha is defined as a period of approximately 13-16 days when the moon changes phases either from new moon (not visible) to full moon (fully visible) or vice versa. The *Paksha* that begins with new moon and ends with full moon is called '*Shukla*' *Paksha* (bright half) and the *Paksha* that begins with full moon and ends with new moon is called '*Vadya* or *Krishna*' *Paksha* (dark half). Combination of these two *paksha*s constitutes one lunar month.

Chandra Kala (Phases of the Moon)

The Moon appears to be a circular disk from any location on the Earth. The Moon is always half illuminated by the Sun. Since the Moon orbits the Earth, we get to see more or less of this half illuminated portion of the Moon. During each lunar orbit, we see the moon's appearance change from not visibly illuminated (*Amawasya*) through partially illuminated to fully illuminated (*Purnima*), then back through partially illuminated to not illuminated, again. New moon day is called *Amawasya* and full moon day is called '*Purnima*' in Indian calendar system. On new moon day, moon's unilluminated side is facing the Earth and thus is not visible, except during a solar eclipse. On the full moon day, the moon's illuminated side is facing the Earth. And the moon appears to be completely illuminated by direct sunlight.

Although full moon occurs each month at a specific date and time, the moon's disk may appear to be full for several nights in a row. This is because the percentage of the moon's disk that appears illuminated changes very slowly around the time of the full moon (also around new moon, but the moon is not visible at all then). The moon may appear 100% illuminated only on the night closest to the time of exact full moon, but on the night before and night after will appear 97-99% illuminated; most people would not notice the difference. Even two days from full moon the moon's disk is 93-97% illuminated.

The phases of the Moon are related to (actually, caused by) the relative positions of the Moon and Sun in the sky. For example, new Moon occurs when the Sun and the Moon are quite close together in the sky. The full Moon occurs when the Sun and the Moon are at nearly opposite positions in the sky - which is why the full Moon rises about the time of sunset, and sets about the time of sunrise, most places on the Earth. The relationship of the Moon's phase to its angular distance in the sky from the Sun allows us to establish very exact definitions of when the primary phases occur, independent of how they appear.

Tithi (Day of the Lunar month)

There are total of 15 *Tithi*s in each *Paksha*. They are named as *Pratipada* (1st day of the *Paksha*), *Dwitiya, Tritiya, Chaturthi, Panchamee, Shashthi, Saptami, Ashtami, Navami, Dashami, Ekadashi, Dwadashi, Trayodashi, Chaturdashi* and 15th day of *Purnima*. The *Krishna Paksha* follows the same nomenclature for *Tithi*s except that the last day is *Amawasya*. *Chandra Kala* (phases of the moon) were employed in counting days of the month. Nomenclature of *Tithi* along with the reference to *Paksha* (*Shukla* or *Krishna*) refers to specific phase of the moon.

Mahabharata method of referring to the day is by referring to the *Nakshatra* closest to the Moon. One can determine the lunar month with reasonable accuracy by knowing the *nakshatra* of the day along with the *Paksha* and the phase of the moon.

In Indian calendar system '*Aha*' may refer to period of time when the Sun is above the horizon, '*Ratra*' may refer to the time when the Sun is below the horizon and '*AhoRatra*' as referring to modern 24 hours day. It is important to note that words '*Aham*' or '*Ratra*' were also used to designate '24 hour day' in Mahabharata times. Day was further divided into *Muhurtas* (30 *Muhurta* = 1 day = 24 hours), which were in turn further divided into smaller units.

Nakshatra (Wives of the Moon)

Predictable rising of the Sun provided the ancients a unit of time. However, in order to track the progress of time, one aspires to monitor the motion of a moving object with respect to non-moving (non- moving only in a relative sense since all astral bodies are in motion) object. Observations of the moon's position (moving) with respect to those of *nakshatras* (not moving) at night provided such an opportunity. Astronomers of Mahabharata time used the system of '*nakshatra Ganana*', developed by their predecessors, to keep track of time. *Nakshatra*, which is loosely translated as 'asterism' could be either a specific star (e.g. *Chitra*) or group of stars (e.g. *Krittika*) along the ecliptic and is employed as reference in stating the positions of astral bodies (sun, moon, planets, comets, etc.).

It appears that the desired number of *nakshatras* were determined based on how long it took the moon to complete one orbital cycle. Since the moon completes one cycle through its orbit in 27.3 days, 27 *nakshatras* were selected. This *nakshatra* system was also used to track positions of other astral bodies. Since the moon visited each *nakshatra* once every month, poetically, it was perceived as moon visiting each of his 27 wives each day of the month, until the moon visited all of them, only to repeat the cycle during the next month. These wives of moon were given specific names, were assigned a devata (deity) and are frequently referred to by the name of their assigned deity. The *nakshatras* along with their Yoga Tara, Deity, Right Ascension and Declination measurements are listed in Table 3.

Some *nakshatras* have synonyms and were recognized by those synonyms, in addition to being referred to by their presiding deity. For example, '*Bhadrapada*' is also called '*Proshtha-pada*', '*Dhanishtha*' is called '*Shravishtha*' and '*Shatabhisaj*' is called '*Shata-taraka*'. Some variations can also be seen while assigning presiding deity to a given *nakshatra*. These variations, fortunately, do not lead to any confusion. Existence of other evidence and cross-references within Indian literature (prior to and after Mahabharata) are sufficient to understand the *nakshatra* referred to. The *nakshatra* closest to the moon on a given day is 'nakshatra of the day' in Indian calendar system. Determination of the nakshatra of any given day based on visual observation can lead to an error of +/- 1 day.

Orbit of the Sun

Orbit of the Sun around the Earth is the reference plane for all Mahabharata astronomical observations made after the sunset (dusk), during the night and before the sunrise (dawn). Nakshatras were employed to track positions of the Sun, the planets and other astral bodies such as comets. Position of the Sun with specific nakshatra gained significance at the points of equinoxes and solstices. Critical point to remember is that the direct observation of the position of the Sun near a specific nakshatra is impossible and is thus inferred from the position and identification of nakshatras before sunrise or after sunset and/or also based on the positions and the phases of the Moon.

Nodes of the Moon

The Sun's orbit is the basic plane of reference and is referred to as the ecliptic of the Earth. The moon's orbit is along this ecliptic and intersects the ecliptic twice. The points of intersection are called nodes and are designated as Rahu (ascending node) and Ketu (descending node). The word Ketu referring to node of the moon does not appear in the Mahabharata text. The word 'Ketu' does appear multiple times, however it appears either as referring to flag/banner/symbol or as referring to a comet (e.g. Dhuma-Ketu), literally smoking flag or banner. The positions of these nodes along with the positions of the Sun and the Moon play critical role in occurrences or predictions of eclipses. The Mahabharata text refers to 'Rahu' in the sense of moon's node whether it refers to solar or lunar eclipse. It is important to think of 'Rahu' as area of the sky as opposed to a specific point.

Nodes of the Planets

All nodes are calculated mathematical points (points are designated using nakshatra close to the mathematically calculated point)

36

where the ecliptic is crossed by the plane of planet's (or the moon's) orbit. All nodes are rather lines instead of points and are thus to be interpreted as an area of the sky, rather than a precise point. Planetary node periods are much longer than the period of the moon's node. The periodicity of the moon's node (e.g. *Rahu*) is ~18 years, which means the moon's node will appear near the same *nakshatra* after ~18 years. Most planetary node periods are of the order of 24000 to 26000 years, about the same time it takes for the precession of equinoxes to complete one cycle. Thus, node of a planet is stationary for all practical purposes, however it will change in the long run as all nodes are moving counter clockwise around the ecliptic through *nakshatras*. All of the planets in our solar system are approximately in the same plane with respect to the background star field and thus all the planets are observed along the ecliptic.

Retrograde & Oblique Motions of Planets

If observed from one night to the next, a planet appears to move from the West to the East against the background stars, most of the time. Occasionally, however, a planet's motion will appear to reverse direction, and the planet will, for a short time, move from the East to the West against the background *nakshatras*. In modern times, this reversal is known as retrograde motion.

Mercury usually turns retrograde 3 times a year and is typically retrograde for 24 days. Venus turns retrograde every 18 months and is typically retrograde for 42 days. Mars turns retrograde once in two years and remain retrograde for 80 days. Jupiter, Saturn, Uranus, Neptune and Pluto go retrograde once each year and for 120, 140, 150, 160 and 160 days respectively. All planets appear much brighter than their usual magnitude during their retrograde motion.

A planet, otherwise seem to be moving parallel to the ecliptic, will cross the ecliptic at an angle (will go from north of the ecliptic to the south and vice versa). This oblique motion of a planet will usually (but not always) be around the node of that particular planet. While this oblique motion is well known to astronomers, I did not think much about it until circumstances led me to it.

All planets have nodes and thus exhibit oblique motion around their respective nodes, however the observed effect is pronounced for Mars and Jupiter. In case of Mercury and Venus, the occurrence of oblique motion is too frequent and may not be visible (especially in case of the Mercury because of its proximity to the Sun) while in case of Saturn, it is too infrequent.

Knowledge of the Planets in Mahabharata Times

It appears that Mahabharata astronomers were aware of all the planets of solar system including Pluto. This may come as a shock and a surprise to the reader, since Uranus, Neptune and Pluto were discovered (or re-discovered) in modern times by Herschel (1781 A.D.), Verrier (1846 A.D.) and Tombaugh (1930 A.D.), respectively.

Thus, instead of assuming that Mahabharata astronomers were aware of these planets, I decided to test my claim (previously made by P V Vartak) of Mahabharata astronomers being aware of these three planets, as part of my book. Mahabharata observations present us with at least 5 opportunities. These opportunities can be explained meaningfully only when we assume Mahabharata astronomers to have knowledge of all 9 planets of the solar system. It is true that Uranus, Neptune and Pluto are referred only few times and only in indirect fashion [18, 21]. One set of Specific Mahabharata observations makes sense, only if one assumes the knowledge of these three planets in Mahabharata times [24, 25]. Another set of specific Mahabharata observations leaves no doubt about the identification and positions of these three planets[23]. What is also interesting is that the references to positions of Neptune and Pluto, planets smaller and farther than Uranus, can be inferred with stronger conviction than that of Uranus.

On the other hand Mercury, Venus, Mars, Jupiter and Saturn are mentioned in the Mahabharata text numerous times and no doubt about their identification exists. The Mahabharata text refers to five planets by names that are consistent with rest of the ancient Indian literature.

While Mercury is referred to as either *Budha* or son of the Moon (Somaputra or *Shashijen*a), Venus is referred to as either Shukra or Bhrigusoon (son of Bhrigu). Mars is identified with multiple names such as Mangal, Angarakha, Parusha *graha* (evil planet), Lohitanga and son of the Earth (*Dharaputra*). Jupiter is predominantly identified with the name 'Brhaspati'. Saturn is identified as Shani, Shanischar or Suryaputra. At times Mahabharata refers to planets simply by adjectives such as Shyama[20] (dark, dark blue), Shweta[19] (white, light blue), *Tikshna* (sharp) or *Tivra*[21] (intense), etc. One has to only guess, in such instances; a planet Mahabharata text might be referring to.

Solstices & Equinoxes

Ancient Indian literature contains references for a new year to begin with Winter solstice, Vernal equinox or Summer solstice however Mahabharata is silent on the beginning of a new year. Solstices are designated in Indian calendar system as '*Uttarayan Bindu*' (winter solstice) and '*Dakshinayan Bindu*' (summer solstice). Equinoxes are designated as *Vasant Sampat* (vernal equinox) and *Sharad Sampat* (fall equinox). Precession of equinoxes affects beginning of new season with respect to Indian lunar calendar. Every two thousand years, the beginning of a season precedes by one lunar month.

Brightness of a celestial object (Star or Planet)

The apparent magnitude (m) of a celestial body is a measure of its brightness as seen by an observer on the Earth, normalized to the value it would have in the absence of atmosphere. The brighter the object appears, the lower the value of its magnitude. The scale for apparent magnitude was initially calibrated by assigning zero value to the magnitude of Vega (*Abhijit*).

Mahabharata descriptions of Planets afflicting *Nakshatras*

The Mahabharata text describes planets afflicting (*pidyate*) or attacking (*akramya*) specific *nakshatras*. Mahabharata researchers, proposing a theory and corresponding timing for the War, are required to interpret these Mahabharata observations. Observations can be interpreted in multiple ways. For example, the Sun and the Moon can be visualized as fighting against each other on the full moon day, at the time of sunset or sunrise. The same analogy might even be used on the day of Amawasya when both of them are next to each other.

Distinguished Stars, Asterisms & Constellations

Specific stars, asterisms or constellations have received greater attention in the Mahabharata text. Beginning with the stars along the ecliptic belt, *Rohini* (Aldebaran) appears to be one of the favorite stars of Mahabharata astronomers. Mahabharata text is at pain to describe various planets or positions of the Moon in the context of *Rohini*. *Chitra* (Spica), *Swati* (Arcturus), *Jyeshtha* (Antares), *Shravana* (Altair), *Krittika* (Pleiades), are some of the other key *nakshatras* besides *Rohini*, mentioned frequently in the Mahabharata text. Mahabharata text mentions *Saptarshis* (seven stars) that form the panhandle of the constellation Ursa Major and specifically *Arundhati* (Alcor) and *Vasistha* (Mizar).

The Mahabharata text refers to *Abhijit* (Vega), *Dhanishtha* (Sualocin), *Rohini* (Aldabaran) and *Krittika* (Pleiades) in a unique context and this very context is the subject of the next chapter.

5

Envious Sister
&
Fall of Abhijit

Sorry, No. The start of the "Julian day" system (4700 B.C.) is the earliest. This is a "pre-historic" date (the world's earliest civilizations date from around 3000 B.C. or so).

- The maker of (sophisticated?) astronomy software (in response to my query asking if software maker had plans to extend the usable timeline of their software to 25000 B.C.)

Year: 1267 A. D.

Roger Bacon, an English Friar, dispatched his faithful servant John, with a manuscript 'Opus Maius' addressed to Pope Clement IV with an urgent appeal to correct the calendar by 9 days. Unfortunately Pope Clement IV died, probably before he had a chance to read 'Opus Maius'. The correction identified by Roger Bacon had to wait additional 300+ years, when Pope Gregory XIII corrected the calendar in 1582 A. D.

Roll back the calendar by 16000 years and roll the Earth some 80^0 in longitude east of Bacon's monastery, to the fertile plains of, now extinct, river Saraswati. It is little wonder that story comes to us only in a mythologized form, but without missing either the urgency or the fervor of Bacon's appeal to Pope Clement IV.

Year: 14602 B.C.

Lord Indra appeared worried and perplexed and conveyed his concern to Lord Skandha. Lord Indra requested Lord Skandha to discuss the matter with Lord Brahma and to come up with a solution.

What was the problem that caused so much grief to Lord Indra? From mythological perspective, Indra is identified with the Sun (in addition to many other designations, e.g. Rain God); Skandha is identified with the axis of Earth while Brahma is identified with the creator of cosmos.

Problem

Abhijit (Vega), younger sister of Rohini (Aldebaran), desiring seniority (over Rohini?) went to the forest to perform austerities. Thus, Abhijit (Vega) slipped/moved from the sky. At that time (as a result) Indra approached Skandha and asked Skandha to discuss the matter with Brahma. Brahma ordained the beginning of time from Dhanishtha (Sualocin), while previous to this incident the beginning of time was from Rohini and the appropriate number of nakshatras existed (for time reckoning). Being told like this by Indra, Krittika (Pleiades), the nakshatra with Agni as its deity and with the shape of a cart (or with seven heads) became happy and went up in the sky[4].

My task is to make sense of the incidents described in this Mahabharata passage.

Solutions proposed by others

C V Vaidya thinks of Abhijit as fictitious nakshatra added to the list of original 27, and states that the meaning of this Mahabharata observation is not quite clear to him. He interprets that when Dhanishtha was considered the first nakshatra, Krittika was pushed at the headship of nakshatras. His interpretation is contradictory since the first *nakshatra* in time reckoning is at the headship of *nakshatras*. In any case, he remains vague on implications of this observation and mentions this observation only to claim that Indians had some knowledge of astronomy during 3000 B.C., the time interval he was trying to justify for the Mahabharata War.

R N Iyengar attempts to interpret this observation, goes all over but really nowhere and fails miserably. He does not use this information anywhere either to make a case for his Mahabharata timeline or to employ it as a corroborative evidence for his timeline. I would hate to force my assertion on my readers and thus reproduce his explanation in the original. R N Iyengar writes,

The above verse appears in all editions of Mahabharata, including the recognized BORI, Pune, critical edition where it appears in Chapter 219. These four verses refer to the four stars *Abhijit, Rohini, Dhanishtha* and *Krittika*. The literal meaning of the first two verses is easy. However, what is meant by *Abhijit* and *Rohini* is not clear. In Vedic literature there is ambiguity as to whether the number of *nakshatras* was 27 or 28. In the much later Siddhantic astronomy whenever 28 stars are mentioned in dividing the ecliptic, *Abhijit* is placed between *U. Ashada* and *Shravana* and is identified with star Vega (α Lyrae). In Taittriya Samhita (4.4.10) only 27 stars are mentioned, whereas in Taittriya Brahmana (1.5.1.3) 28 stars with *Abhijit* placed between *U. Ashadha* and *Shravana* are listed. Again, even though *Rohini* is popularly identified with Aldebaran, there is indication in the above text that Jyeshtha was once called by the same name *Rohini*. *Abhijit's* competition with her elder sister *Rohini* and eventual vanishing from the sky should be an allegory for brightening followed by dimming beyond recognition. If we take the traditional position of *Abhijit* as the correct position since ancient times, its relative brightening would have been with respect to Antares (*Jyeshtha Rohini*). There is an indirect allusion to the missing *Abhijit* in Taittriya Samhita (Brahmana 3.3.6.4) also. In the available ancient Chinese, records on supernovae, there is reference to a star near Antares that vanished in 1400 B.C. Could this be the vanishing star referred as *Abhijit* in Mahabharata? The statement that this happened when time (year) began with star *Dhanishtha* lends support to this possibility. Winter solstice at *Dhanishtha* was the period of Vedanga Jyotisha, which has been dated to 1400 B.C. The meaning of the last three lines of the above verses, in relation to the previous ones is not clear as noted by S.B. Dikshit, a scholar of great repute.

Notwithstanding the meaningless chatter of this passage, I want to highlight few precious nuggets quoted by R N Iyengar before I move on. Taittriya Samhita mentions only 27 *nakshatras* while Taittriya Brahamana mentions 28 including *Abhijit* and also the fact that there is an indirect allusion to the missing *Abhijit* in Taittriya Samhita/Brahamana. These three observations provide corroborative support for my solution to the problem of 'Fall of *Abhijit'*. Since I have not established the solution as yet, I leave the subject as is for now. I may mention while passing that my solution to 'Fall of *Abhijit'* could be used to determine the timing of Taittriya Samhita and Taittriya Brahmana.

P V Holay refers to 'Fall of *Abhijit'* in one of his papers on Dating of the Mahabharata War and claims that both *Jyeshtha* (Antares) and *Rohini* (Aldabaran) were understood to be '*Rohini*' during Mahabharata times. He does not use this information anywhere in his paper. In effect Holay is saying what Iyengar said and both of them are at loss as to why even they mention this reference.

P V Vartak interprets this observation in two different ways. I learnt of this observation from his book "*Swayambhu*' and I understood the implications of this observation because of him. My interpretation is different from his and I claim mine to be more consistent. I provide his translation with the aim of making clear the distinction between my interpretation and his. Vartak's literal translation is from one of his papers, written some time after '*Swayambhu*',

Contesting *Abhijit* (Vega), the daughter-like younger sister of *Rohini* (Aldebaran) went to *Vana* (i.e. water) for heating the summer (*tapa*) because she was desirous of seniority. I do not understand anything. I wish you good luck, but I must tell that the star *Abhijit* has slipped down from the sky. This is a distant time but you (Skandha) think of it with Brahma. At that time Brahma had reckoned the time, placing *Dhanishtha* at the top of the list of *nakshatras*. *Rohini* was also given first place in the past. I have gathered this much knowledge (*Sankhya*). When Indra talked like this, *Krittika* went to the heaven (i.e. attained the highest respectable

44

position). That seven-headed constellation whose deity is fire (*Agni*) is still glittering.

Vartak has provided additional explanation and I paraphrase it,

> The daughter like younger sister of *Rohini* (Aldebaran) is *Krittika* (Pleiades). *Krittika* wanted seniority so she contested with *Abhijit* (Vega). Vartak considers this as poetic idea to give an explanation to the fact that *Abhijit* slipped down and infers that writer of Mahabharata assumed *Abhijit* slipped down because of *Krittika* and thus were held responsible. He interprets that it was *Krittika* who went to *Vana* (meaning water or forest) for *tapa* (meaning summer or penance), but it also means *Krittika* went to water for heating the summer. He wonders about his own interpretation of 'water' and then suggests that *Krittika* went to rainy season, i.e. to summer solstice, when rainy season starts in India. Since *Krittika* were at summer solstice around 21000 B.C., he infers that slipping of Vega was observed around this time and hence the plausible correlation in Mahabharata writer's mind. To Vartak, Brahma's reckoning of *Dhanishtha* in the first place refers to the time when *Dhanishtha* was at the vernal equinox, which is around the same time as 21000 B.C. And since *Rohini* was also in the first position in further antiquity, Vartak surmises that this was the time period of around 22500 B.C. when *Rohini* was at summer solstice. Vartak thinks that by exposing these two ancient facts, Indra reveals to Skandha the two methods in vogue at that time, to list the *nakshatras*. One method that gave the first place to the *nakshatra* at Vernal equinox, and the other that gave the first place to the *nakshatra* at summer solstice. Vartak suggest that this dialogue took place between Indra and Skandha around 13000 B.C. when there was a complete fall of Vega. And why would Indra tell this story to Skandha around 13000 B.C? Vartak asks the question and then answers that this was probably due to the fact that around 13000 B.C. summer solstice was around *Abhijit* and some scholars might have suggested that *Abhijit* be given first place, however to oppose this proposal, Indra describes the past incident and brought to notice the fact that *Abhijit* had fallen to the horizon to become celestial North Pole and so it was not useful as *nakshatra* for reckoning time.

I consider myself lucky that Vartak retained his true discovery (i.e. *Abhijit* becoming Pole Star) in spite of the confusing explanation he entangled himself into. I provide straightforward and consistent interpretation of this observation.

Where is *Abhijit* now?

At present *Abhijit* has Declination of $+39^0$, i.e. as far to the south as it gets from the celestial North Pole. Another time *Abhijit* was so close to the ecliptic was in 25000 B.C. *Abhijit* started moving away from the ecliptic, towards the north and became North Pole star around 12000 B.C. This is the phenomenon of the 'Fall of *Abhijit*'. After 12000 B.C. *Abhijit* began moving away from the celestial North Pole and towards the ecliptic to attain its present position.

My Interpretation

All modern calendars require additional corrections, in addition to the protocol of periodic corrections. Assigning leap year every 4 years plus additional rule of not taking century year as a leap year unless it is evenly divisible by 400 or adding of extra lunar month (*Adhika* masa) to every 2.5 lunar years are examples of periodic corrections. Slow movements caused by phenomenon such as 'the precession of equinoxes' make it necessary to apply major correction(s) in order to make sense of the calendar with the expectation of seasons, beginning of a new year and their connection with religious celebrations or rituals. It is not unusual for these sporadic but necessary corrections to get delayed until someone feels the urgency to fix the issue; he may be Roger Bacon who is worried about devout Christians celebrating their religious festivals on wrong days or he may be Indra who is worried about the mismatch between the beginning of the year and the first *nakshatra*.

Nakshatras along the ecliptic are used in keeping track of time by noting down positions of the Moon (each day) and positions of the Sun during solstices and equinoxes. Allegorically speaking, functional *nakshatra* is a *nakshatra* that is useful in demarking the position of the moon (e.g. close to the ecliptic) and thus assist in keeping track of time and can be considered to be one having a social life. In this context, *Abhijit* moving towards the celestial North Pole can be visualized as going to the forest (into seclusion and away from social life). As *Abhijit* approached the celestial pole, contemporary

46

observers would have perceived *Abhijit* as being stationary. Allegorically speaking, slipping/movement of *Abhijit* towards the celestial pole and its position close to the celestial pole can be visualized as going to the forest (away from social life) to do *tapa* (penance) by being stationary in one place.

Abhijit began slipping towards the celestial pole after 25000 B.C. and over time was becoming useless for the purposes of time keeping. Since this slipping of *Abhijit* was an extremely slow process, the required correction of eliminating *Abhijit* as *nakshatra* and replacing her with another appropriate star or asterism was delayed, until the problem had to be faced head on. When correction became imminent, Indian astronomers took the opportunity to make all necessary corrections. Indian astronomers made three specific corrections to their calendar,

1. Removed *Abhijit* from the list of *nakshatras* as *Abhijit* lost its utility in keeping track of time, i.e. *Abhijit* lost its status as functional *nakshatra*
2. Replaced *Krittika* in place of *Abhijit,* as new *nakshatra,* in order to have desired number (27) of *nakshatras* for time reckoning
3. Replaced *Rohini* based time reckoning with *Dhanishtha* based time reckoning

Rationale for assigning *Dhanishtha* as the first *nakshatra* is same as that of why *Rohini* was considered the first *nakshatra* prior to this correction. Ancient Indian literature contains numerous references to a year, beginning with summer solstice, winter solstice or vernal equinox.

If one wants to estimate the timing of this correction, one should look for 'the time' when,

1. *Dhanishtha* would be at one of the cardinal points (equinox or solstice), considered plausible for the beginning of a year
2. *Abhijit* would be approaching the Celestial North pole, with its position close enough to be considered North pole star or soon to attend such a status, i.e. in effect sig-

47

nificantly away from the ecliptic and unable to act as functional *nakshatra*

3. *Rohini* should have been at this cardinal point prior to this event

Requirement of *Abhijit* approaching the celestial North Pole is critical. The requirement is critical as the timing of crisis created by loss of *Abhijit* (as *nakshatra*) was approaching and was getting worse with time and had to be squarely faced. On the other hand, *Abhijit* moving away from the celestial North Pole would mean that the crisis should have been resolved long time ago.

Error Elimination: Experiment 1

At present, *Dhanishtha* is located between the points of winter solstice and vernal equinox,

(1) If we turn the clock backward, we reach the point of winter solstice near *Dhanishtha* in 1600 B.C.
(2) Declination of *Abhijit* was around $+40^0$.
(3) *Abhijit* was going away from the celestial pole.
(4) Winter solstice was near *Rohini* in 9500 B.C.

If winter solstice is assumed to be the reference point when *nakshatra* was given the first status, then progression of winter solstice from *Rohini* to *Dhanishtha* is consistent with Mahabharata observation. Winter solstice is indeed a plausible point to begin a new year.

On the other hand, the position of *Abhijit* was nowhere close to Celestial North Pole and is rather as far as it gets to the south, close to the ecliptic, and thus away from Celestial North Pole. In addition, *Abhijit* was moving away from celestial North Pole. *Abhijit* moving away from the celestial North Pole and the fact that its position was far away from the celestial North Pole are decisive observations in support of rejecting this date as the timing of the 'Fall of *Abhijit*'.

I want the reader to understand that it is possible to predict the timing of equinoxes or solstices near a specific Nakshatra with accuracy.

Error Elimination: Experiment 2

(1) The autumnal equinox was near *Dhanishtha* in 8500 B.C.
(2) Declination of *Abhijit* was around +68°, significantly closer to the celestial North Pole.
(3) *Abhijit* was moving away from the celestial North Pole.
(4) Autumnal equinox was near *Rohini* in 16000 B.C.

The fact that *Abhijit* was moving away from the celestial North Pole (8500 B.C.) is decisive observation in support of rejecting this date as the timing of the 'Fall of *Abhijit*'.

Error Elimination: Experiment 3

(1) Summer solstice was near *Dhanishtha* in 14500 B.C.
(2) Declination of *Abhijit* was around +74°.
(3) Position of *Abhijit* was the closest (among positions tested for 4 plausible time periods) to the celestial North Pole and *Abhijit* was moving towards the celestial North Pole.
(4) Summer solstice was near *Rohini* in 22500 B.C.

Summer solstice is indeed a plausible time to begin a new year based on numerous references in ancient Indian literature including word for the year - *Varsha* (rain) that begins (in India) at the point of summer solstice.

Abhijit had attained a position closer to the celestial North Pole and was moving towards the point of celestial North Pole. After additional 2500 years (12048 B.C.), Abhijit was closest to the point of North Celestial Pole. This combination presents consistent scenario that would corroborate Mahabharata observation. I will return to outcome of this experiment after explaining one last scenario.

Error Elimination: Experiment 4

(1) Vernal equinox was near *Dhanishtha* in 20000 B.C.
(2) Declination of *Abhijit* was around +46°
(3) *Abhijit* was moving towards the celestial North Pole but *Abhijit*'s actual position was far away from the Celestial North Pole

49

(4) Vernal equinox was near *Rohini* in 29000 B.C.

While Vernal equinox is a plausible point to begin a new year and while *Abhijit* is indeed moving towards the celestial North Pole, the position of *Abhijit* (Declination = 46^0) cannot justify the crisis described by 'Fall of *Abhijit*'. It will be useful to remember that Declination attained by *Abhijit* when it is closest to the ecliptic (and thus farthest from the celestial North Pole) is around $+40^0$.

Critical Discussion

I noted down the direction of the movement as well as the position of *Abhijit* when specific solstice or equinox was near *Dhanishtha*. Requirement of *Rohini* to be at the critical point of solstices or equinoxes, prior to *Dhanishtha* reaching the very same point (equinox or solstice) provided 'arrow of time'.

The Mahabharata text is not explicit when it comes to the beginning of a year. India has multiple time reckoning systems coexisting at present. New Year, per western calendar, begins with 1st of January, while another New Year, per Hindu calendar, begins with new moon day in the lunar month of *Chaitra* in some parts of India, while with new moon day of the lunar month of *Vaishakha* in other parts, and still another year beginning with new moon day in the lunar month of *Kartika*. These are not the only systems of time reckonings in vogue, however my point being to illustrate more than one system of time reckonings coexisting at any given time. It could be the case during Mahabharata times. Fortunately, uncertainty surrounding the beginning of a year during Mahabharata times does not affect our ability to select the time for the 'Fall of *Abhijit*' from four plausible alternatives. Summer solstice near *Dhanishtha* around 14500 B.C. corroborates all criteria for the 'Fall of *Abhijit*'.

Abhijit began moving away from the ecliptic and towards the celestial North Pole after 25000 B.C. and astute astronomers would have noted the slipping away of *Abhijit* (away from the ecliptic) when the summer solstice was in *Rohini* (22500 B.C.). For a star or asterism to become a *nakshatra*, its position should be at or close to the ecliptic, in order to be useful for time reckoning. *Abhijit* is not at or even close to the ecliptic and the only rational, I presume, ancient astronomers might have had for her inclusion into the *nakshatra* list is her conspicuous presence in the sky, partly due to her brightness (magnitude =0.07).

Swati (Arcturus) or Shravana (Altair) might have been included in the nakshatra list for the same reasons as that of Abhijit. Swati is bright (magnitude= 0.16) however her Declination has changed from +20^0 (at present) to +60^0 around 7000 B.C. Shravana has magnitude of 1.02 and her Declination has changed from +5^0 (200 B.C.) to + 54^0 around 13000 B.C.

It is important to note that the choice of Abhijit as a nakshatra is not an ideal choice. Even when Abhijit is closest to the ecliptic, its position is still far away from the ecliptic (+40^0). As Abhijit moved towards the celestial North Pole, astronomers would have faced difficulties in employing Abhijit as functional nakshatra, for tracking positions of the Moon and/or the Sun, a necessary step in reckoning of time. With every passing century (or millennium) the difficulty would have turned into a problem that eventually turned into a crisis and thus had to be addressed. It was finally addressed around 14500 B.C., when Abhijit had slipped far away from the ecliptic and had attained Declination of around 74^0. Indian astronomers made three corrections,

1. They removed Abhijit from the list of nakshatras
2. Added Krittika to the list of nakshatras making a total of functional nakshatras back to 27
3. They acknowledged the shift in the point of summer solstice (and hence the beginning of a year), which was now near Dhanishtha and assigned the first rank, among nakshatras, to Dhanishtha.

Rationale for selection of Krittika

Krittika was added to the list of nakshatras and this selection of Krittika could have taken place for any number of reasons. What follows is my conjecture (cupiditas speculandi) for selection of Krittika. I was validating work of S B Dikshit where he determined the timing of an astronomy observation, 'Krittika rising due east' from Shatapatha Brahmana and my simulation (using Voyager 4.5™) confirmed his proposed time period (~ 2927 B.C.). I realized that 'Krittika rising due east' was a repetitive phenomenon and I was curious to find out its occurrence prior to 2927 B.C. I simulated Declination coordinate of *Krittika* past 3000 B.C., until *Krittika* were rising due east – again! *Krittika* were rising due east in 14963 B.C., previous to 3000 B.C. *Krittika* had deviated by only 2^0 when summer solstice coincided with *Dhanishtha* (14602 B.C.). I speculate that *Krittika* rising due east around the time of summer solstice coinciding with Dhanishtha was the reason for the selection of Krittika to the list of *nakshatras*.

Implications: Fall of *Abhijit*

The 'Fall of Abhijit' reference occurs in *Vana Parva*, where Sage Markandeya talks about it while instructing the Pandavas, towards the end of their exile in the forest. Sage Markandeya is narrating an incident of the past, of times ancient with respect to Mahabharata itself. Author of Mahabharata has used multiple digressions while telling the story of Kuru dynasty to achieve his aim of including knowledge of various subjects, as available and understood during the time of Mahabharata. It is not always easy to figure out, while reading the Mahabharata text, when the factual story ends and discourse on knowledge begins, often in a garb of a metaphor, myth or allegory.

The Mahabharata observation and my interpretation of it asserts that Indian astronomers were meticulously documenting motions of stars and the *nakshatras* for a long period of time, at least as far back as 22500 B.C. When one has records of a phenomenon observed in 22500 B.C., one can easily infer that not only the science and discipline of observation must have begun in further antiquity but also the tools required to transferring such knowledge.

Outcome of this observation indicates that Indian astronomers were observing and recording motions of key stars for a long period, at least amounting to the cycle of precession of equinoxes (26000 years) and more likely far beyond. It may be helpful to think of the movement of our current North Pole star – Polaris. Observation of *Rohini* at summer solstice takes us back to the time when Polaris was North Pole star (24000 B.C.) some 26000 years ago. The observation then establishes ancient, if not the oldest known tradition of visual astronomy, based on internal Mahabharata references.

6

The Epoch of Arundhati

If 'Arundhati' does not qualify as the most unambiguous astronomical evidence in determining the date of Mahabharata War, let's stop talking about astronomical evidence in Mahabharata.

- Nilesh Oak

You have to be an asshole to quote yourself

- Anonymous

Vyasa tells Dhritarashtra, day before the Mahabharata War[1],

> My dear King, *Arundhati* (saintly wife of *Vasistha*) who is revered by the righteous all over the three worlds, has left her husband *Vasistha* behind.

Arundhati (Alcor) and *Vasistha* (Mizar) are two well-known stars from the panhandle of the constellation Ursa Major. I was fascinated by this astronomy observation when I read it for the first time in the Rutherford library of University of Alberta. My fascination was simply driven by the reality that for the first time I came across an astronomical observation within the Mahabharata text that I could comprehend. I had heard of Mahabharata text being full of astronomical observations made around the time of Mahabharata War, however, I was convinced that the subject was beyond my capabilities.

Missing observation of *Arundhati* & Mahabharata Research

Mahabharata researchers, who considered Mahabharata as fiction, did not give a second thought about astronomical evidence in the Mahabharata text. On the other hand those who believed in factual nature of Mahabharata and exhibited faith in astronomical observations were also puzzled by *Arundhati* observation. Many dealt with the dilemma by simply ignoring it, as if the *Arundhati* observation did not exist. I came across, directly and indirectly, works of 20+ researchers on dating of the Mahabharata War using astronomical observations. I was astonished to find that only four researchers mentioned '*Arundhati*' observation while rest of them ignored it altogether. I assert that this lack of inclusion of '*Arundhati*' observation in their research is not due to oversight. *Adhyaya* 2 of Bhishma *Parva* has 4 astronomy observations,

1. The full moon of *Kartika* appearing coppery red[28]
2. *Arundhati* walking ahead of *Vasishtha*[1]
3. Saturn afflicting *Rohini*[9]
4. Mark on the surface of the moon invisible[9]

My assertion for deliberate omission of '*Arundhati*' observation by these researchers can be deduced from the fact that these researchers, without exception, refer to 3 out of 4 observations while conveniently ignoring the remaining observation of *Arundhati*.

Fanciful & Absurd Observation

The observation, specifically *Arundhati* walking ahead of *Vasistha*, is/was considered impossible and ridiculous to the extent it has been used by many to prove their conjecture of how the Mahabharata text is filled with rubbish and why astronomical observations within Mahabharata should not be taken seriously. The observation is at least acknowledged by 4 researchers and I summarize their interpretations.

C V Vaidya, in his book 'The Mahabharata: A Criticism' proposes that all astronomical references were added by Sauti 'to swell the list of evil omens' which presumably included *Arundhati* observation. In his words,

> We, on our part, believe that most of these references are of doubtful authenticity, in other words that they do not belong to the original Mahabharata of Vyasa but to its latest edition. It will be admitted by all that some of them are fanciful and absurd. The last editor probably wished to accommodate the number of evil omens, which preceded the war and tried to put in such impossible combinations as he could bring together. For instance we may safely put aside as absurdities the statement that the Sun and the Moon were eclipsed at the same time or the statement that *Arundhati* went beyond *Vasistha* among the *Saptarshis*.

Vaidya misunderstood the reference of the Sun and the Moon eclipsing at the same time and I have provided straightforward explanation of the solar and the lunar eclipses in Chapter 8. Vaidya thought 'Arundhati' observation absurd because he could not, with the technology available in his times, design experiments to test it. I would also add that mere availability of technology is never enough; we also need little ingenuity, little creative thinking and lot of luck. Elsewhere, in the same book, Vaidya essentially repeats his above argument, and refers to *Arundhati* observation' as a proof of absurdities introduced in the Mahabharata text by Sauti. He presents 'Arundhati' observation as justification for his theory of interpolation of astronomical observations by later writers, especially Sauti.

P V Kane provides detailed discussion of astronomical observations and does mention 'Arundhati' observation. He mentions *Arundhati* to emphasize how the author of Mahabharata, in describing the evil portents of an impending tragic event, often assemble together all kinds of astronomical phenomena irrespective of the fact whether some of them are possible in the very order of nature. He refers to 'Arundhati' observation as one of those impossible events in the very order of nature along with 'mare giving birth to a cow' or 'a dog giving birth to a jackal' or the descriptions such as 'images of gods trembled, laughed and vomited blood'.

P V Vartak attempted to solve the mystery behind *Arundhati* observation. He stated few conjectures and asked pertinent questions however in the end, realizing inadequacy of his explanation, and in the true spirit of a researcher, requested astronomy community to research it further. He offered various conjectures and requested experts in astronomy to test them. His conjectures are as follows,

1. He wondered if *Atreya* (Alkaid) was considered *Vasistha* in ancient times as opposed to the current identification of star Mizar with *Vasistha*.
2. He interpreted current position of *Arundhati* as ahead of *Vasistha*, based on astrological convention, since *Arundhati* (Alcor) is <u>east</u> of *Vasistha* (Mizar) and then wondered when *Arundhati* would have moved east of *Vasistha*.
3. He referred to a data source (specific data source is not mentioned) according to which *Vasistha* made an angle of 20^0 with a line defined by Alioth and Megrez, 100,000 years ago. Referring to the same data source, he explained that in our times, the same angle is down to 14^0. He inferred (I do not understand how he does it) that *Arundhati* may not be part of *Saptarshi* (Big dipper) cluster and assuming independent motion for *Arundhati*, he speculated that it is conceivable for *Arundhati* to go ahead of *Vasistha*.

His first conjecture amounts to shifting the problem somewhere else. It would involve searching through enormous ancient Indian literature looking for validation of his conjecture and supposing one finds corroborative support for his conjecture, one is left with the task of identification of the timing of supporting document, and still the question of the year of Mahabharata War will remain unanswered. The second conjecture is easy to test. I have also tested his third conjecture in a modified form, i.e. without worrying whether *Arundhati* is part of *Saptarshi* cluster or not.

R. N. Iyengar offers an ingenious and admirable explanation however his conclusions are decidedly false. I mention his effort to express my appreciation of his creativity, much desired, but characteristically lacking among many others. He combines second couplet of

Arundhati observation[1] with another unrelated couplet[14], both of them from different *Adhyayas* of Bhishma *Parva*. In the absence of my discovery, I would have failed to notice his novel combination of couplets and curious aspect of his interpretation. I do not believe that combining of partial statements from two different *Adhyayas* is either warranted or justified. His combination of couplets from two different *Adhyayas* is as follows,

> *Arundhati* has gone ahead of (her husband) *Vasishtha*[1]
> Dhruva, the Pole Star blazing and fierce, is moving anti-clockwise[14]

I will return to this innovative combination and interpretation of R N Iyengar, in the light of my discovery, at the end of this chapter.

Importance of *Arundhati* observation

Arundhati observation made my theory of 'visual observations of the sky' a falsifiable and an empirical theory. I did not of course think of my theory in this language when I stumbled on *Arundhati* observation. I was attracted to *Arundhati* observation for a simple reason. I could understand it and I felt, naively so, that I could easily test it. I was equally intrigued by other astronomical observations where a specific planet was described in the vicinity of multiple *nakshatras* however my knowledge of *nakshatras* was limited. I could neither identify them in the night sky nor identify them by corresponding star/asterism in a star atlas. On the other hand, I knew *Arundhati* (Alcor) and *Vasistha* (Mizar) from my childhood and had observed them for hours in the night sky when I was barely ten years old. I could observe them during most part of the year if I wished to, as long as the sky was clear.

Did *Arundhati* go ahead of *Vasistha* and assuming she did, when did she do it? This is what I termed the 'Mystery of *Arundhati*'. If I could solve this problem, I reasoned, I would be willing to put extra efforts to understand *nakshatras* and positions of planets, in order to comprehend remaining Mahabharata observations. On the other hand, if I could convincingly prove that *Arundhati* observation was not a mystery after all, but rather an absurd statement introduced by either the original or later authors, I would be saved from the torture of understanding and/or interpreting remaining Mahabharata observations. Intuitively I felt that *Arundhati* was a factual observation since I could not come up with a rationale on the part of original author of Mahabharata (or on the part of later authors) to write or insert something that would be impossible, as they could have always gotten away with mentioning few conjunctions of planets with each other or with *nakshatras*. I found it fascinating that my approach to this problem was very much along the lines of 'testability', 'falsifiability' and 'simplicity' as espoused by Karl Popper.

Falsifiability is the only criteria for the empirical character of certain statements such as Mahabharata astronomical observations. Falsifiability originates only in the context of 'testability of the statement'. Falsification of a theory occurs, only when basic statements, accepted in building a theory, contradict the very observations theory is trying to explain. Thus a statement 'mare giving birth to a cow' is not a testable statement in the context of my theory and thus not empirical. On the other hand one can still evaluate a theory with the help of testable observations from the pool of testable and non-testable Mahabharata observations. P V Kane and C V Vaidya have made a case for Mahabharata passages containing astronomical statements getting mixed with non-astronomical statements. I agree with their claim however I differ from both of them in the following respect. While both of them claim 'mixing of statements' as evidence for the absurdity of astronomical observations such as that of *Arundhati*, I claim that all astronomical statements are testable while all non-astronomical statements are not; at least not with our current knowledge of Mahabharata conventions, current interpretation of non-astronomical passages and current advances in technology at our disposal.

Where is *Arundhati* now?

Imagine yourself sitting under the sky with a clear view of the sky at Kurukshetra, battlefield site of the Mahabharata War, 100 miles north of New Delhi in northern India. Imagine a day of your choice during a pleasant autumn season of past 1000 years. Sometime after midnight, you would see *Vasistha* rise from the horizon in the northeast direction, *Arundhati* following immediately behind.

Vasistha and *Arundhati* were circumpolar stars for millennia with respect to Kurukshetra. Both of them ceased to be circumpolar with respect to north-central India around 800 A. D. Circumpolar or not, when visible, *Vasistha* could be seen making rounds around the point of celestial North Pole and *Arundhati* following behind *Vasistha*. Today, position of *Arundhati* is north of *Vasistha* (Declination coordinate) and east of *Vasistha* (Right Ascension coordinate). One standing on the Earth will perceive *Arundhati* as walking behind (and not ahead of) *Vasistha* and such perception is due to,

(1) The Earth rotates from the west to the east
(2) Position of *Arundhati* is east of *Vasistha*.

Problem & Potential Solution

The question I had to answer was,

(1) Was *Arundhati* ever walking ahead of *Vasistha*?

In other words, was position of *Arundhati* ever west of *Vasistha* based on Right Ascension measurements? In addition, assuming answer to the above question in affirmative, the next question I had to answer was,

(2) When did such an event take place?

In other words, my problem was to determine if *Arundhati* ever appeared as walking ahead of *Vasistha* and if so, to determine the year or time interval, when *Arundhati* would have been perceived as walking ahead of *Vasistha*. This year or time interval then would be probable year or time interval of the Mahabharata War.

Canadian Rockies & Critical Tests

I moved to Calgary, Canada in 1997 A.D., two years after I stumbled on *Arundhati* observation. I started reading books on astronomy and found that stars, although they appear stationary, do have motion with respect to their neighboring stars. This motion is called 'proper motion'.

I approached one of the professors of physics working in Astronomy and his graduate group at University of Calgary. I do not know if they understood what I was after but they were helpful. They explained what proper motion meant, taught me about 'Declination' and 'Right Ascension' coordinates and allowed me access to their small library. I noted down Proper motion Declination - PMD (north-south) and Proper motion Ascension – PMA (east-west) measurements for *Arundhati* and *Vasistha*.

Positive PMD signifies that the star is moving in northwardly direction with respect to the ecliptic while positive PMA signifies that the star is moving in eastwardly direction with respect to the point of Vernal Equinox. My research notes from year 1999 A.D. confirm that I consulted at least three different reference books looking for PMD and PMA: Hipparcos & Tycho Stellar database, Hubble stellar library and Millennium Star Atlas. The proper motions were listed along with their standard errors. I performed calculations using mean values as well as values adjusted for standard errors.

Error Elimination – Experiment 5

At present (1928 A.D.), *Arundhati* is east of *Vasistha* based on Right Ascension measurements, and thus *Arundhati* appears to walk behind *Vasistha*. I noted down PMA values for *Arundhati* and *Vasistha*, and difference between their Right ascension coordinates.

> **Vasistha- PMA = 0.0141 arc-sec/year**
> **Arundhati – PMA = 0.0135 arc-sec/year.**
>
> **Delta-RA (Arundhati – Vasistha),**
> **= 1082.6 arc-secs (1928 A.D.)**
>
> **Year when Vasistha would have identical RA as Arundhati**
> **1082.6 / (0.0141-0.0135)**
> **= 1,971,000 Years (~ 2 million years in the future)**

Positive values of PMA for *Arundhati* and *Vasistha* signify that both of them are moving eastward. *Arundhati* is to the east of *Vasistha* and since *Vasistha* is moving faster, albeit marginally, *Vasistha* will reach a position east of *Arundhati* some two million years into the future. This means *Vasistha* was never east of *Arundhati* (i.e. walking behind *Arundhati*) based on PMA calculations and RA coordinates. Thus, the test employing PMA and RA measurements failed to corroborate *Arundhati* observation.

Error Elimination – Experiment 6

Next, I considered proper motions in North-south direction. This proposal requires many more assumptions and justifications in order to imagine *Arundhati* either ahead or behind *Vasistha*. I wanted to test my conjecture against all plausible combinations in order to feel confident that I had exposed the conjecture to most severe tests. I was trying to interpret *Arundhati* observation and observation could be interpreted in multiple fashions, specifically a statement of the type 'X walking ahead of Y'. How does one determine, while considering the positions and motions of *Arundhati* and *Vasistha* in North-South direction, if *Arundhati* is walking ahead without introducing another ad hoc hypothesis? This was indeed a serious problem. I decided to postpone the problem of finding adhoc hypothesis but wanted to find out if *Vasistha* was ever north of *Arundhati* in the past, considering its current location south of *Arundhati*.

PMD values for *Arundhati* and *Vasistha* are negative, implying that both of them are moving south. *Vasistha* is moving faster than *Arundhati*, based on magnitude of their PMDs. Current position of Vasistha is to the south of Arundhati. I concluded that sometime in the past they had same Declination, and that *Vasistha* was north of *Arundhati* prior to them attaining same Declination. I performed the calculations using range of values for their PMD's however demonstrate calculations based on mean values alone.

> **Vasistha- PMD = - 0.02 arc-sec/year**
> **Arundhati – PMD = - 0.009 arc-sec/year.**
>
> **Delta-Dec (*Arundhati – Vasistha*),**
> **=222.2 arc-secs (1928 A.D.)**
>
> **Year when,**
> **Declination of *Vasistha*= Declination of *Arundhati***
> **222.2 / (0.02 - 0.009))**
> **= 20,200 B (efore) P (resent), Where, Present = 2010 A.D.**

I could not think of visual and/or objective basis for *Arundhati* going ahead of *Vasistha*, based on output of this experiment. In summary,

1. No visual basis existed for interpretation of *Arundhati* north or south of *Vasistha* as either ahead or behind *Vasistha*, even before I conducted this experiment
2. The results of the experiment failed to establish objective criteria for
   a. *Arundhati* ahead of *Vasistha*
   b. Minimum difference in their Declination coordinate that would justify *Arundhati* ahead of *Vasistha*

3. Relative motions of *Arundhati* and *Vasistha* in North-South directions are/were so slow (0.011 arc-sec/year) that the phenomenon is practically useless for determining the year of the Mahabharata War with resolution (accuracy) of 1, 10, 100 or even 1000 years.

I had an opportunity to repeat these experiments with the help of SkyGazer™ and Voyager™ in 2009 A.D., ten years after my first attempt and conclusions remained unchanged (Error Elimination – Experiment 8). One significant difference was the timing of both stars attaining same Declination. Instead of 20,200 BP, the number calculated using mean values of PMD (from Star databases); the SkyGazer™ simulation resulted in 44,320 BP. The difference in number of years is due to the followings reasons,

(1) PMD and Declinations measurements from Astronomy reference books were accurate only to the second decimal places. Although this error may sound trivial, it adds up when calculations are performed over a long period of time.
(2) The calculations ignored the effect of 'precession of equinoxes' on the positions of stars (Declination and Right ascension coordinates of the stars)

Estimates of 20000 BP or 44000 BP as plausible time of the Mahabharata War did not bother me at all. If the estimates were wrong, they would be falsified by other observations. I considered this experiment (Error Elimination - Experiment 6) using PMD motions, as a failure rather due to subjective interpretation (as opposed to visual interpretation) the results led to. I could not come up with an objective criterion to explain why one would have perceived *Arundhati* as walking ahead of *Vasistha*. In addition, the results did not provide finite interval for the timing of Mahabharata War. In short, experiments performed using PMD neither defined specific time interval nor ruled out any time interval for the plausible year of Mahabharata War.

Error Elimination – Experiment 7

Some astronomers have speculated extremely slow motion of *Arundhati* around *Vasistha*. The motion suggested is indeed speculative in nature. I will name this conjecture 'motion of *Arundhati* around *Vasistha*'. If such a motion does exist, astronomers predict that it will take some 750000 years for *Arundhati* to complete one circle around *Vasistha*. If so, for certain time period during its orbit around *Vasistha*, *Arundhati* could be envisioned as walking ahead of *Vasistha*. All the problems discussed in the context of North-south movement of *Arundhati* and *Vasistha* (Error elimination - Experiment 6) also apply to this scenario, in addition to the fact that the motion of *Arundhati* around *Vasistha* remains highly speculative.

Error Elimination – Experiment 8

After my dismal failure in establishing the plausibility of '*Arundhati* walking ahead of *Vasistha*', I had to stop testing since I could not envision any new experiments to test this observation. I decided to give this subject a rest but was determined to revisit it in future. In fact the subject never left my mind however I changed the focus to other hobbies of mine. Occasionally I conducted random searches on *Arundhati/Vasistha* or looked for the latest version of astronomy software. I played a bit with Skyglobe, DOS based software program and later with 'Voyager II'. In early 2009 A.D., my interest was rejuvenated and I began exploring latest versions of astronomy software. I ran into SkyGazer 4.5™, astronomy software developed by Carina Software.

I began testing conjectures of P V Vartak on 'Fall of Abhijit' using SkyGazer 4.5™. I accepted his interpretation of *Abhijit* observation as referring to the time when *Abhijit* became a North Pole Star however I felt that his overall interpretation was inconsistent. I began experimenting with the help of Sky Gazer 4.5™. The outcome of my work on the 'Fall of Abhijit' is presented in chapter 5. I realized what a significant change in Declination of some stars (e.g. *Abhijit*) could be caused by the precession of equinoxes. I wondered what that might mean to the relative Declinations of *Arundhati* and *Vasistha*.

I devised an experiment to measure the effect on relative Declinations of these two stars, not only due to their proper motions but also due to the precession of equinoxes. I repeated experiments, carried out manually some ten years ago, using Sky Gazer 4.5™. The conclusions remained unchanged. Measurements using Sky Gazer showed that *Arundhati* and *Vasistha* would have had attained same Declination in 44320 BP, instead of my earlier crude calculations of 20200 BP.

I began measuring Declinations and Declination difference between these two stars, beginning with the present (2009 A.D.), and going back at an interval of 1000 years. I planned to carry out these measurements for the time span of one complete cycle of precession of equinoxes (26000 years) and beyond to ~44000 BP.

I defined Declination Delta (DD) as,

DD = Declination (Arundhati) – Declination (Vasistha)

I defined DD such that the formula yielded positive values for the current period (2009 A.D.) by taking into account the fact that *Arundhati* has higher declination than *Vasistha*, i.e. *Arundhati* is north of *Vasistha*. I was keenly interested in identifying year or time interval when DD had negative values between now and 44000 BP. In other words, I was looking for a possibility of *Vasistha* being north of *Arundhati* due to the effect of the precession of equinoxes. DD started declining as experiments progressed into the past, advancing with a jump of 1000 years, however only after few data points the trend reversed and DD began to increase. DD never changed from positive to negative, a scenario I was eagerly hoping for. The magnitude of 'Declination Delta' did show oscillations during simulation, nonetheless DD never turned negative.

Error Elimination – Experiment 9

It was 2 AM of Friday night, 8 May 2009 A.D., when I completed my simulations and measurements (Error elimination - Experiment 8). I was disappointed, tired, frustrated and mildly delirious. I was ready to throw the towel. I realized that I had to perform one more set of experiments, at least for the sake of completeness. I got up from my chair, prepared a large pot of strong ginger tea and sat down. At this point, I was doing it merely as an obligation, i.e. obligation to my conjecture and without expectation of any reward. I aimed to record the output and file the papers away forever, unless of course I could come up with another idea in future to test the observation.

I defined Right Ascension Delta (RAD) as,

RAD =RA (Arundhati) – RA (Vasistha)

I defined RAD in such a way so as to yield positive values for the current period (2009 A.D.). I simulated measurements for RAD, advancing with a jump of 1000 years, beginning with the present, and going backward in the past. Lady *Arundhati* was finally pleased with my efforts. As soon as I completed measurements and calculations for my 8th data point, I had found the treasure! I could not believe my eyes, my measurements, my calculations, my computer or Sky Gazer! RAD measurement had crossed the barrier Zero, and entered the territory of negative RAD! I continued my simulation and measurements in a mechanical fashion. Each new data point confirmed what I intuitively felt for 12+ years but could not confirm until this day. Yes! *Arundhati* did walk ahead of *Vasistha* in the past and had stopped walking ahead of *Vasistha* sometime after 5000 B.C. As I progressed with my experiments, I found out that *Arundhati* did stop walking ahead of *Vasistha* sometime around 13000 B.C. This meant during the recently completed cycle of the precession of equinoxes (cycle of precession with Polaris as pole star twice), *Arundhati* was walking ahead of *Vasistha* during the approximate time interval bounded by 4000 B.C. and 13000 B.C. I conjectured that the phenomena would have repeated itself during each cycle of the precession of equinoxes. I estimated such time interval for the previous cycle of the precession of equinoxes, jumped to that period (e.g. 30000 B.C. - 39000 B.C.), ran my simulation and confirmed what I had expected.

Although I could nail down neither a single year nor unique time interval for *Arundhati* walking ahead of *Vasistha*, at least I had found time interval that possibly repeated during each cycle of the precession of equinoxes, when *Arundhati* walked ahead of *Vasistha*. I called this repetitive time interval 'Epochs of *Arundhati*', when *Arundhati* walked ahead of *Vasistha*. It was 5:30 AM when I completed this experiment. I was elated, exhausted and delirious. I went to bed happy.

Next day, I got up as fast as I could. I refined my search along the lower bound of the latest 'Epoch of *Arundhati*' and found that *RAD* went from positive to negative sometime between 4380 B.C. and 4390 B.C. I inferred 4380 B.C. as the lower limit on the year of the Mahabharata War. The significance of this discovery was thrilling! This discovery meant that the Mahabharata War did not take place anytime after 4380 B.C.! The discovery carried with it a great deal of force and even if this were the only observation from the Mahabharata text I could produce, it would render the unavoidable conclusion that the Mahabharata War took place sometime before 4380 B.C.!

My work of previous night had also alluded to the fact that these 'Epochs of *Arundhati*' lasted for few thousand years during each cycle of the precession of equinoxes. Although I could state that the Mahabharata War did not take place anytime after 4380 B.C., I could not say with confidence that it indeed took place during the time interval bounded by 4380 B.C. and 13000 B.C. In principle, the Mahabharata War could have taken place during any one of the multiple 'Epochs of *Arundhati*'.

Imagine interpreting and testing 100+ astronomical observations from the Mahabharata text for multiple instances (years) within an 'Epoch of *Arundhati*' which lasted approximately nine thousand years; and here I was faced with one such time interval every twenty six thousand years! What I stumbled on was progress indeed, especially because the outcome had falsified 96+% of all existing proposals for the year of Mahabharata War. On the other hand, the plural aspect of this 'Epoch of *Arundhati*' presented enormous mental and practical roadblock in my ability to search for the year of Mahabharata War.

I began re-reading the Mahabharata text and noted down additional astronomical observations. I contacted Carina Software, makers of SkyGazer™ to find out more about the settings and assumptions behind Sky Gazer simulations. Tim DeBenedictis, an extremely knowledgeable and kind employee of Carina Software wrote back, informing me that Sky Gazer™ did not take into account 'proper motion' of stars however their professional version of the software –Voyager 4.5™ did incorporate 'proper motion' of stars.

I repeated my experiments using Voyager 4.5™ and realized that Lady (Luck) *Arundhati* had not left me yet. Epochs of *Arundhati* turned into the Epoch of *Arundhati*!

When I re-simulated RAD calculations, taking into account proper motions of stars, the length of epoch shortened. I could define the Epoch of *Arundhati* as time interval between 11091 B.C. and 4508 B.C. This is the time interval when RAD had negative values, which also meant *Arundhati* would have appeared to walk ahead of *Vasistha* during this ~6500 years time interval. This interval of 6500 years is the interval where one should search for the year of Mahabharata War. I assert that the Mahabharata War did not happen even a day late than year 4508 B.C.!

If humanity survives for another 11000 years (13000+ A.D.), it will witness another 'Epoch of *Arundhati*' however as far as the past is concerned, there was only the Epoch of *Arundhati*.

Explanation for *Arundhati* walking ahead of *Vasistha*

The placement of *Arundhati* 'west' of *Vasistha*, during the Epoch of *Arundhati* was caused by,

1. The precession of equinoxes, which result in the movement of the celestial North Pole, such that location of celestial North Pole made peculiar orientation with respect to relative positions of *Arundhati* and *Vasistha*.
2. Proper motions of *Arundhati* and *Vasistha* also contributed to changes in Right Ascension and Declination in addition to the changes in the Right Ascension and Declination measurements of *Arundhati* and *Vasistha* caused by the movement of the celestial North Pole.

Negative Value of RAD refers to the position of *Arundhati* west of *Vasistha* with respect to an observer on the Earth. In this case, an observer will perceive *Arundhati* walking ahead of *Vasistha*!

Position of the celestial North Pole moves very slowly and traces a circular trajectory, and completes a circle in about 26000 years. This movement of the celestial North Pole is due to 'the precession of equinoxes'. All the stars appear to go around the position of the celestial North Pole and the effect is pronounced for circumpolar stars. Distinct star close to the position of the celestial North Pole is designated as North Pole star for a period of time. For example Polaris is North Pole star in our times and thus we see circumpolar and near-circumpolar stars making rounds around Polaris. During the 'Epoch of *Arundhati*', position(s) of celestial North Pole and those of *Arundhati* and *Vasistha* made such a peculiar combination, where an observer on the Earth would have perceived *Arundhati* walking ahead of *Vasistha*.

Positive values of RAD refer to the position of *Arundhati* east of *Vasistha* in the sky with respect to an observer on the Earth. An observer on the Earth will perceive Arundhati walking behind *Vasistha* since the Earth rotates from west to east. This is the scenario today and had been the scenario for the extended period in the past, except during the Epoch of *Arundhati*.

Figure 4 shows values of RAD over a period of ~42000 years, beginning with the present (2010 A.D.) and going back to ~40000 B.C. The Epoch of Arundhati is shown by section of the curve when RAD is negative. This is the time interval when *Arundhati* was west of Vasistha and thus appeared to walk ahead of *Vasistha*. My proposed year for the Mahabharata War (5561 B.C. or 7571 BP) occurs close to a point when *Arundhati* was as far to the west as she could reach with respect to *Vasistha*.

Figure 5 provides visual demonstration of change in the east-west orientation of *Arundhati-Vasistha* due to the movement of North celestial Pole. Table 4 provides Delta (RAD) between Right Ascension coordinates of Arundhati (Alcor) and Vasistha (Mizar). While Figure 4 graphically depicts RAD over an extended period of 40000 years, Table 4 provides RAD values for 15000 years beginning with the present and for the entire epoch of Arundhati. I have presented multiple values around 5561 B.C. to emphasize that Arundhati's position was ahead of Vasistha, as far as she could go, during the Mahabharata War.

I would encourage readers to run their own simulation to validate my findings. The Epoch of Arundhati began when the Celestial North Pole was near Star HR6767 (Magnitude 6.37) in Hercules constellation (11091 B.C.) and lasted for ~6500 years (until 4508 B.C.) when the Celestial North Pole was near Star HR 133666 (Magnitude 6.85). Celestial North Pole was close to Star HR 5715 at the time of Mahabharata War. I have provided the nomenclature and magnitudes of pole stars only as a reference and to aid readers in their simulation.

Revisiting interpretation of R N Iyengar

Before I conclude, I want to go back to the ingenious work of R N Iyengar. He combined portions of two couplets, one from Bhishma[1] *Adhyaya* 2 and another from Bhishma[14] *Adhyaya* 3. I consider such combination neither required nor justified. For fun and only as hypothetical exercise, I want the reader to recall it and apply it to my results.

Arundhati, who was otherwise always walking behind *Vasistha*, began walking ahead of *Vasistha*, during the Mahabharata War and during the time interval defined by the 'Epoch of *Arundhati*'. I could imagine an observer in Mahabharata times, interpreting the phenomenon described by 'ingenious combination' of R N Iyengar. I have borrowed his combination but not his explanation for my hypothetical exercise, on the part of an observer in Mahabharata times. An observer, noticing *Arundhati* walking ahead of *Vasistha* (who otherwise was walking behind *Vasistha*) may visualize the celestial North Pole (and North Pole star if there was one available) blazing and fiercely moving in reverse direction, as an explanation for the miraculous walking of *Arundhati* ahead of *Vasistha*!

My interpretation of the synthetic couplet of R N Iyengar is a hypothetical exercise and not to be taken seriously. My interpretation of his synthetic couplet corroborates well with my explanation of *Arundhati* observation, however neither my usage of his couplet nor his combining of couplet is rational and justified.

R N Iyengar has done admirable job of identifying numerous astronomy observations from ancient Indian literature.

Implications: The Epoch of *Arundhati*

I enumerate implications of the discovery of 'the Epoch of Arundhati' less the significance is lost,

(1) The observation corroborates my theory of 'visual observations of the sky'

(2) Testing of *Arundhati* observation and its corroboration leads to the prediction of time interval for the year of Mahabharata War, 11091 B.C. – 4508 B.C.

(3) This is an illustration of the validity of *'Shabda Pramana –* Verbal Testimony' corroborated by *'Pratyaksha Pramana –* Empirical Proof'

(4) This is the first time an astronomical observation and its testing resulted in prediction of time interval, clearly bound on both sides for the plausible year of Mahabharata War

(5) *Arundhati* observation and my explanation of it falsified 96%+ (121 out of 125) of all previously proposed years for the Mahabharata War

(6) Anyone claiming a year for the Mahabharata war that falls after 4508 B.C. (or before 11091 B.C.) has onus to explain how *'Arundhati'* observation corroborates with one's proposed timeline

(7) *Arundhati* observation asserts the date for Ramayana and Vedas to be before 4500 B.C., in further (and unknown) antiquity, since Ramayana is before Mahabharata, and Vedas even before Ramayana

(8) Mahabharata states that Vyasa expanded the Vedas, hence his name – Vyasa[5]. Assuming current version of Vedas to be the one edited, expanded/recasted by Vyasa, the Vedas we know today are at least older than 4500 B.C.

(9) *Arundhati* observation provides corroborative support for the ancient tradition of meticulous astronomy observations, as inferred by 'Fall of *Abhijit'*. Mahabharata author is implying his awareness of the time when *Arundhati* was NOT walking ahead of *Vasistha*. The timing of such observation could not have been after 11000 B.C., rather long before 11000 B.C.

(10) If I were allowed to research only one Mahabharata observation, I would have considered myself lucky to research on

'*Arundhati*' observation. I was lucky in that I happen to stumble on *Arundhati* observation and, fortunately, not let it go for 15+ years.

Significant advances in our knowledge have occurred due to falsification of an existing theory rather than due to identification of additional corroborative evidence. While one may desire (or demand) observations and/or experiments that lead to falsification of a theory, one definitely needs appropriate tools, background knowledge, little ingenuity and lots of luck to stumble on such findings. Ptolemy's theory of epicycles survived for 1500 years, and while Copernicus could raise valid doubts about Ptolemy's theory, Copernicus was still forced to employ assumptions of 'epicycles' and 'uniform circular motion'. Both of these assumptions did not go away until Kepler falsified assumption of circular orbits of planets. Kepler's work falsified Ptolemy's theory and became the basis for dramatic growth of knowledge in Cosmology.

My demystification of *Arundhati* observation instantaneously falsified 96% of all proposals (121 out of 125) for the year of the Mahabharata War. All past proposals for the year of Mahabharata War, where proposed year falls after 4508 B.C., are instantaneously falsified by *Arundhati* observation. The fate of all future proposals would be similar to those of the past, if the year proposed is after 4508 B.C.

The reader may consider such claim audacious and I am in 100% agreement. In fact I define The Epoch of *Arundhati* as the only time interval within which the Mahabharata War took place and compare its importance with discoveries of Copernicus (geocentric to heliocentric), Kepler (circular to elliptical orbits) or Galileo (celestial = terrestrial).

71

7

The Planets Were Aligned
Searching for the Year of Mahabharata War

Facts which at first seem improbable will, even on scant explanation, drop the cloak which has hidden them and stand forth in naked and simple beauty.

- Galileo Galilei

After the success of *Arundhati* observation, I began to learn *nakshatras* and their corresponding stars/asterisms. I came across a paper by BNN Achar, which listed Indian *nakshatras* along with corresponding stars or asterisms. My work on the 'The Epoch of *Arundhati*' and 'Fall of Abhijit' had made me aware of not only the motions and the positions of stars with respect to the celestial North Pole, but also the movement of the solstices and equinoxes, caused by the precession of equinoxes, through the *nakshatras*.

Searching for the Year of Mahabharata War

Searching for the year of Mahabharata War was indeed identical to searching for the needle in a haystack. *Arundhati* observation

72

significantly reduced the quantity of haystack nonetheless the iso-lated quantity of haystack was still large. My task was to identify the year of Mahabharata War from the time interval of 6500 years, which is what I termed the Epoch of Arundhati.

I had collected, by this time, numerous observations of pla-nets from the Mahabharata text. Mercury, Venus, Mars, Jupiter and Saturn are mentioned explicitly among planetary observations. Sa-turn and Jupiter are the slower moving planets of these five planets. I built my search strategy using Mahabharata descriptions for the posi-tions of Saturn and Jupiter, a strategy to explore the Epoch of Arundhati looking for a probable year of the Mahabharata War. For example, the Mahabharata text states that Jupiter and Saturn were settled near Vishakha for a year and dimmed the brightness of Sap-tarshis[6]. Position of Vishakha is next to Swati and Swati was understood to be in the vicinity of Saptarshi by Mahabharata astro-nomers[7]. Saturn was afflicting (pidayati) Rohini around the time of War [8, 9]. Saturn is also described as afflicting (akramya) Uttara Phal-guni (Bhaga) [10]. Jupiter is described as going vakri near Shravana[11]. Final mention of Jupiter occurs after the death of Karna, when Jupiter began afflicting (sampra-pidya) Rohini, similar to the Sun and the Moon, after the sunset on the 17th day of War[12].

Jupiter has orbital period of 11.86 (~ 12) years and Saturn has orbital period of 29.42 (~ 30) years. Jupiter and Saturn combination and their positions, whatever they might be, provide a periodic inter-val of ~ 60 years (12 x 5 = 30 x 2 =60), when both of them would be approximately in similar combination, i.e. combination that would corroborate descriptions of their positions as stated in the Mahabha-rata text. Search for such Saturn/Jupiter combinations within The Epoch of Arundhati, spanning 6500 years (11000 B.C. − 4500 B.C.), resulted in ~ 110 instances for the plausible year of Mahabharata War (6500/60 ~ 110). I was gung ho on using information related to posi-tions of Mars, Venus & Mercury, as described in the Mahabharata text, to narrow down the timing of Mahabharata War from these ~110 possibilities.

When I re-read Vartak's Swayambhu, I realized that the prob-able instances for the Mahabharata War, to be tested within the Epoch of Arundhati, can be reduced to less than 40, when one takes into account orbital period of Rahu (one of the two nodes due to in-tersection of moon's orbital path with the ecliptic). Orbital period of

Rahu is ~18 years (or 9 years considering two nodes) and thus periodic interval for testing a year, for the Mahabharata War, increased from 60 to 180 years (12 x 15 = 30 x 6 = 9 x 20 = 180). The calculations are approximate and one has to search +/- 3 years in the vicinity of a probable year, estimated using interval of 180 years. This was an afterthought and I mention it only as a useful tip for future researchers who might be interested in exploring the year of Mahabharata War either within the Epoch of *Arundhati* or otherwise.

Later on, as my work progressed (Chapter 9), observations related to *Bhishma Nirvana* allowed me to define a 3000 year time interval for the plausible year of Mahabharata War (3500 B.C. through 6500 B.C.) and combining this knowledge with the Epoch of *Arundhati* provided a compact time interval of 2000 years (4500 B.C. - 6500 B.C.) for the plausible year of Mahabharata War. Nonetheless at the time, I was not aware of these additional observations of *Bhishma Nirvana* and their consequences for the plausible year of Mahabharata War.

Mars is described as traveling through space of 13 *nakshatras* beginning with *Magha* and ending with *Shravana/Abhijit*. Mars has orbital period of 686.93 days (~1.88 years) and this means the Mahabharata text has recorded observations of Mars for a period of more than one year. Mars went *vakri* near *Magha*[11] and then settled between *Chitra* and *Swati*, while shining brightly, and was seen going in abnormal (*apasavya*) direction[14]. Mars was seen afflicting *Chitra*[13]. Mars went *vakri* near *Jyeshtha* while pleading for friendship with *Anuradha*[13]. After completing this *vakra-anuvakra* journey, the red planet approached bright *Shravana* and settled along *Brahmarashi* (*Abhijit*)[14].

Venus and Mercury are seen before the sunrise or immediately after the sunset. Venus is easier of the two to observe. Mercury is described as moving through all the nakshatras[15] and the observation does not provide any useful information except perhaps additional corroborative support for the duration of Mahabharata observations (more than one year). This is because Mercury will indeed take around a year's time to go through all *nakshatras*. Mercury is described as rising '*Tiryak*' (unusual, oblique or unnatural) in the sky after the sunset on the 17th day of War[16]. Mercury is also described as seen in the western part of the sky, along with Mars and Venus, on the 18th and the last day of War[17]. Venus is described as

74

making a *'parikrama'* (moving in a close loop) by turning north near *Purva Bhadrapada*, and in the presence of another planet[18].

Three planets with no clear identification are also described. *'Shweta'* planet settled near *Chitra*[19], *'Shyama'* planet appeared fiery and smoky and was shining brightly while settled near *Jyeshtha*[20] and *Tivra* planet and/or *nakshatra* was in the vicinity of *Krittika*[21]. Great comet[22] and/or spread of great comet[21] settled near *Pushya*. Seven planets were seen along with the Moon during the evening/night on the 14th day of War[23]. Seven planets were also seen near the Sun on the first day of War[24]. Seven planets were seen going away from the Sun on the 17th day of War[25]. The Sun and the Moon together, afflicted *Rohini* on the first day of War[26].

The Mahabharata text also records observations of eclipses and are useful in narrowing down search for the year of Mahabharata War, when combined with numerous observations of planets. Marks on the moon were covered [9, 27] and *Rahu* was approaching the Sun [19, 27]. *Rahu* approaching the Sun is indicative of solar eclipse in the near future. The full moon of *Kartika* was devoid of effulgence; the moon appeared coppery red and so did rest of the sky[28]. The Mahabharata text refers to pair of eclipses, solar and lunar, separated by only 13 days[29]. The conversation between Vyasa and Dhritarashtra occurred one day before the War, based on the observation that showers of blood (water) and flesh (hail) occurred on the 14th day of 'Krishna Paksha'[30]. Thus there are total of 27 observations related to eclipses and positions of planets around the time of Mahabharata War.

I agree with the hypothesis of P V Kane that Mahabharata author had, at his disposal, multiple sets of astronomical observations, more likely prepared by multiple observers around the time of Mahabharata War. Usefulness of this hypothesis can be judged by its ability to make sense of available astronomical data. This hypothesis explains multiple descriptions of the positions of planets, however, with different twists/analogies as well as different time durations for each set of observations. For example, while astronomical observations of Udyoga *Parva* are made over a relatively shorter period of time (8 months), those of *Bhishma* are made over an extended period of time (~ 30 months), before and after the War.

I grouped multiple references of same phenomenon, e.g. Saturn afflicting Rohini, comet in the vicinity of Pushya, Marks on the moon getting covered or Mars afflicting Chitra. The summary of planetary observations is as follows,

1. Saturn near *Vishakha* for a year (along with Jupiter) [6]
2. Saturn near *Uttara Phalguni* [10]
3. Saturn afflicts *Rohini* [8, 9]
4. Jupiter near *Vishakha* for a year (along with Saturn) [6]
5. Jupiter goes *Vakri* near *Shravana*[11]
6. Jupiter afflicts *Rohini*, after the sunset on the 17th day of War, similar to the Sun and the Moon[12] (i.e. as the Sun and the Moon were afflicting *Rohini*, on the first day of War[23])
7. Mars goes *vakri* near *Magha* [11]
8. Mars goes *vakri* near *Jyeshtha/Anuradha*[13]
9. Mars traveling in *apasavya* (reverse, unnatural) direction by becoming steady between *Chitra* and *Swati*, while shining brightly with fearful and cruel appearance [14]
10. Mars afflicts *Chitra*[13]
11. Mars heading straight to *Shravana/Abhijit* region[14]
12. Mercury traveling through all *nakshatras*[15]
13. Mercury seen rising '*Tiryak*' (oblique, unnatural, unusual) after the sunset on the 17th day of War[16]
14. Venus (*Bhrugusoon*), Mercury (*Shashijen*) and Mars (*Dharaputra*) seen in the western part of the sky, at the end of 18th day of War [17]
15. Venus making a *parikrama* (around another planet) while turning north near *Purva Bhadrapada*, in the company of another planet [18]
16. '*Shweta*' (or *Budha*) planet settled near *Chitra* [19]
17. '*Shyama*' (or *Shweta*) planet shining brightly and settled near Jyeshtha [20]
18. '*Tivra*' planet and/or *nakshatra* in the vicinity of *Krittika* [21]
19. Great comet and/or spread of great comet settled near *Pushya* [21, 22]
20. Seven planets seen along with the Moon in the sky – the evening/night of the 14th day of War [23]
21. Seven Planets seen near the Sun (first day of the War) [24]
22. Seven Planets seen going away from the Sun (17th day of the War) [25]

23. The Sun and the Moon, together afflicts *Rohini* (on the first day of War) [26]
24. Moon's mark was covered and *Rahu* was approaching the Sun [9, 19, 27]
25. The full moon of *Kartika* was devoid of effulgence. The moon appeared coppery red and so did rest of the sky [28]
26. Two eclipses (solar & lunar) within an interval of 13 days [29]
27. Up to 3 eclipses – 2 lunar and one solar based on reference to 14th day of Krishna *Paksha* (of *Kartika*) [28, 29]

Dynamic Visual Astronomy – DVA™

I found it exhausting to test 27 observations for each plausible year (of the Mahabharata War) from 110 instances. My challenge involved testing each of these 27 observations using Voyager 4.5™. The testing was tiresome, as tiresome as *'samudramanthan'* might have been however I was rewarded with at least one precious gem.

I invented a technique – Dynamic Visual Astronomy, DVA™, while trying to make sense of Mahabharata observations of Mars. DVA™ is a simple technique and although I am claiming myself as its innovator in the context of Mahabharata research, all credit goes to the team at Carina Software who designed and developed Voyager 4.5™. DVA™ involves simulating movement of the object of interest, as seen from a specific location on the Earth, and is far superior to observing or analyzing static images of the sky. The object of interest could be a planet, a comet, the Sun, the Moon or a *nakshatra*. Estimating optimum time interval between adjacent static images is critical to the success of DVA™, and the desired time interval depends on the objective of the search.

DVA™ was of immense help in understanding Mahabharata descriptions of Mars and I applied the technique in understanding and/or corroborating other Mahabharata observations as well. DVA™ was critical to my understanding of Mahabharata observations of Venus and of comet (*Dhumaketu*). I utilized DVA™ to explain 'Fall of *Abhijit*', 'The Epoch of *Arundhati*', 'Jupiter & Saturn near *Vishakha* and journey of Mars through 13 *nakshatras* during the time of Mahabharata War.

I was curious to find out interpretations of other researchers for these 27 observations. I began my search for the year of Mahabharata War with criticism of the works of other researchers. Fortunately the process was not as excruciating as it might appear. When I solved the mystery of *Arundhati*, the solution led to a time interval, bounded on both sides, for the year of Mahabharata War. The 'Epoch of *Arundhati*' made my search easier.

I am humbled by this realization and would assert that while one holds the key to creative imagination, one only has to depend on 'luck' for successful creative imagination. Had I began researching with some other Mahabharata observation, I only wonder where I would have landed! I found that only 4 out of 20 researchers had proposed year of the Mahabharata War that fell within the 'Epoch of *Arundhati*'. Modak proposed 5000 B.C. and Dikshit proposed 7300 B.C. Both dates were proposed as an approximate time period rather than a specific day or year, and for this reason I decided to eliminate them from further testing. Lele proposed 5228 B.C. and Vartak proposed 5561 B.C.

I developed critical tests to see if Mahabharata observations corroborated the timing proposed by either Lele or Vartak. I tested observations of the Mahabharata text using DVA™ and Voyager 4.5™ for the year 5228 B.C. and could immediately eliminate this year as a possible year of the Mahabharata War. On the other hand, year 5561 B.C., proposed by P V Vartak, proved resistant to my falsification attempts. Specifically Mahabharata observations of Saturn afflicting *Bhaga*, Jupiter & Saturn near *Vishakha*, Saturn afflicting *Rohini* and Jupiter afflicting *Rohini* on 17th day of the War and their corroboration for the year 5561 B.C. was promising. While the timing proposed by Vartak was promising, all of his explanations of astronomy observations were not. I began testing of his proposed day and year of the War by simulating the positions of various planets on the first day of Mahabharata War.

Vartak proposed 16 October 5561 B.C. as the first day of Mahabharata War. While I accepted the first day of Mahabharata War proposed by Vartak, I have not accepted his proposed positions of planets for that day.

The view of the sky on 16 October 5561 B.C., simulated using Voyager 4.5™, shows Saturn near *Chitra*, Jupiter near *Shravana*, Mars, Venus and Uranus near *Dhanishtha*, Neptune near *Purva Bhadrapada*, Pluto near *Krittika/Rohini*, Mercury near *UttaraAshadha*, the Sun and the Moon near *PurvaAshadha/Mula*.

Error Elimination – Experiment 10

Jupiter & Saturn near *Vishakha* [6]

My first simulation begins on 16 October 5562 B.C., one year before the first day of Mahabharata War. Jupiter is near *Mula* (Shaula) and Saturn is near *Hasta* (Algorab), positions nearly equidistant, in *nakshatra* space, east and west of *Vishakha* (Zubeneschamali), respectively. I employed DVA™ technique with *Vishakha* at the center, and simulated the sky view with single day as a step change, for a year, until 16 October 5561 B.C., the first day of War. Jupiter stayed in the region of *Mula-UttaraAshadha*, Saturn stayed in the region of *Chitra-Uttara Phalguni*. I treated this as satisfactory corroboration of this Mahabharata observation[6]. I may mention that this was merely a verification of Vartak's explanation.

Error Elimination – Experiment 11

Saturn near *Bhaga* (*Uttara Phalguni*) [10]

Voyager simulation shows that Saturn is near *Bhaga* (*Uttara Phalguni*) for a period of more than two years leading to the first day of Mahabharata War, when it began approaching *Chitra*.

Error Elimination – Experiment 12

Mercury traveling through all *nakshatras*[15]

Mercury traveling through all the *nakshatras* over a period of one year is a trivially true observation and no verification is required[15]. The observation certainly corroborates my conjecture for the time interval over which astronomy observations were made during, before and after the Mahabharata War.

Some versions of the Mahabharata text are interpreted to suggest that Mercury was located in the space of 3 previous (previous to the position of the Sun) *nakshatras*. Mahabharata researchers have interpreted such reference in multiple fashion and such interpretations have caused lot of unnecessary confusion. Only Vartak has attempted, albeit unsuccessfully, an explanation.

Error Elimination – Experiment 13

Mars through *Magha, Chitra/Swati, Jyeshtha/Anuradha* & *Shravana/Abhijit* [11, 13, 14]

Observations of Mars are the most intriguing. Mars is described as,

1. Going *vakri* near *Magha*
2. Afflicting *Chitra*
3. Becoming steady, while moving in reverse (*apasavya*) direction between *Chitra* and *Swati*
4. Going *vakri*, again, near *Jyeshtha/Anuradha*
5. Heading straight (after traveling *vakri-anuvakri*) to *Shravana/Abhijit*.

This journey of Mars through 13 *nakshatras* amounts to a time period of, per my crude calculations, approximately one year. Modern Indian astronomy/astrology interprets *'vakri'* in the sense of 'retrograde' motion and thus I was looking for the evidence of retrograde Mars near *Magha* and near *Jyeshtha/Anuradha*. I observed neither.

I began researching 'retrograde' motions of Mars, since *'vakri'* is translated as 'retrograde' in modern Indian Astronomy and astrology. All Mahabharata researchers have interpreted *'vakri'* in the sense of 'retrograde'. I found it curious and perplexing to read Mars going *vakri* near *Magha*[11] and again going *vakri* near *Jyeshtha/Anuradha*, especially because Mars goes retrograde only once in two years. I conjectured that *'vakri'* meant something different if Mars was doing 'it' twice within a span of 6-7 *nakshatras*, i.e. between *Magha* and *Jyeshtha/Anuradha*. Mars stays in one *nakshatra* for approximately twenty days and thus the time interval between *'vakri'* motions of Mars, per the Mahabharata text, was only about four months (20 x 6 = 120 days ~ 4 months).

I hypothesized that *'vakri'* meant something else, instead of 'retrograde' motion, however I could not think of what that would be. DVA[TM] came to my rescue. I simulated journey of Mars through *nakshatra* space beginning with few *nakshatras* before *Magha* and

80

ending with the first day of War. I felt confident that I had truly discovered the meaning of 'vakri' as intended by Mahabharata author.

As simulation progressed, Mars began crossing the ecliptic and was clearly on the other side (north) of the ecliptic when it reached Magha[11], it traveled straight passing Chitra on its way to the region of Swati when it turned back and approached Chitra for the second time, and after spending ~ 6 months in the region of Chitra/Swati, traveled east [13, 14]. Mars began crossing the ecliptic again, was on the other side (south) of the ecliptic near Anuradha, traveled towards Jyeshtha[13] and then straight to Shravana and settled along Brahmarashi (Abhijit) by the first day of War[14].

Past researchers were deceived in their interpretations mainly because they, uncritically I think, stuck to interpretations of pervious commentators of Mahabharata. No wonder straightforward references to Mars deceived them.

I interpreted Brahmarashi as referring to Abhijit since Brahma is the nakshatra-deity of Abhijit. My interpretation of Brahmarashi as referring to Abhijit (Vega), and position of Mars along Brahmarashi (Abhijit) can be further corroborated by RA coordinates of Shravana, Abhijit, Dhanishtha and Mars on the first day of War.

	RA
Shravana	13h, 48 min
Mars	14h, 21 min
Abhijit	14h, 32 min
Dhanishtha	14h, 52 min

Description of the motions and the positions of Mars make it ample clear that Mahabharata astronomers referred to oblique crossing of the ecliptic by a planet as 'vakri' motion while the true retrograde motion of a planet was described as being steady (dhruva or sthayi), or traveling in reverse (apasavya) direction.

There is indeed something intriguing about Mars. Small discrepancy (between prediction and actual observation) in the measurement of Mars led Kepler to his marvelous theory of elliptical orbits of planets. Intriguing descriptions of Mars in the Mahabharata text and my explanation provide high degree of corroboration to the proposed year of 5561 B.C.

Error Elimination – Experiment 14

Jupiter going *vakri* near *Shravana*[11]

I translated observation[11] of Mars and Jupiter as 'Mars goes *vakri* near *Magha* <u>while Jupiter (goes *vakri*) near *Shravana*</u>'. All researchers including Vartak translated the same observation as 'Mars goes *vakri* near *Magha* <u>and Jupiter is in *Shravana*</u>'. I did not agree with their translation however I neither knew what '*vakri*' meant nor could I verify retrograde motion of Mars near *Magha*. On the other hand Jupiter was near *Shravana* during the time of War and thus accepted, albeit tentatively, Vartak's translation.

When I realized the significance of '*vakri*' as demonstrated by the simulation of the motions of Mars, observation of 'Jupiter traveling *vakri* near *Shravana*' presented itself as 'falsification test' for my interpretation of '*Vakri*' motion. DVA^{TM} simulation of Jupiter corroborated '*vakri*' motion of Jupiter as it traveled obliquely across the ecliptic near *Shravana*[11]. Figure 9 and Table 7 provide additional details related to *vakri* motion of Jupiter near *Shravana*.

Error Elimination – Experiment 15

Venus near *Purva Bhadrapada*[18]

Venus was between *Dhanishtha* and *Shravana* on the first day of the War. I wondered why Venus in *Purva-Bhadrapada* was mentioned in the context of the Mahabharata War. There was no need to guess though, not when you have DVA^{TM} and Voyager 4.5^{TM}! I simulated Venus journey beginning with the first day of War. Venus turned north and began '*parikrama*' (circular journey) around Neptune, near *Purva Bhadrapada*. Venus turned north and then west, as far as *Shatabhisaj* (Sadalmelik) before turning east. The simulation corroborated Venus turning north as if to do *parikrama* (around Neptune) near *Purva Bhadrapada*.

While retrograde motion of Venus is described as 'Venus making a *parikrama* by turning north', those of Jupiter and Saturn are described as being steady (*Stayi*) for a year. Retrograde motion of Mars is described moving in abnormal (*apasavya*) direction while burning brightly.

82

Error Elimination – Experiment 16

Tivra or *Tikshna*, Planet or *nakshatra* near *Krittika*[21]

The Mahabharata text has 3 planetary observations where planets are simply listed as *'Shyama'*[20], *Shweta*[19], *'Tivra'* or *'Tikshna'*[21]. Such generic names can provide open field for researchers. Researchers can imagine these planets to be planets that suit their fancy but more likely those that suit their timeline.

Mahabharata observation of a *'Tikshna'* or *'Tivra'* planet near *Krittika* was intriguing[21]. It was intriguing because Mahabharata author referred to the planet as both *'graha'* (planet) and *'nakshatra'*. Vartak has interpreted this observation, correctly I think, as referring to Pluto. *'Nakshatra'* literally refers to one that does not move however Mahabharata author referring to a *'nakshatra'* with respect to *Krittika*, another *nakshatra*, was the intriguing part! Vartak inferred that the word *'nakshatra'* might have been used to mean 'extremely slow moving planet'. He did his calculations assuming this *'Tivra'* or *'Tikshna'* planet/*nakshatra* to be Pluto and corroborated his hunch.

My task was then simply to re-confirm what Vartak has already figured out. Pluto is seen between *Rohini* and *Krittika*, rather closer to *Rohini* on the first day of War. This is sufficient corroboration of this Mahabharata observation[21]. I want to bring it to the attention of the reader that the Mahabharata text has observations made over an extended period of time around the Mahabharata War. Pluto was between *Rohini* and *Krittika* during its retrograde motion as well as prior to reaching *Rohini*. This observation demands telescopic ability, i.e. access to such instruments in Mahabharata times. This ability is also required to explain few other Mahabharata observations.

Error Elimination – Experiment 17

The Sun and the Moon together afflicting *Rohini*[26]

The Mahabharata observation states that the Sun and the Moon, together, were seen afflicting *Rohini*[26]. Vartak assumed this observation to be on the first day of War. Since he conjectured this day to be *Amawasya*, he interpreted the observation where the Sun and the Moon together, as is the case on *Amawasya* day, afflicted *Rohini*. He interprets this observation astrologically since he states that the Sun and the Moon near *Jyeshtha* can afflict *Rohini* with 7th *Drishti*.

Voyager 4.5™ shows that, as the Sun and the Moon, together, were setting on the western horizon, *Rohini* was rising on the eastern horizon. I conjectured that Mahabharata author visualized the Sun and the Moon together, on the *Amawasya* day, afflicting *Rohini* with their rays. I assert this observation to be a visual observation of the sky, at the time of sunset, on the first day of War. Vartak provided me a reasonable assumption for the timing of this observation and my conjecture allowed me to explain two other Mahabharata observations [8, 9, 12].

Error Elimination – Experiment 18

Jupiter, similar to the Sun and the Moon, afflicting *Rohini* after the sunset on the 17th day of War[12]

Arjuna killed Karna on the 17th day of War and in describing situation of the battlefield; Mahabharata observation states that after the sunset, Jupiter became bright and began afflicting *Rohini*, similar to the Sun and the Moon[12].

After sunset, on the 17th day of War, Jupiter was on the western horizon, same position occupied by the Sun and the Moon on the first day of War while afflicting rising *Rohini* on the opposite (east) horizon. The Sun and the Moon were not together on the 17th day of War and thus I assert that Mahabharata reference of 'similar to the Sun and the Moon' is referring to the observation of first day of War[26], when they were afflicting *Rohini*.

Vartak, Kane and Iyengar have acknowledged this Mahabharata observation, but have not corroborated it for their proposed timeline, while all other researchers have simply ignored it as if it did not exist.

Vartak did explain this observation as 'exaggerated descriptions' by Mahabharata author, in describing impossible things (e.g. death of Karna). His explanation made his theory irrefutable and therefore non-testable and thus un-scientific. It is still unclear to me why Vartak missed correct interpretation of this observation.

Error Elimination – Experiment 19

Saturn afflicts *Rohini* [8, 9]

Vartak explains this observation in two ways. First he uses his theory of Sayan-Nirayan method and claims that Saturn in Nirayan *'Uttara Phalguni'* is same as Sayan *'Rohini'* and interestingly offers alternate and second explanation of Saturn afflicting *Rohini* through a phenomenon known as *'Rohini-Shakat Bheda'*. I consider both explanations utterly unsatisfactory. Vartak had anticipated simple and consistent explanation for *Rohini*- Jupiter[12], and *Rohini*-Saturn [8, 9] observations, when he explained the Sun and the Moon, together, afflicting *Rohini* on the first day of War[26] however he missed on both counts. I already explained one of these two observations anticipated by him, i.e., Jupiter, similar to the Sun and the Moon, afflicting *Rohini*[12]. It is easy to understand Mahabharata observation(s) of Saturn [8, 9] in the light of explanation of *Rohini* afflicted by the Sun and the Moon on the first day of War and again by Jupiter on the 17th day of War.

Vyasa was observing the sky not only after sunset but also before dawn[31], and what he would have seen at dawn, days before the War, is *Rohini* on the western horizon and Saturn being the only other planet in the eastern part of the sky. This observation is then described as Saturn afflicting *Rohini* [8, 9]. The scene could also be imagined as *'Yuddha'* or *'Bheda'* between *Rohini* & Saturn, *Rohini* & Jupiter, *Rohini* & the Sun/Moon', and the alternate reading of Mahabharata verse (critical edition) in the context of 'Saturn afflicting *Rohini*' as *'Akashe Rohini bhettum'* is thus significant.

Error Elimination – Experiment 20

Unusual (*Tiryak*) rising of Mercury on the 17th day of War (after the sunset) [16]

I would be willing to assert that most readers have not seen the planet Mercury, at least knowingly. Mercury is plenty bright, brighter than *Abhijit* (Vega) or Saturn. Difficulty of observing Mercury is due to its elusiveness. Mercury orbits so close to the Sun that even when the Earth and Mercury are ideally aligned in their orbits and

Mercury is at aphelion, Mercury is still never more than ~ 27^0 from the Sun. This means observing Mercury is confined to a narrow band of dawn and twilight hours when the glare of the rising or setting sun inevitably interferes with observation. Mercury orbits the Sun in ~88 days, which means its position in the sky shift rapidly and thus a favorable window of time to observe Mercury does not last long.

I was pleasantly surprised to note two distinct observations of Mercury in the Mahabharata text. Both observations occur at the tail end of War, i.e. the 17th and 18th day of War and provide 'falsifying tests' of higher degree. Mercury is described as rising in an unusual, oblique or abnormal fashion (*Tiryak*) after the sunset on the 17th day of War [16]. The observation requires that the position of Mercury is east of the Sun and have enough separation from the Sun in order for Mercury to be visible, in spite of the glare of the setting Sun.

Voyager simulation shows position of Mercury, on the first day of the War, to the east of the Sun and separation of 8.4^0 between them. This separation continued to increase and reached 16.2^0 on the 17th day of War. An observer, observing western horizon every day, during the Mahabharata War, at sunset, would have observed Mercury as if rising from the west due to Mercury attaining higher altitude each passing day. This is then the explanation for the unusual or abnormal (*Tiryak*) rising of Mecury[16].

Error Elimination – Experiment 21

Mars, Venus & Mercury in the western part of sky[17]
After sunset, 18th day of the War

Mars, Venus and Mercury appeared behind the Pandavas on the 18th day of War[17]. The Pandava army had taken position to the west of the Kaurava army[32] and thus when the War took place, the Pandava army was facing eastward[33]. The observation is thus describing the positions of planets – Mars, Venus and Mercury in the western part of the sky.

Voyager simulation confirmed positions of these planets in the western part of the sky after sunset. The separation angles between planets and the Sun were 46.6^0, 43.1^0 and 16.5^0 for Mars, Venus and Mercury respectively. Reader should note that visible area of the sky at any given time corresponds to 180^0.

Error Elimination – Experiment 22

Seven planets seen near the Sun[24]
(First day of the War)

Seven planets were seen near the Sun[24]. I assert that the observation belongs to the first day of War. Initially, I was not sure whether the observation referred to the factual information that there were seven planets in the sky along with the Sun or that these seven planets were *seen* along with the Sun in the sky.

I speculate that the planets were seen along with the Sun, during the solar eclipse, on the first day of War. Whether they were seen or not, Voyager does confirm presence of seven planets from east to west: Neptune, Uranus, Mars, Venus, Jupiter, Mercury and Saturn. Positions of all planets, with respect to the position of the Sun, were to the east, only with the exception of Saturn which was to the west of the Sun.

Error Elimination – Experiment 23

Seven planets seen attacking the Moon[23]
(Evening/night – 14th day of the War)

Observation refers to seven planets attacking the Moon[23] and employs this analogy to describe the war scene of seven Kaurava brothers attacking Bhima. The observation is of the evening/night sky on the 14th day of War. Voyager simulation shows the full Moon rising in the east and seven planets lined up to attack the Moon, from east to west: Pluto, Neptune, Mars, Venus, Uranus, Mercury and Jupiter.

Error Elimination – Experiment 24

Seven planets going away from the Sun[25]
(17th day of the War)

Seven planets were seen going away from the Sun on the 17th day of War[25]. While it is possible that the planets might have been seen along with the Sun during the eclipse on the first day of War, the planets could be seen only before sunrise or after sunset on the 17th day of War. Voyager simulation of the first day of the sky showed six planets to the east of the Sun and one planet (Saturn) to the west. The Sun and the Moon, of course, were together on the first day of War due to solar eclipse/*Amawasya*. Voyager simulation shows seven planets, after the sunset, on the 17th day of War. They were, from east: Pluto, Neptune, Mars, Venus, Mercury and Jupiter.

The fact that seven planets could be seen in the sky immediately after the sunset is sufficient corroboration for this Mahabharata observation[25], however I would like to add that the statement 'going away from the Sun' might refer to the fact that these seven planets were moving to the <u>east</u>, i.e. away from the Sun, unless of course any one of them were in retrograde motion.

Voyager simulation showed that all planets were going away from (towards east) the Sun, with the exception of Pluto. Pluto was retrograde. The reader may keep in mind that movement of Pluto is extremely slow, whether normal or retrograde, and will appear practically stationary over a short period of time.

Error Elimination – Experiment 25

Brightly Shining Comets (!) in the Sky

Jupiter, Saturn and Mars are described as shining brightly. While Jupiter and Saturn[6] are described with an adjective '*Prajwalita*', Mars[14] is described with an adjective '*Prajwalita ghora*'. *Shyama*[20] planet is also described with an adjective '*Prajwalita*'. I could not identify this '*Shyama*' planet based on its generic identification '*Shyama*' and its position near *Jyeshtha*[20] (Error Elimination - Experiment 26).

Three planets (Jupiter, Saturn & Mars) are bright, distinct and easy to spot in the sky and as a result I did not pay much attention to their adjectives with respect to specific Mahabharata observations until I came across an interesting hypothesis (by BNN Achar and also by Mohan Gupta) that these Mahabharata observations were referring to comets! Rational criticism of the works of other researchers, including Achar and Gupta, would fill another book and thus I will limit my discussion to their specific claim of these observations being that of comets. While Achar treats all observations of 3rd *Adhyaya* of

Bhishma *Parva* as either observations of comets or purely poetic imagination in describing horrifying situation before the impending War, Gupta treats all observations of planets from this *Adhyaya* as comets.

I want to emphasize that scientific criticism does not (and should not) try to show that the theory in question has not been proved or demonstrated. It does not try to show that theory in question has not been established or justified. In short, scientific criticism does not attack the arguments, which might be used to establish, or even support the theory under examination. Scientific criticism attacks the theory itself, i.e. solution of the problem it tries to solve. It examines and challenges consequences of the theory, its explanatory power, its consistency, and its compatibility with other theories.

My point is that while theory for identification of Jupiter, Saturn, Mars and all other planets described in *Adhyaya* 3 of Bhishma *Parva* with that of comets (as proposed by Achar or Gupta) may sound bizarre, one should not consider anything objectionable in such a theory. After all theories of Aristarchus, Copernicus, Galileo, Kepler, Newton, Einstein & others were thought equally bizarre when they were proposed. Rather one should examine theories of Achar and/or Gupta by evaluating their ability to solve the problem, their explanatory power and their consistency.

Specific aspect of their theory, never mind their entire theory, generated problems even worse than their theories claimed to solve. In addition, their approach has many characteristics of a bad theory; subjective interpretation, inconsistency, ad-hoc hypotheses that explained away rather than explained observations and inability of their theories to solve the problem they set out to solve!

Achar's theory is false because he could not show presence of two comets (in apparition) settled for a year in the vicinity of *Vishakha,* for his proposed year of the Mahabharata War (3067 B.C.). When Achar could not produce his two comets near *Vishakha*, he tried to save his theory, first, by suggesting need for additional research, and secondly, by trying to explain planetary observations as merely poetic fancy. While the former suggestion for future research left the issue unresolved, the latter approach simply resulted in explaining away Mahabharata observations, rather than explain them! Worse still, Achar clings to both conjectures (comets and poetic fancy) not realizing that these theories, either of them individually or both of them together, are incapable of explaining anything. His theory runs into contradictions when he accepts astronomy observations of Udyoga *Parva* [8, 13] and of *Adhyaya* 2 of Bhishma *Parva* as factual, but considers astronomy observations of *Adhyaya* 3 (Bhishma *Parva*) as product of poetic imagination! To top it off, he considers, selectively I might add, 3 out of 4 observations [9, 28] from 2nd *Adhyaya* of Bhishma *Parva*, and ignores, conveniently I think, the observation of *Arundhati*[1]. I may mention that the only observation Achar could corroborate, notwithstanding his claims to contrary, is that of Saturn near *Rohini*!

Gupta treats all observations of planets from the 3rd *Adhyaya* of Bhishma *Parva* as comets, quotes *VarahaMihir*'s Brihat-samhita for list of comets and proposes a grammatical theory to identify specific Mahabharata observation as either a comet or a planet, i.e. a theory of Indicative power (*Lakshana Vritti*), one of the three powers of words (the other two, according to him, being *Abhidha* and *Vyanjana*, i.e. narrative and suggestive powers). His theory has additional details, however I could not understand a word of his theory and I would request curious readers to read his work in the original. Of course my inability to understand his theory is no disqualification criteria of his theory. Rather his theory is false for the same reason Achar's theory is false. Gupta neither shows comets named *Brihaspati* (Jupiter) and *Sanaishchara* (Saturn) near *Vishakha* for his proposed year of the Mahabharata War (1952 B.C.) nor any of the other comets (with familiar names of planets) he refers to! Gupta interprets some observations [8, 9, 13] as planets and claims that Saturn was near *Rohini*, however Voyager 4.5™ simulation shows than Saturn is nowhere close to *Rohini* and is rather 5 *nakshatras* away (between *Purva* and *Uttara Bhadrapada*) from *Rohini,* during his proposed year of 1952 B.C. He claims Mars going retrograde near *Anuradha/Jyeshtha* however Voyager 4.5™ shows that Mars did not go retrograde anywhere close to *Anuradha/Jyeshtha*. Gupta proposed 17 October 1952 B.C. as the first day of the Mahabharata War. Mars went retrograde near *Ashlesha/Punarvasu*, a year before his proposed date of the Mahabharata War, and again went retrograde one year after his proposed date of the Mahabharata War, this time near *Purva Phalguni*.

I will now turn to corroboration of specific observations [6, 14] with my theory and my proposed timing of the Mahabharata War. As I wrote earlier, Jupiter, Saturn and Mars are plenty bright and distinctly visible planets and I did not think much about the words '*Prajwalita*' and '*Prajwalita ghora*'. However, once I explained these observations as retrograde motions of Jupiter, Saturn and Mars, it dawned upon me that Mahabharata observations might be more accurate and precise than I had thought. In the absence of 'theory of comets' by Achar and Gupta, I would have easily missed significance of specific descriptions (Prajwalita, ghora) of planets.

Prajwalita could be translated as begin to blaze, flame forth, burst into flames or burns/shines brightly. Ghora could be translated as dreary, horrible, dreadful, awful, frightful, scary or terrific.

Jupiter and Saturn are described as shining brightly and settled near *Vishakha* for a year before the Mahabharata War. Keep in mind that the brighter the object appears, the lower the value of its magnitude. Saturn had magnitude of 1.1 on 16 October 5562 B.C., one year before the War, its brightness increased and was as high as 0.6 during latter half of January 5561 B.C. Saturn had magnitude (brightness) of 1.0 on the first day of War (16 October 5561 B.C.). Jupiter had magnitude of -1.8 one year before the War, became brighter (magnitude = -2.7) during April-May 5561 B.C. and dimmed back to -1.9 by the first day of War.

Mars is described as settled between *Chitra* and *Swati*, began moving in *apasavya* (abnormal, unusual) direction, shined brightly and would have been perceived as shining with dreadful appearance. Mars (along with Saturn) are considered planets with evil influences in our times and that may be the case in Mahabharata times. In fact we have at least one Mahabharata observation[14] where Mars is referred to as *Parusha* (harsh, cruel, unkind) *graha*. Voyager 4.5™ confirmed that Mars became retrograde between *Chitra* and *Swati*, began moving backwards (west) and by the end of February 5561 B.C. and became very bright (Magnitude = -2.1). It is worth remembering that at this level of brightness, Mars would have shined brighter than anything else in the sky except the Sun, the Moon and Venus.

Venus turned retrograde near *Purva Bhadrapada* and, as expected, it became bright during retrograde. Mahabharata observation does not specifically refer to brightening of Venus during retrograde. Venus is as such plenty bright and the change in brightness during retrograde would not have been noticed or considered worthy of mention (from average magnitude of -3.9 to -4.6). In fact beginning with the first day of the Mahabharata War through its *parikrama* (retrograde) around Neptune in the region of *Purva Bhadrapada* and then resuming its normal movement, Venus had shown small variation in brightness, i.e. from -4.4 (16 October 5561 B.C.) to its brightest value (-4.6) during December 5561 B.C. and back to -4.3 by March 5560 B.C.

Error Elimination – Experiment 26

Shweta (near *Chitra*) [19] & *Shyama* (near *Jyeshtha*) [20]

At the outset, I want to make it clear that I have no clue whatsoever regarding the identification of two planets, based on limited information, as simply *Shyama*[20] and *Shweta*[19] along with their positions near *Jyeshtha*[20] and *Chitra*[19], respectively. Here is my feeble attempt and speculation, with the help of Voyager 4.5[TM] and Mahabharata descriptions, to identify these planets.

Shweta[19] planet described in the vicinity of *Chitra* also appears as *Budha* (Mercury) in some manuscript(s) of Mahabharata. Voyager simulation shows that Saturn, after staying in the region of *Chitra-Uttara Phalguni* for a long period, approached *Chitra* around the first day of Mahabharata War. I speculated that this *'Shweta'* planet could be Saturn. Saturn was approaching *Chitra* (RA = 6 h 42 min) and was very close to *Chitra* (Saturn RA = 6 h 26 min) on the first day of War (16 October 5561 B.C.). Why Saturn would be called *'Shweta'* is beyond me. I present this observation of Saturn near *Chitra* to document one of my feeble attempts to corroborate Mahabharata observation of *'Shweta* near *Chitra'*[19].

Shyama[20] planet (whatever that means) is also described as shining brightly and in the vicinity of Jyestha[20]. Observation refers to a planet near Jyeshtha however the Mahabharata text does not specify its identity other than referring to it by an adjective *'Shyama'*[20]. This Shyma[20] planet also appears as *'Shweta'* in some manuscript(s) of Mahabharata, not to confuse with another observation[19], which also refers to a planet as *'Shweta'*. Not surprisingly, Mahabharata researchers had field day with this observation. Researchers have spent time interpreting *'Shyama'* or *'Shweta'* to mean a specific planet. To me any planet will do if one can be found in the position as described by the Mahabharata text, provided all other observations can be corroborated. I could not find any planet near *Jyeshtha*, at least not on the first day of War. My speculative hunch is that the description is of Jupiter, based on the fact that it was also described as 'Shweta' but also 'Prajwalita', smoky (sadhuma) and fiery (saha-Pawaka) and in the vicinity of Jyeshtha (nakshatra of Indra). The only planet that went retrograde near Jyeshtha during my proposed time-line for the Mahabharata War was Jupiter. Beginning December 5563 B.C. (~2 years before the Mahabharata War) through July 5562 B.C., Jupiter was in the vicinity of Jyeshtha, went retrograde near Jyeshtha, and attained magnitude as bright as -2.6. It is important to remember that Jupiter is plenty bright (-1.8 to -1.9) even when it is not retrograde.

Once I speculated that this Shweta/Shyama graha near Jyeshtha[20] could be Jupiter, I thought of revisiting Mahabharata observation 'Shweta near Chitra'[19]. This latter observation[19] appears as 'Budha near Chitra' in some manuscript(s) of Mahabharata. Mercury (Budha), Venus and Jupiter can be identified with the objective 'Shweta' because of their brightness and visual appearance to the naked eye. Mars appears as red and Saturn (at least to me) appears as red to yellowish-brown. I wanted to test the possibility of Mercury (Budha) near Chitra, and Voyager 4.5™ simulation suggested a corroborative scenario for 22nd July 5562 B.C., after sunset. Similar scenario also existed for 2nd September 5562 B.C. (before Sunrise) and for 22nd July 5561 B.C., after sunset. Venus was near Chitra on 12 July 5561 B.C., after sunset or on 23 September 5562 B.C., before sunrise. I have presented multiple scenarios to emphasize the point that unless we have additional information, we should consider the identification (and consequently corroboration) of the planets described in these Mahabharata observations [19, 20] as unresolved.

Error Elimination – Experiment 27

Comet attacking Pushya [21, 22]

The Mahabharata text has two instances of observations related to a fearsome comet [21, 22]. One observation states that 'great fierce comet has settled near Pushya'[22] and another observation states that 'the spread of the comet is settled near Pushya'[21]. There are numerous comets and their visibility from the Earth depends on their proximity to the Earth during their visit to the inner portion of the solar system. Comets with well-known orbits that have orbital period of less than 200 years are called Short-Period comets. As of 2008 A.D., less than 200 short-period comets are known.

Mahabharata Observation does not specify additional information, other than stating that the comet and/or spread of the comet were settled near *Pushya*. This information is not sufficient to identify a comet from the known comets today. I ran a simulation with step change of a day, using DVA™ by locking the position of *Pushya* and observing the view of the sky near *Pushya* for a period of two years before and after 5561 B.C. No specific comet appeared and/or settled near *Pushya*, an observation that would corroborate Mahabharata description.

Vartak interpreted Mahabharata observations [21, 22] as referring to Haley's comet; performed calculations based on orbital period of Haley's comet and inferred that Haley's comet must have been seen during the War. Voyager simulation shows that this is not the case. I had noticed the error in Vartak's assumptions and his subsequent orbital calculations, long before I did this simulation, and I was not expecting Haley's comet to show up during 5561 B.C.

Many more simulations later and based on my conjecture of 'visual observation', I postulated that whatever this comet might be, it should be seen either traveling near or settled near *Pushya*. I postulated that Mahabharata observation of the comet is not referring to the time of comet's apparition, since during apparition, comet would more than likely (usually, but not always) occupy lot more space than space of one *nakshatra* (*Pushya*). In addition, a comet would travel through multiple *nakshatra* space within a span of few days and thus specific reference to *Pushya* would be meaningless and cannot be corroborated. This postulate tuned out to be a useful one and led me to design another experiment.

I activated the settings for all known short-period comets (known to NASA), and with the help of DVA™ began noticing moving stellar objects (comets) in the vicinity of *Pushya*. Lo and Behold, I found Haley's comet in the vicinity of *Pushya*! Haley's comet stayed in the vicinity of *Pushya* until it was ready for its next apparition. In fact it is during the apparition that the Haley's comet started moving away from *Pushya*. It did not take me long to appreciate the meaning of Mahabharata observation, assuming of course the comet referred to in the Mahabharata text is indeed Haley's comet. Mahabharata text is stating that the fearsome comet is not in its apparition and

94

thus rather settled near *Pushya*[19] and comet that is not in apparition can be visualized as one whose spread has collapsed on itself [21]. Haley's comet has orbital period of ~75 years and at apparition it remains visible for few weeks/months at most. Thus my interpretation appears trivial at first glance since one would wonder what would be the purpose of Mahabharata author in stating such a phenomenon of non-apparition, which is the reality for some ~75 years out of orbital period of ~75.3 years. The objection raised is entirely valid. On the other hand, while trivial, this interpretation of mine corroborates Mahabharata observations [21, 22] and corroboration is easy to demonstrate using DVA[TM] with step function of one year. Voyager simulation shows Haley's comet in its non-apparition state and in the vicinity of *Pushya* for 99% of its orbital period and goes away from *Pushya* only during apparition.

My explanation requires two distinct assumptions: (1) Ability to see objects far smaller and distant in the sky, the ability as such already assumed during the discussion of Uranus, Neptune and Pluto, (2) Ancient astronomical tradition of meticulous observations and their documentation, the assumption already corroborated by 'Fall of *Abhijit*'.

Implications: Planetary & Cometary Evidence

I began with the ambitious plan of testing some ~110 instances within the Epoch of *Arundhati* for the year of Mahabharata War. I searched for works of other researchers and their proposals for the year of Mahabharata War. The Epoch of *Arundhati* defined time interval for the plausible year of Mahabharata War, which in turn eliminated 96% of all existing proposals. I was left with 4 proposals that fell within the Epoch of *Arundhati*: Dikshit (7300 B.C.), Vartak (5561 B.C.), Lele (5228 B.C.) and Modak (5000 B.C.). I decided not to include proposals of Dikshit and Modak in my critical analysis and/or testing as they proposed approximate time intervals rather than a specific year. I was left with two dates: 5561 B.C. and 5228 B.C. I could easily eliminate 5228 B.C. however 5561 B.C. turned out resistant to my falsification attempts. Voyager simulation corroborated, for year 5561 B.C., twenty-five Mahabharata observations of planets and comets, falsified none and could not explain and/or corroborate two observations [19, 20].

95

While I did not test all 110 potential instances within the Epoch of Arundhati for the year of Mahabharata War, I did test 38 potential instances (based on relative positions of Saturn near *Bhaga* and Jupiter near *Shravana*) over a shorter period of 6500 B.C. - 3500 B.C. The reader will understand the significance of this compact time interval after reading Chapter 9.

The year, 5561 B.C., proposed by Vartak is the only year that could meaningfully corroborate twenty-seven planetary and cometary observations. I want to emphasize the requirement for any theory and corresponding prediction for the year of Mahabharata War to corroborate these 27-30 Mahabharata observations, instead of explaining them away! Many researchers are/were aware of these planetary observations and they had documented these observations, however, all of them ended up developing ad hoc theories with the goal of explaining away, rather than explain these observations. Good number of these researchers decided to include only those Mahabharata observations, which corroborated their proposed year for the Mahabharata War and ignored rest of the observations.

Are you convinced that the year of Mahabharata War was 5561 B.C.? If answer is yes, then let's find out the first day of Mahabharata War. Determination of the first day of Mahabharata War is the subject of next chapter.

8

The First Day of Mahabharata War
Phases & Positions of the Moon

All truths are easy to understand once they are discovered; the point is to discover them.

- Galileo Galilei

Is it possible to predict the first day of Mahabharata War?

The question is irrelevant since Mahabharata researchers have already advanced proposals for the first day of Mahabharata War. I have classified all these proposals into two categories,

1. *Amawasya* as the first day of War
2. The first day of War being 0 to 4 days before full moon day

Raghavan, Achar, Karandikar and few other researchers have proposed the beginning of Mahabharata War (the first day) near full moon day (*Margashirsha Shuddha* 11/12 through Margashirsha Purnima). These researchers invoke following observations in support of their theory,

1. Traditionally celebrated day of *Gita Jayanti*. *Gita Jayanti* is celebrated on *Margashirsha Shuddha 11*.
2. Late moonrise on the 14th day of War
3. *Shravana nakshatra* on the last day of War, based on statement of Balarama

I consider traditional belief worthless, as primary evidence, in support of any theory however I am willing to allow it as corroborative evidence for an established theory, i.e. established based on independent empirical evidence. I have dealt with remaining two observations in the next chapter.

The lunar day (*Tithi*) and *nakshatra* of the day is not exactly the same as the day defined by rising and setting of the Sun. The lunar day (*Tithi*) and/or *nakshatra* of the day could be determined by simply noting down the phase of the moon and/or *nakshatra* close to the position of the moon. The lunar day (*Tithi*) can also be calculated mathematically. The timing of an observation and an error on the part of an observer may lead to an error of +/- 1 day (i.e. Lunar day or *nakshatra*) in stating the phase or position of the moon.

Since I began with criticism of the year proposed by P V Vartak, it was natural for me to criticize/test his proposal for the first day of War. He proposed *Amawasya* as the first day of War. Many other researchers have also proposed *Amawasya* as the first day of Mahabharata War. Vartak provided multiple Mahabharata observations in support of '*Amawasya*' as the first day of Mahabharata War, specifically Mahabharata observations alluding to the solar eclipse on the first day of War. In addition Vartak provided alternate explanation for the late moonrise on the 14th day of War [93]. Vartak's explanation of Balarama *Tirthayatra* [88], its duration, and *nakshatra* of his arrival is a mixed baggage. I have borrowed Vartak's explanation of Mahabharata observations related to the solar eclipse however, have provided alternate explanations for the late moonrise [93] as well as *Tirthayatra* of Balarama [88] (Chapter 9).

In this chapter, my objectives are,

(1) To test the conjecture of '*Amawasya*' as the first day of Mahabharata War

(2) To propose timeline for pre-war events, beginning with Krishna leaving for Hastinapur (from Upaplavya) on peace mission and ending with Vyasa meeting Dhritarashtra, day before the War

(3) To corroborate my proposed timeline (for pre-war events) with Mahabharata observations

(4) To corroborate passing away of Krishna, 36 years after the Mahabharata War.

If my conjecture about the first day of War as *'Amawasya'* is correct, I reasoned, that I should able to find observations to corroborate my conjecture. To be fair, I also wanted to search for observations, which would falsify my conjecture. I began re-reading the Mahabharata text, looking for any and all observations with astronomical flavor. I realized that, in addition to the descriptions of the planets and eclipses, Mahabharata author was equally happy employing specific astronomical events happening around him in comparing the War scenes. Eclipses are indeed dramatic, but Mahabharata author is equally happy comparing warriors with mid-day sun or with the positions and the phases of the Moon and/or stars.

Error Elimination – Experiment 28

Lunar Eclipses [9, 27, 28, 29, 64]

The Mahabharata text has up to 5 observations, considered by other researchers as referring to lunar eclipse(s). The observations 'moon's mark has disappeared'[9, 27], 'the full moon of *Kartika* was devoid of effulgence and appeared coppery red'[28], and 'the lunar eclipse and the solar eclipse are happening within an interval of 13 days and such an occurrence is rare indeed!'[29] may allude to lunar eclipse(s) however it is not clear whether the observations refer to one or more (lunar) eclipses. Observations stating 'moon's mark has disappeared' occur twice in the Mahabharata text and I conjecture that they refer to the observations of moon close to *Amawasya* day, when significant portion of the moon' surface is dark and when the mark on its surface is not clearly visible.

I ran Voyager 4.5™ conjunction search as well as simulations for lunar months (specifically full moon days) of *Ashwin* through *Pau-*

sha in 5561 B.C. Conjunction search showed a possible lunar eclipse on *Kartika* full moon, with separation angle of 2.726^0, at 9:58 PM on September 30, 5561 B.C. Another lunar eclipse was shown on 30 October 5561 B.C., with separation angle of 0.127^0, at 12:19 PM. I request experts to determine if separation angle of 2.726^0 for the conjunction of 30th September qualifies as lunar eclipse and, assuming an affirmative answer, also to determine the type of lunar eclipse. The time of the second eclipse, the lunar eclipse of October 30 is around noon and thus the eclipse would not have been visible at Kurukshetra (~Delhi). Voyager simulation, however, showed that the Moon, still eclipsed, was above the horizon at 7 PM and Mahabharata observer would have seen eclipsed Moon for at least ~90 min, albeit in final stages of the eclipse, before the Moon became free from the Earth's shadow.

Description of 'the full moon' on *Kartika Purnima* is generic enough and cannot be used as decisive description of the lunar eclipse. On the other hand, if someone confirms this lunar eclipse (*Kartika Purnima*) by other means, the Mahabharata description could be used to corroborate such an instance. The reader should keep in mind that when the Moon does not enter into the umbra, the darkest part of the Earth's shadow, it does not darken completely, and we get a partial eclipse. These are hard to notice; the moon just darkens a bit, but does not disappear completely into the night. Of course it is important to remember that the moon does not disappear even during the total lunar eclipse, but rather turns dark red. I request readers to re-read section on 'Lunar Eclipse' of chapter 3 for the causes of the moon turning red. The Lunar eclipse of 30 October 5561 B.C. is corroborated by two Mahabharata observations [29, 64] along with Mahabharata observations related to solar eclipse [34, 35, 36].

Most researchers have considered only two eclipses, i.e. the lunar eclipse on *Kartika Purnima*, followed by the solar eclipse on *Kartika Amawasya*. For example, Vartak has not given any consideration to the lunar eclipse of 30th October 5561 B.C. My point being he did not arrive at his proposed year based on this lunar eclipse. Eclipses are critical in order to validate and corroborate any specific proposal for the year of Mahabharata War. On the other hand, many researchers depended too much, incorrectly I think, on presence of solar and lunar eclipses in predicting their proposed year of the Mahabharata War.

Error Elimination – Experiment 29

Two eclipses separated by only 13 days[29]

Many researchers have voiced their frustration with the Mahabharata reference[29] of either *Amawasya* occurring within 13 days or the lunar and the solar eclipses occurring on the same day. The frustration and confusion is caused by existence of multiple versions (due to transcription and transliteration errors) for this reference[29]. Critical edition lists one version (not employed by any past researchers) which reads, '*chaturdashi panchadashi **kadachidapi** shodashim, imam tu nabhijanami **bhutaPurva** trayodashim*' and when this version is combined with the next verse of the lunar and the solar eclipses separated by only 13 days, the translation and interpretation becomes straightforward. The time interval of 13 days is not referring to *Amawasya*, but rather to the time interval between the lunar and the solar eclipses.

The lunar eclipse of 30th October is hardly in doubt and I assert that Mahabharata observation of seeing two eclipses (the lunar and the solar eclipses) separated by only 13 days refers to the solar eclipse of 16th October and the lunar eclipse of 30th October. The solar eclipse occurred mid-day on 16th October while the lunar eclipse occurred on 30th October (lunar eclipse occurred around mid-day but was visible at Kurukshetra only in the evening for less than 2 hours), and thus these two eclipses are separated by 13 days, i.e. not counting the days of eclipses themselves[29].

Error Elimination – Experiment 30

Solar Eclipse – The First day of War

Voyager conjunction search shows that the solar eclipse of 16th October 5561 B.C. occurred at 12:57 PM and with a separation angle of 1.8^0. I request experts to shed some light on the type of solar eclipse this would have been. The Mahabharata text does not specifically state the occurrence of the solar eclipse on the first day of War. Vartak identified Mahabharata observations [34, 35], which allude to the occurrence of the solar eclipse on the first day of War. I identified additional observations alluding to the same phenomenon.

Error Elimination – Experiment 31

The Sun appeared as if split in two parts[34]

Solar eclipse seen from the Earth may be perceived as 'the Sun appearing as if split in two parts'[34].

Error Elimination – Experiment 32

Flames of the Sun were visible[34]

This observation is from the same couplet where the Sun is described as split in two parts. During the solar eclipse, two phenomenons are observed – Baily's beads and solar corona and I think the description of 'visible flames' of the Sun is referring to one or both of these phenomena.

Error Elimination – Experiment 33

Morning Sun with its splendor lost[35]

Mahabharata observation states that while army was waiting for the sunrise, wind started blowing and raindrops appeared without clouds in the sky. Soon the war field was covered with darkness. Big meteor fell from the sky and crashed (appeared as if it crashed) into the rising Sun and made a loud noise. The Sun appeared with its splendor lost[35]. I consider this as corroborative evidence for the occurrence of the solar eclipse.

Error Elimination – Experiment 34

Disappearance of the Sun in the middle of the battle[36]

As two armies engaged in bloody fight, on the first day of War, the Sun disappeared [36]. It is true that Mahabharata observer suggests dust raised by the armies as the cause of Sun's disappearance. The time of the disappearance of the Sun was sometime around noon, but before the end of the first half of the first day's War and it corroborates well with that of the time of solar eclipse.

102

Error Elimination – Experiment 35

The Sun and the Moon seen on *Amawasya* [38]

Satyaki and Abhimanyu were forced to fight from the same chariot with the Kaurava army on the third day of War and Mahabharata author compares them to the view of Sun and Moon, together, as seen on the past/recent (*Gatau*) *Amawasya* day[38]. The reader may recall that the Moon can be seen (edges of the moon) along with the Sun only during the solar eclipse, which occurs on *Amawasya*. I present observations related to the solar eclipse [29, 34, 35, 36, 38] as corroborative evidence for '*Amawasya*' as the first day of Mahabharata war.

Error Elimination – Experiment 36

First 11 days of the War

The moon is conspicuous by its absence in Mahabharata descriptions during the first 7 days of War. The battlefield at the end of the third day of War is described as similar to the autumnal star-studded sky[40]. Mahabharata author describes distinguished warriors troubling armies of the opposite side with that of the scorching sun or the autumnal sun throughout the War. The battlefield is described as similar to the sky, which was filled with planets and *nakshatras*[41].

One has to wait until the 8th day of War to read description of the war scenes and their comparison with the moon. Duryodhana who was surrounded by his servants with oil lamps in their hands, on his way to meet Bhishma, is compared with the Moon surrounded by planets[43].

The first mention of the full Moon appears on the 10th day of War where Arjuna troubling Dusshasan, during the fight, is compared with angry *Rahu* troubling the full Moon[47]. Arjuna sitting in his chariot and surrounded by various jewels of his chariot, on the 11th day of War, is compared with the Moon surrounded by *nakshatras*[49].

It appears that both parties engaged themselves in a fight on any given day, either until they were severely exhausted or until severe darkness forced them to stop the fight. The fight stopped on the first day of War with the sunset and the darkness was such that it was impossible to decipher anything[37]. The fight continued for some time after the sunset on the 6th day of War[40]. The fight continued into the night on the 8th day of War until fighters on both sides were utterly exhausted[42] and until leaders of both sides ordered to stop the flight, when some fighters had run away from the battlefield and many others were feeling sleepy and could not see each other [42]. The fierce fight began when the Sun was ready to set on the western horizon, on the 9th day of War[44]. The Sun set while Bhishma was fiercely killing the Pandava army and the entire army, utterly exhausted, was hoping for the fight to cease[45]. It is not clear if fight indeed stopped at this time, for all Sanjay tells Dhritarashtra is that he did not <u>observe</u> the fight after this time[46].

This then is the chronological account of the first 11 days of the War, which includes 'absence of moon references' for the first 8 days and accounts of fighting continuing into the night with each progressing day of the War, as corroborative evidence for 'Amawasya' as the first day of War.

Error Elimination – Experiment 37

The moon rising with its pointed ends down[48]

The planets were described, on the 10th day of War, as circling either the Sun (or the Moon) in an abnormal direction signifying inauspicious omens, while the Moon was described as rising with its pointed ends directed downwards[48].

I could not interpret the circling of planets around either the Sun (or the Moon) however the rising of the Moon with its pointed (non-smooth) ends downward corroborates well with the rising (or visible) moon during 'Shukla Paksha' of any month, i.e. bright half of the lunar month. I present this observation in support of 'Amawasya' as the first day of War.

I encourage the reader to observe the phases of the moon, through both Shukla and Krishna Paksha, to understand the significance of this otherwise ordinary phenomenon. I was indifferent and insensitive to changing phases and positions of moon, before I began writing this book, in spite of my keen interest in visual astronomy. Mahabharata observations of moon changed my attitude towards observations of moon from ancient Indian literature.

Error Elimination – Experiment 38

The moon appearing like the full moon
Last 7 days of the war

The descriptions of the war scenes during the final 7 days of Mahabharata War are rich in full moon analogies, i.e. analogies of the sky with the full moon in it! The reader may find it useful to recall that during few days preceding and following the full moon day, the Moon's surface facing the Earth is 90%+ illuminated and thus an observer from the Earth would visualize the Moon as full Moon, during this period. There are five distinct observations of the moon during these 7 days that provide corroborative support for the conjecture of 'Kartika Amawasya' as the first day of the War and therefore I treat them separately. The remaining observations are equally critical and form a common theme of the full moon during the latter half of the War.

The face of King Neel, killed by Ashwatthama on the 12th day of War, is compared with the full moon[51] and so is the face of fallen Abhimanyu on the 13th day of War [52]. This observation also provides another peculiar analogy: the scene is described as if the moon had eclipsed [52]! Voyager simulation shows that the Moon was near the node (Rahu) on the 13th day of the War. Voyager conjunction search also confirmed the lunar eclipse two days after the fall of Abhimanyu. The battlefield with fallen Abhimanyu is compared with the star-studded sky along with the full moon [53]. Description of the battlefield on the 16th day of War compares faces of fallen heroes with the full moon[54], and compares the faces of kings, fallen on the war field, with that of the full moon [55]. Faces of fallen kings are compared with lotuses and other flowers and also with the sky, filled with the stars of the Sharad season [56]. Bhima killed Vivitsu on the 17th day of War and the face of fallen Vivitsu is compared with the full moon[60]. Arjuna killed another distinct warrior on the 17th day of War and the face of this warrior is compared with the full moon [61]. The canopy of Karna's chariot is compared with the full moon [62] and so is Bhima surrounded by his enemies [63]. The face of Karna, fallen on the ground, is compared with the mid-day Sun of Sharad season[65] and also with the full Moon[66]. Arjuna killed many warriors of the Kauravas and generated a pile of their faces on the ground and these faces appeared like the full moon[71]. The fallen faces on the battlefield, which had appearance of the full moon, also appeared similar to the stars spread in the sky[72]. Duryodhana was standing in the middle of the battlefield, surrounded by his bodyguards, on the last day of the War, and canopy of his chariot appeared similar to the full moon[67]. Duryodhana, fallen on the battlefield and surrounded by dust, is compared with the full moon surrounded by ring of darkness[68]. Gandhari and other royal women visited the battlefield a day after the War was over. Gandhari compares faces of fallen Shalya[69] and Balhik King[70] with the full moon. The fight continued throughout the night at the end of the 14th day of the War. The fight also continued into the night on the 18th (and the last) day of War. I present these Mahabharata observations and their comparison with that of the full moon, during last the 7 days of War as corroborative evidence in support of 'Amawasya' as the first day of War.

Error Elimination – Experiment 39

The full moon near *Krittika*

I had predicted additional observations and the potential nature of these observations, when I first proposed my theory. Of course I could not say if such observations existed in the Mahabharata text, however, what I did say is that if new observations were discovered, my theory and theories of others must able to corroborate them. I meant, by additional observations, those observations existing in the Mahabharata text but not evaluated or employed by past researchers in determining the year of Mahabharata War.

While I had to depend on Mahabharata author for recording additional Mahabharata observations, I felt confident that if additional observations were found, they would corroborate my theory of visual observations. I have shown, in this chapter, newly identified observations to be consistent with the idea of Mahabharata War beginning on *Amawasya*. P V Vartak has mentioned some, but not all, of the observations presented by me in Error Elimination – Experiment 38. I was not expecting specific observations, specific enough to provide high degree of testability and falsifiability. I was pleasantly surprised to discover observations discussed in Error elimination experiments 35, 36, 37 and 38.

The reader would then understand my joy when I came across the observation of the full moon near *Krittika* on the 12th day of War. This observation presents, in my mind, decisive corroborative evidence for *Kartika Amawasya* (per *Amanta* reckoning) as the first day of the Mahabharata War. The Mahabharata text describes white canopy on the chariot of King Bhagadatta as similar to the full moon near *Krittika*. This was on the 12th day of the War [50]. While I was overjoyed to discover this observation, little did I know that this was only the beginning!

Error Elimination – Experiment 40

The Moon between two *Vishakhas* [57]

All observations are theory laden. This means one may not even notice them unless one is expecting them, based on predictions of one's theory. It also means that the theory determines the interpretation of an observation or the specifics of an observation one should be looking for.

After I stumbled into 'the full moon near *Krittika*' observation[50], I ran the simulation for the position of the moon for each day of the War, beginning with the first day (my proposed date), and noted down *nakshatras* in the vicinity of the moon. I had these descriptions in the back of my mind as I re-read the Mahabharata text beginning with the first day of War. The partial outcome of this exploration is summarized under descriptions of the moon and the duration of the fight through eighteen days of the War (Error Elimination – Experiments 35-38). These observations of the moon point to '*Amawasya*' as the first day of War. Observation of 'full moon in *Krittika*' on the 12th day of the War points to '*Kartika Amawasya*' as the first day of War, per *Amanta* reckoning (Error Elimination – Experiment 39).

Pandyaraj, another warrior, was killed on the 16th day of War and the Mahabharata text compares his face with the full moon. The same observation also mentions that the face of Pandyaraj was looking beautiful, similar to the moon between (two) *Vishakhas*[57]!

Voyager simulation had shown the Moon to be near '*Punarvasu*' during the 16th day of War. I had employed star Pollux as YogaTara for *Punarvasu*, which is next to another star Castor and I

107

knew that Pollux and Castor together represented 'two *Punarvasus*'. I wondered if Mahabharata author would have referred to Pollux and Castor as two *Vishakha*s! Although I could not see the Moon between these two stars (*Punarvasu*s) in Voyager simulation, I was still intrigued by mention of '*Vishakhas*' in an unexpected place, unexpected because nakshatra *Vishakha* being at least 9 days away from the position of moon on the 16th day of War.

I began reading literature on identification of specific stars with *nakshatras* and found that nakshatra *Vishakha* is described with two stars and *Punarvasu* is described sometime with 2 stars and at other times with 4 stars.

When *Punarvasu*s are described as made up of 4 stars, the *nakshatra* include two stars on each side of the ecliptic. The description of the (full) moon between *Vishakha*s was for the 16th day of War, only 4 days removed from the description of the full moon near *Krittika,* which convinced me that the description indeed referred to the moon near *Punarvasu*s. However since nakshatra '*Vishakha*' also existed (among the list of *nakshatras*) and was identified with two stars, I did not want to interpret this observation as referring to the full moon near *Punarvasu*s.

I still want to state my suspicion! I suspected that observation referred to the full moon between the two branches (*Vishakha*s) of *Punarvasu*s; one branch to the north of the ecliptic formed by Castor and Pollux and the second branch to the south of the ecliptic formed by Procyon and Gomeisa, four stars of *Punarvasu*s. The full moon was indeed between these two branches of *Punarvasu*s on the 16th day of War.

I request readers to bring it to my attention if they come across references within ancient Indian literature referring to two branches (*Vishakha*s) of *Punarvasu*s. Numerous simulations of mine confirmed that the Moon would take a minimum of 8 days and as long as 11 days to reach *Vishakha* and thus I was convinced that above observation could not have referred to *Vishakha*, however, in the absence of additional evidence, I do not want the reader to accept my claim for this observation as corroborative evidence for my conjecture, at least not until I present next two Mahabharata observations [58, 59].

Moon would be indeed near Vishakha for the year proposed by Raghavan /Achar on the 16th day of the War, however, the day was less than 4 days removed from the day of Amawasya (30% illumination) and thus the observation cannot be corroborated with full moon description of the Mahabharata text. Theory and proposed date of Raghavan/Achar has been falsified by every single observation (except Saturn near Rohini and comet near Pushya) discussed in this book. Although Raghavan or Achar have not claimed it, they would have been justified in claiming this observation of 'moon between *Vishakhas*' as corroborating their timeline. On the other hand, mention of the full moon is problematic for their timeline.

Error Elimination – Experiment 41

Five sons of Draupadi protecting Dhrishtadyumna[58]
&
Five bright stars protecting the Moon

I noticed this observation in the Mahabharata text only because I knew what I should be looking for. In the absence of specific expectation, this is a generic observation and may not carry much value.

Five sons of Draupadi are described as protecting Dhristadyumna, their maternal uncle, by surrounding him, on the 17th day of War and Mahabharata author compares this military arrangement with the Moon protected by (5) bright stars in the sky [58]. I conjecture that the (5) bright stars (referring to five sons of Draupadi) protecting Dhristadyumna are 4 stars of *Punarvasu* (Pollux, Castor to the north & Procyon, Gomeisa to the south) along with Alhena to the west. The full moon is to the east of these stars and can be visualized as protected by these five stars.

Error Elimination – Experiment 42

Two Panchal warriors behind Yudhishthir
&
Two *Punarvasus* behind the Moon[59]

Two Panchal warriors protected Yudhishthir, from behind, on the 17th day of War and Mahabharata author compares this military arrangement with the moon protected by two *Punarvasus*[59]! This observation is another distinct observation that corroborates the position of moon on the 17th day of War, but also *'Kartika Amawasya'* as the first day of War.

The observations (Error Elimination – Experiments 41 & 42) corroborate well with identification of Vishakhas (Error Elimination – Experiment 40) with that of Punarvasu. The observation of 'full moon near Krittika (Error Elimination – Experiment 39) provides corroborative support to such a conjecture. I do not deny the possibility that Mahabharata author might have simply used the analogy of 'full moon between Vishakhas', without any intent of comparing it with actual situation in the sky.

Error Elimination – Experiment 43

Yudhishthir free from misery
&
The moon free from *Rahu*[64]

Yudhishthir was injured on the battlefield, on the 17th day of War, and his protectors removed him from the battlefield. Expert medical practitioners removed the arrows from Yudhishthir's body and in no time Yudhishthir was back on the battlefield.

Mahabharata author compares the return of joyous Yudhishthir, free from misery, with the full Moon freed from the torture of *Rahu*[64], i.e. the full moon coming out of the lunar eclipse.

Mahabharata observer could witness the lunar eclipse on the 15th day of the War for some 90 minutes after the sunset. Although 90 min is sufficiently long time interval to notice an eclipse, it is also important to remember that objects below and close to the horizon can be seen due to refraction of light.

Problem of Pre-War timeline

The problems posed by observations related to the timeline before the War and leading to the first day of War, have implications for adjusting the timeline of events before the War, but does not affect either the first day & the year of the War or the timeline of events after the War. Any timeline, proposed for the events before the War, has to satisfy the following,

1. Krishna leaves for Hastinapur (from Upaplavya) early morning on *Anuradha Muhurta* and on Revati *nakshatra* during the lunar month of Kartika or *Kaumudi* (month of lotuses)
2. Krishna and Karna meet 7 days before *Shakra* (*Jyeshtha*) *Amawasya*
3. Krishna returns to Upaplayva before the arrival of Balarama to the Pandava camp
4. Balarama arrives at the Pandava camp and then leaves for Saraswati *Tirthayatra* on *Anuradha nakshatra*
5. Rukmi visits the Pandavas and the Kauravas and then returns to his kingdom
6. Yudhishthir holds secret meeting, after the departures of Balarama and Rukmi, but before the visit of Uluka. This meeting appears to be near the full moon day
7. Uluka visits the Pandava camp, with the message from Duryodhana, and returns to the Kaurava camp with the message from the Pandavas
8. Both the Kauravas and the Pandavas leave on *Pushya* day
9. Both armies arrive at Kurukshetra on *Magha* day
10. Balarama spends 42 days doing Saraswati *Tirthayatra*, before arriving on the last day of War, to attend the fight between Bhima and Duryodhana
11. Balarama leaves for *Tirthayatra* on *Pushya* (*Shravana* or *Anuradha*) and arrives on the last day of the War on *Shravana* (or *Pushya*)

According to Vartak, Krishna left Upaplavya on 27th September (Revati) and arrived at Hastinapur on 30th September. Krishna conducted few rounds of negotiations. Duryodhana asked his fellow kings to leave for Kurukshetra on *Pushya*, while Krishna was still in Hastinapur. Krishna met with Karna on 9th October (*Uttara Phalguni*), 7-8 days before Jyeshtha *Amawasya*, and left for Upaplavya on the same day. Krishna requests Karna to tell Bhishma and Drona of his intention to begin the preparations for the War (or the War) in seven days, i.e. on 16th October, the day of *Amawasya*.

There are numerous pre-war Mahabharata observations that directly contradict compressed timeline of 7 days (7 days between Krishna-Karna meeting and the first day of War) proposed by Vartak. They are,

111

(1) Balarama meeting with the Pandavas and Krishna, upon Krishna's return from Hastinapur, and then traveling around Saraswati for 42 days before returning on the last day of War, to witness the dual between Bhima and Duryodhana

(2) Krishna leaving for Kurukshetra, along with the Pandavas on *Pushya* and both armies reaching Kurukshetra on *Magha*

(3) Balarama leaving for Saraswati (from the Pandava camp) on *Anuradha*, *Shravana* or *Pushya*

(4) Balarama beginning his *Tirthayatra* on *Anuradha*, *Shravana* or *Pushya*

(5) Seven days is insufficient time for war preparation, building of war camps, tents, fortification and movement of the army. This period of seven days also appears extremely compressed when one takes into account time required for Krishna to return to Upaplavya, assignment of generals, arrival and departure of Balarama followed by that of Rukmi and finally visit of Uluka to the Pandava camp and his return to the Kaurava camp

Elaboration of problems posed by timeline of Vartak

I simulated position of moon near *Jyeshtha* on 16th October and then counted backwards for 8 days. The day is 9 October 5561 B.C. This is the day, according to Vartak, when Krishna requested Karna to communicate to Bhishma and Drona of his plan to begin the war on upcoming *Amawasya* day. This *Amawasya* day (*Shakra Amawasya*) was only seven days away. This timeline poses problems in explaining numerous Mahabharata observations,

(1) Assuming Krishna returned to Upaplavya the same day (9th October) and Balarama arrived at the Pandava camp also on the same day and left the same day, it still means Balarama had only 25 days for his Saraswati *Tirthayatra*. I should also mention that even this analysis assumes unrealistically compressed timeline, i.e. assumption of Krishna reaching Upaplavya the same day and so is the arrival and departure of Balarama. It also means Balarama left for Saraswati on *Uttara Phalguni* and no corroborative evidence exists to justify such an assumption.

112

(2) Vartak has also conjectured in one place that Krishna returned to Upaplavya on the *Pushya* day, same *Pushya* day
when Duryodhana encouraged his side to proceed to Kurukshetra. This conjecture contradicts rest of Krishna's stay in
Hastinapur that involved multiple meetings in the Hastinapur
court, meeting with Kunti and finally meeting with Karna,
seven days before the *Amawasya* day.

(3) Balarama could leave for *Tirthayatra*, based on the timeline
proposed by Vartak, neither on *Pushya* nor on *Shravana*. Vartak has made an ingenious case for Balarama leaving for
Tirthayatra on *Anuradha*, but more on that in Chapter 9.

(4) Rukmi visited the Pandava camp, after departure of Balarama.

(5) Yudhishthir held a secret meeting, after departure of Balarama and Rukmi, with his allies to determine the war strategy
and this meeting appears to have taken place around the full
moon day. Vartak's compressed timeline does not allow full
moon descriptions between Krishna-Karna meeting and the
first day of War.

(6) Uluka visited the Pandava camp after this secret meeting.
Uluka conveyed the message of Duryodhana and returned to
the Kaurava camp with message from the Pandavas.

(7) Arrival of Balarama on *Pushya*, i.e. 18th and the last day of
War, per Vartak, contradict Mahabharata observation. Since I
have accepted Vartak's timeline for the 18 days of the War,
my assertion for Balarama arriving on *Pushya*, 18th day of the
War also contradicts Mahabharata observation. I have dealt
with this issue in Chapter 9.

(8) Neither army has time to leave for Kurukshetra on *Pushya*
and arrive at *Magha*, per Vartak's timeline. Beginning with
9th October, the Moon is in *Uttara Phalguni, Hasta, Chitra,
Swati, Vishakha, Anuradha, Jyeshtha, Mula* & *Purva-Ashadha*,
leading to the first day of Mahabharata War, per the timeline
proposed by Vartak. Neither *Pushya* nor *Magha nakshatras*
appear during the 7 days between Krishna-Karna dialogue
and the first day of War, per Vartak's timeline.

(9) Udyoga Parva contains elaborate descriptions of war preparation and movement of army. Time interval of 7 days is too
compressed to allow for these activities.

113

Error Elimination – Experiment 44

Insertion of an additional month
(Between Krishna-Karna dialogue & the first day of War)

I conjecture that a period of not only seven days but also a lunar month in addition to 7 days passed between Krishna-Karna dialogue and the first day of Mahabharata War. Krishna left Upaplavya, per this proposal of mine, on the morning of 31st August 5561 B.C., reached Hastinapur on 2-3 September and stayed at Vidura's house. Duryodhana encouraged his fellow kings to leave for Kurukshetra on 7-8 September. The day was *Pushya*. Krishna- Karna dialogue occurred on 9-10 September, some 7-8 days before *Shakra Amawasya*. The War preparations at Kurukshetra began on 17-18 September on *Shakra (Jyeshtha) Amawasya*. Balarama arrived at the Pandava camp sometime between 9 and 17 September, and left the Pandava camp on 17 September, on *Anuradha (Maitri) nakshatra* and began Saraswati *Tirthayatra* around 21st September, on *Shravana nakshatra*. Balarama subsequently arrived on the last day of the War, on 2nd November and on *Pushya nakshatra*, after traveling along Saraswati for 42 days.

This modified timeline also provides sufficient time interval, albeit still compressed, for the war preparation and movement of the armies on both sides. I have noted down the *nakshatra* when Balarama began his *Tirthayatra* and there is no Mahabharata reference that supports my conjecture of Balarama beginning his *Tirthayatra* on *Shravana nakshatra*. My conjecture for the period of a lunar month + 7 days, is ad hoc, and has no corroborative support of specific Mahabharata observation, however, I want readers (and researchers) to judge the merit of my conjecture based on its ability to explain numerous Mahabharata observations prior to the War.

Error Elimination – Experiment 45

Yujyate vs. Yojante[73]

Numerous researchers (e.g. Vartak) have taken Krishna's statement as referring to the beginning of War[73]. I interpret Krishna's statement as referring to 'war preparation and planning' and not referring to the beginning of War itself. I translate *'Yojante'* of critical edition as 'plan or prepare' for the War rather than 'engage' in the War[73]. Some researchers (Raghavan, Achar, Holay) have interpreted Krishna's statement as referring to worship (*yajante*) of weapons (Lohabhihar ritual) before the War and I consider their explanation as equally valid.

Error Elimination – Experiment 46

Jyeshtha (Shakra) Amawasya[73]

Once I modified the timeline before the War, I wondered if *Amawasya* of 17-18 September qualified as *Shakra (Jyeshtha) Amawasya*. I ran Voyager simulation and found that *Amawasya* day; of 17-18 September or that of 15-17 October would qualify as 'Jyeshtha' *Amawasya* based on visual observations of the Moon. Too many Mahabharata researchers quote this reference but only to forget it altogether in their analysis. I simulated position of the Moon near *Jyeshtha* during these two *Amawasya*s,

Amawasya 1: 16 September 5561 B.C. (9:56 PM)

Nakshatra/Sun	RA
Jyeshtha (Antares):	9 hr, 47 min
Sun	9 hr, 5 min
Anuradha	9 hr, 23 min
Vishakha	8 hr, 42 min

Amawasya 2: 16 October 5561 B.C. (1:30 PM)

Nakshatra/Sun	RA
Jyeshtha (Antares):	9 hr, 47 min
Sun	11 hr, 2 min
Mula (Shaula)	10 hr, 29 min
Purva Ashadha	11 hr, 11 min

I interpret, based on RA measurements, *Amawasya* of 16 September to be *Jyeshtha Amawasya*, however, request readers, experts in astronomy, to provide criticism of my interpretation.

I also want to point out that *Amawasya* of 16 September, based on relative position of Sun and *Vishakha*, can also be consi-

115

dered *Amawasya* near *Vishakha* whose *nakshatra* deity include both Indra (*Shakra*) and Agni.

Error Elimination –Experiment 47

Krishna leaving on Revati *nakshatra*[74]

Krishna left Upaplavya, early morning, on 31st August. The Moon is near Revati *nakshatra*. I do not know the significance of '*Maitri Muhurta*', however, if it refers to '*Maitri*' *nakshatra* being on the eastern horizon, then *Anuradha* (*Maitri*) *nakshatra* was on the eastern horizon around 7:30 AM.

Error Elimination – Experiment 48

Balarama leaving the Pandava camp on *Anuradha*[75]

Balarama left the Pandava camp on 17 September. The *nakshatra* was *Anuradha* (*Maitri*). In few days, after leaving the Pandava camp, he began Tirthayatra of Saraswati. King Rukmi visited the Pandavas after Balarama had left the Pandava camp.

Error Elimination – Experiment 49

Secret meeting of Yudhishthir near full moon day[76]

After Balarama and Rukmi departed, the Pandavas sat down in secrecy, along with their allied kings, for the discussion of war tactics. Mahabharata author describes this assembly as beautiful and compares it with the sky filled with the moon and *nakshatras*.

No explicit mention is made of the full moon however I conjecture that this meeting took place near the full moon of *Kartika*, i.e. around 30th September. My conjecture for the timing of this meeting (near full moon) is based on description of this meeting and its comparison with moon surrounded by stars in the sky.

I conjecture that Uluka came to the Pandava camp around this time, probably after the secret meeting of the Pandavas and returned to the Kaurava camp before 4th October. Both armies left for Kurukshetra after Uluka returned to the Kaurava camp.

116

Error Elimination – Experiment 50

Both armies leaving for Kurukshetra on *Pushya* [(77), 78, 79]

Both armies left for Kurukshetra on 4th October, *Pushya nakshatra*. Mahabharata researchers, who make a big deal of the *nakshatras* of Balarama Tirthayatra, interestingly remain silent on this Mahabharata observation.

Error Elimination – Experiment 51

Both armies arriving at Kurukshetra on *Magha*[80]

Both armies arrived at Kurukshetra on 6-7 October. The Moon was near *Magha nakshatra*.

Error Elimination – Experiment 52

Krishna Nirvana [81, 82, 83]

I have included timing of Krishna Nirvana in this chapter only because astronomy observations related to *Krishna Nirvana* are of eclipses and are compared with that of the Mahabharata War. Otherwise, it is my considered opinion that many researchers have made a big deal of this observation for nothing.

Other ancient texts refer to sightings of comet (Haley's comet) before the Mahabharata War, but also after the Mahabharata War and before Krishna Nirvana. These observations have significance for the timing of Mahabharata War however, in keeping up with my promise of restricting to only Mahabharata observations I have not discussed these extraneous observations, extraneous to the Mahabharata text, in this book.

Krishna passed away 36 years after the Mahabharata War. The only Mahabharata observation is that of the solar eclipse and reference to the circumstances similar to that of the Mahabharata War. This observation is trivial as there could be up to two solar eclipses per year in any given year.

I found one instance each for 5525 B.C. and 5524 B.C., where the lunar and the solar eclipses took place within the interval of 13 days and were visible from Dwarka. In year 5525 B.C., the solar eclipse took place on 7th November and the lunar eclipse took place on 21st November. In year 5524 B.C., the solar eclipse took place on 27th October and the lunar eclipse took place on 10th November.

Conclusions

Numerous Mahabharata observations corroborated the conjecture of 'Amawasya' as the first day of Mahabharata War and four distinct observations corroborated 'Kartika Amawasya day' as the first day of Mahabharata War. Eighteen-day timeline of the Mahabharata War, 16 October through 2 November 5561 B.C., as proposed by Vartak, withstood numerous falsification tests, i.e. tests provided by Mahabharata astronomy observations. No astronomy observation within the Mahabharata text falsified this timeline. Mahabharata observations regarding Krishna Nirvana corroborate well with the simulations of Voyager 4.5[TM] for years 5525 B.C. and/or 5524 B.C.

I conjectured 'additional month', i.e. additional to only 7 days proposed by Vartak between Krishna-Karna meeting and the first day of Mahabharata War. My conjecture of 'additional month' could explain 10 out of 11 pre-war incidents. The only pre-war observation that is not explained is the nakshatras of arrival (Shravana) and departure (Pushya), as stated by Balarama[88], related to his Saraswati Tirthayatra. Next chapter (Chapter 9) addresses this observation along with 6 other Mahabharata observations that appear to conflict with my proposed timeline.

9

Conflicting Observations

I have always adhered to the habit of praising what in my opinion others have done well, of rejecting what they have done badly. Never do I scorn or conceal other people's knowledge when I lack my own. Never do I feel servile to others or forget myself when I have done something better or discovered it sooner with my own power.

- Johannes Kepler

In this chapter, I discuss specific Mahabharata observations that contradict my proposed timeline (the year and the first day) of Mahabharata War. I want to point out two distinct astronomical Mahabharata observations, one related to *Tirthayatra* of Balarama and other related to late moonrise on the 14th day of War, both of them directly contradicting my timeline.

Numerous researchers quote only one or two specific observations, from the Mahabharata text, in the context of *Bhishma Nirvana* and these observations, often quoted, directly contradict my proposed timeline. I identified 20+ additional Mahabharata observations, while attempting to resolve apparent contradictions related to *Bhishma Nirvana*. Some of these additional observations have been identified or acknowledged by likes of P V Vartak or P V Kane however ignored by all other Mahabharata researchers. These additional observations not only corroborated my timeline but also decisively falsified all other proposals for the year of Mahabharata War! Numerous researchers insist on observations related to *Bhishma Nirvana* being critical in building their proposed timeline however all of them have forgotten, conveniently I think, to corroborate these observations with their proposed year of the Mahabharata War. I have shown that all researchers, whose work I am aware of and who considered observations related to *Bhishma Nirvana* as critical observations, have failed to corroborate these observations with their proposed timings of the Mahabharata War.

I also address traditional notion of the timing of Mahabharata War, i.e., 36 years before the beginning of *KaliYuga*. And how the traditionally assumed time interval for the Mahabharata War, based on the beginning of *KaliYuga,* contradicts my Mahabharata timeline.

There are two additional astronomical observations that do not contradict, but pose exceptions to my theme of employing Mahabharata observations to corroborate my timeline.

Finally, I want to highlight one Mahabharata reference, which contradicts the season of Mahabharata War. Thus there are six specific Mahabharata observations and one traditional belief (*KaliYuga* and the Mahabharata War) conflicting with my theory and/or proposed timeline and are summarized as follows,

1. The *nakshatra* (*Pushya*) when Balarama left for *Tirthayatra* and the *nakshatra* (*Shravana*) when he returned, after 42 days, to witness the club-fight between Bhima and Duryodhana, on the last day of War.

2. Drona *Parva* refers to late moonrise at the end of 14th day of War and this phenomenon, if interpreted in certain way, directly contradicts my 18-day war timeline.

3. Mahabharata observation records Bhishma passing away during the lunar month of *Magha* and when 3/4th of the month (or *Paksha*) was still remaining, after being on the bed of arrows for 58 nights. The day of his death was the day of winter solstice. Some manuscripts contain a verse that states Bhishma passing away on *Magha Shuddha Ashtami* and that

the Moon was near *Rohini*. These Mahabharata observations contradict my proposed year of the Mahabharata War.

4. Tradition assumes 3102 B.C. as the beginning of *KaliYuga*. Tradition also assumes that the Mahabharata War happened 36 years before the beginning of *KaliYuga*. My proposed timeline of the Mahabharata War is more than 2000 years before the traditionally assumed beginning of *KaliYuga*.

5. Bhishma is compared with the full moon on the first day of War. This analogy conflicts with my timeline since the first day of War is *Amawasya,* per my proposed timeline.

6. The Mahabharata text states analogy of the solar eclipse, during Bhima-Duryodhana fight, on the 18th and the last day of War. This day was closer to the full moon day and nowhere close to Amawasya. Thus the analogy of the solar eclipse appears to conflict with my timeline.

7. When Krishna left for Hastinapur, the Mahabharata observation states that it was the end of *Sharad* season. This observation, suggesting the season when Krishna left on a peace mission, directly contradicts my timeline. The Mahabharata War took place, per my timeline, during the *Sharad* season. In addition, I conjectured time interval of an additional lunar month and 7 days between the first day of Mahabharata War and the end of Krishna's visit to Hastinapur (i.e. Krishna-Karna meeting).

1. Balarama *Tirthayatra*

Krishna returned to Upaplavya (from Hastinapur) after a failed attempt of peace negotiations. Balarama arrived at the Pandava camp when the war preparations were underway[85]. Balarama declared his intention not to participate in the War and decided to go on Saraswati *Tirthayatra*. Krishna returned to the Pandava camp after accompanying Balarama for some distance[85].

Krishna told the Pandavas, after returning from Hastinapur, that the Kauravas did not listen to his advice. Krishna asked the Pandavas to proceed with him towards Kurukshetra on *Pushya nakshatra*[79]. Balarama left the Pandava camp, along with Yadavas, on *Maitri (Anuradha) nakshatra* to begin *Tirthayatra* of Saraswati[75]. Bhoja joined Duryodhana while Yuyudhan (Satyaki), along with Krish-

121

na joined the Pandavas. Krishna left for Kurukshetra along with the Pandavas, after departure of Balarama, on *Pushya*[78, 86].

When Balarama heard the details of the Mahabharata War, he interrupted his *Tirthayatra* and immediately proceeded to Kurukshetra, eager to witness the fight between his two disciples, Bhima and Duryodhana[87].

The Problem

The problem of Balarama *Tirthayatra,* in the context of Mahabharata War, begins when Balarama states, upon arrival at the site of dual between Bhima and Duryodhana, that "42 days have passed since I began the *Tirthayatra* of Saraswati; I left on *Pushya* and am returning on *Shravana*" [88]. The *nakshatra* on the last day of War, according to my timeline, is 'Pushya' and not 'Shravana'.

There are 6 Mahabharata statements related to the *Tirthayatra* of Balarama,

(1) Balarama left the Pandavas on *Anuradha nakshatra*[75]
(2) Balarama began his *Tirthayatra* on *Pushya*[88]
(3) Balarama arrived on the 18th day of War, and witnessed the dual between Bhima & Duryodhana
(4) Balarama arrived on the 18th day of War and the *nakshatra* was *Shravana*[88]
(5) The duration of his *Tirthayatra* was 42 days[88]
(6) Balarama was surrounded by surviving Kings, and the arrangement appeared similar to the full moon surrounded by *nakshatras* [89, 153].

Statements (1), (3) & (5) do not contradict my timeline. Statement (6) provides corroborative support for my assertion that the last day of War was close to the full moon day. Statements (2) & (4) directly contradict my proposed timeline. In fact my timeline reverses the sequence of the *nakshatras*; i.e. Balarama began his *Tirthayatra* on *Shravana nakshatra* (21st September) and returned on the last day of War when the moon was near *Pushya* (2nd November), 42 days after he began his *Tirthayatra*.

The reader may keep in mind that no Mahabharata researcher has successfully corroborated *nakshatras* of arrival and departure of Balarama *Tirthayatra* and total duration of 42 days, without getting into serious difficulties.

Error Elimination – Experiment 53

Transposing Error & Degrees of Freedom

I ran simulation for my proposed timeline, beginning with *Pushya* on 2nd November and going backwards 42 days. The Moon was near *'Shravana'* on 21st September. These simulations made me realize that Mahabharata reference in Shalya *Parva*[88] was not providing three independent pieces of information,

1. Balarama leaving on Pushya (for *Tirthayatra* or from the Pandava camp)
2. Arriving on Shravana (18th and the last day of War)
3. Total duration of *Tirthayatra* = 42 days

My simulation showed that given any two, the third automatically follows. This relation is not only valid for *Pushya-Shravana* combination, but practically for any two *nakshatras* separated by 13-14 *nakshatra* spaces.

Daftari proposed theory of transposition of two *nakshatras* in the fashion **'Shravanae samprayotosmi pusheyna punaragatah'**. P V Kane mentions this effort of Daftari in his 'History of Dharmashastra'. My timeline would certainly agree with transposition suggested by Daftari however I do not want to propose such a theory. My reservation is due to the fact that once one starts taking liberties with such modifications, there is no stopping and the very spirit of rationality and scientific method is undermined. I would rather be content to accept the observation as not corroborating my theory.

Error Elimination – Experiment 54

Transliteration Error
('Sampryatosmi' instead of 'Samproptosmi')

Vartak proposed that **'Samprayatosmi'**[88] was a transliteration error and the correct word should have been **'Sampraptosmi'**. I searched for alternate readings within the critical edition of Mahabharata and realized that had he looked into alternate readings, he would have realized that one of the alternate readings indeed suggests 'Sampraptosmi'! It is safe to say that he did not consult critical edition for this observation[88], for he goes on to suggest various ways of splitting 'Samprayatosmi', which would lead to the meaning of 'arrived at' instead of 'departed on'.

Fortunately, we have no need for such maneuvers to coax the desired meaning. The desired meaning is also the natural outcome, if one accepts Amawasya as the first day and Margashirsha as the lunar month of Mahabharata War. I accept the alternate reading from the critical edition, and now the first part of the second line[88] translates as 'arrived on *Pushya*' as opposed to 'departed on *Pushya*'.

Error Elimination – Experiment 55

'Samagatah' instead of 'Punaragatah'[88]

I found one of the alternate readings for '***punaragatah***' in critical edition was '***samagatah***'. The word translates as 'came to the assembly (Sama – assembly, gatah – returned, came to)' instead of 'returned again (punar-again, gatah – returned, came to)'. This modification by itself leads to only a minor change of meaning and the reader may not think much about it since the problem of arriving on two *nakshatras* (*Shravana* and *Pushya*) is hardly solved.

Error Elimination – Experiment 56

Shravane: '*Shravana nakshatra*' or 'Listening'? [88]

Vartak had already solved the problem of 'arriving on two different *nakshatras*' and I restate his explanation.

Narada met Balarama on the bank of Saraswati and curious Balarama expressed his desire to hear (*shravane*) details of the War[90]. When he heard (shravane) of the impending fight between Bhima and Duryodhana, he left *Tirthayatra* in a hurry and riding his chariot, arrived at the assembly of surviving warriors to witness the fight[87]. Kurukshetra, the site of Mahabharata War was located between Saraswati and Drishtavati. The Mahabharata observation[88] can be re-translated, as follows,

> It has been 42 days since I (Balarama) began *Tirthayatra* of Saraswati. I am arriving at the assembly (of kings) on *Pushya nakshatra* after listening (details of the War).

I would like to point out that this translation corroborates all 6 Mahabharata statements, related to the *Tirthayatra* of Balarama, with my timeline of the Mahabharata War.

2. Late Moonrise (14th day of the War)

The Mahabharata War began, per my proposal, on *Amawasya* day and thus the 14th day of War would be close to the full moon day. The moon will rise, on the full moon day, at the time of sunset and will set around the time of sunrise next day. Voyager simulation of rising and setting of the moon, on 29th October – the 14th day of War, shows that the moon rose around 6 PM (evening of the 14th day of War) just before the sunset. The moon went down the horizon around 6 AM (morning of the 15th day of War – 30th October).

The Problem

Mahabharata observation describes late moonrise, which directly contradicts my proposed timeline. Ghatotkacha was killed around the midnight of the 14th day. The fight continued and the soldiers of both sides were injured by arrows and were exhausted, long before half of the night was over[91]. Arjuna noticed this condition of the army on both sides and said to the fighting armies, "You and your animals are exhausted and are overpowered with sleep. The battlefield is covered with darkness due to enormous dust in the air. If you consider it appropriate, stop the fight and rest for a while[92]. **After the moonrise** *(or when the moon is visible again),* you may resume the fight"[93]. Both sides accepted the proposal, warriors retired from fighting and slept for some time [94]. **After sometime the Moon appeared in the sky[95].**

Late moonrise on the 14th day of War necessitates that the War began around the full moon day. Raghavan/Achar and few others have attempted such proposals. All such proposals run into difficulty while corroborating observations of the night of 14th day of War and numerous additional observations.

This late moonrise on the night of the 14th day of War is impossible for my proposed timeline, since the 14th day of War, per my timeline, is near the full moon day. This is then the problem of late moonrise. I have borrowed a lot from P V Vartak in solving this problem. However I have proposed a different solution and have also corroborated descriptions of the moon, which in turn removed the need for additional ad hoc conjectures employed by Vartak.

Error Elimination – Experiment 57

Timeline of the events – 14th day of the War

The time of the appearance of the moon (either reappearance or moonrise), although approximate, can be estimated. The fight resumed, sometime after 'moonrise', when only 3 out of 15 *Muhurtas* (*Muhurta* = 48 min) of the night were still remaining[96].

Voyager simulation shows the sunrise at 6:30 AM on the 15th day of War. This would mean the fight resumed 3 *Muhurtas* before 6:30 AM, which would be around 4 AM. The Mahabharata text refers to time of approximately 2 *Muhurtas* between moonrise or reappearance of the moon, and resumption of the fight [97, 98]. This would mean the moonrise occurred around 2 AM.

The Mahabharata text does not explicitly mention the time when Arjuna made the suggestion to stop the fight. After the death of Ghatotkacha, fight resumed when half of the night was already over and the fight continued until Arjuna requested both parties to stop it[91]. Assuming that the fight continued for another hour, until 1 AM, the duration of sleep for the warriors could not be more than 3 hours (1 AM – 4AM).

The fight resumed after the appearance of the Moon or its reappearance, and continued until the sunrise, when the warriors of both sides took a short break to worship the Sun [99].

Mahabharata researchers (Raghavan, Achar, Karandikar) who have included the observation of late moonrise, either to build their timeline or to explain it in an alternate fashion, have translated the observation - "after taking rest and becoming alert resume the fight when the moon rises"[93].

Error Elimination – Experiment 58

Description of the Moon on the 14th day of War

Assuming late moonrise around 2 AM, the phase of the moon is such that the moon is only 5 days away (~34% illumination) from the *Amawasya* day. Late night moonrise is expected during the time of the lunar month close to but before *Amawasya* day.

On the other hand the rising Moon is described as similar to the bow of Kamadev (Cupid) and the Moon was shining with full brightness[100]. In no time, rays of the moon dimmed the brightness of *nakshatras* and exhibited first signs of the dawn[97]. After exhibiting signs of the dawn, the moon started spreading broad light, similar to the golden rays and began destroying the darkness[101]. Within one *Muhurta*, the battlefield was bright and the darkness completely vanished [98]. The battlefield was bright like a day, once the moon started shining [102]. The warriors woke up with the touch of the rays of the Moon, similar to the waking up of lotuses due to the rays of the Sun. The excitement arose within the army similar to the turbulence of the ocean due to the rising of the moon, and the fight resumed [103].

I assert that descriptions of the moon presented here are suggestive of the time of the full moon or near full moon, rather than of a time close to *Amawasya*.

Error Elimination – Experiment 59

Delirious state of warriors

The fight continued after the sunset on the 14th day and Ghatotkacha was killed around midnight. The fight resumed with fresh attack from the Pandava warriors, and soon the warriors and animals (horses, elephants, etc.) of both sides were totally exhausted. The warriors were becoming blind with sleep and were unable to do their duties to the extent they perceived this night of 3 *prahara* as equivalent to 1000 *prahara*. The warriors spent half of the night in that exhausted state while being hurt by others and injured by arrows.

127

Both armies were devoid of energy to fight and weapons began to fall from their hands [91]. The warriors were unable to fight properly, however, out of the sense of duty and to avoid embarrassment could not leave the battlefield.

Many in the army dropped their weapons and slept right on the battlefield; some on chariots, some on elephants and still others on horses. They were incapable of comprehending attack from others, due to overwhelming fatigue and sleep, and thus were being killed. The warriors were killing those who were unconscious and dreaming. Many warriors were delirious and were talking to themselves, even injuring themselves, at times killing members of their own side and also those of the opposite. Many were standing, in spite of sleep, with the desire to kill, and their eyes had become red due to lack of sleep. Few of them were roaming in the battlefield in spite of being overwhelmed by sleep and were killing warriors of the other side. Many warriors, on both sides, were incapable of comprehending their own death by warriors of the other side [104].

Error Elimination – Experiment 60

Exhausted state of Warriors and Descriptions of their Sleep

The warriors on both sides began to praise Arjuna for his suggestion, praised him profusely and went to sleep. Some slept on back of horses, some on chariots, some on elephants and others on the ground itself, while holding on to their weapons. Elephants slept on the ground while horses began resting, still standing and tied to the chariots [106].

Error Elimination – Experiment 61

Darkness on the battlefield
(Common phenomena during the Mahabharata War)

'Darkness on the battlefield' was becoming a common affair during the War, irrespective of whether it was day or night. The Mahabharata text has numerous references of battlefield being covered with darkness to the extent the sun became invisible. On multiple occasions, raising of the dust due to war activities is mentioned as the cause of this darkness. The Mahabharata text describes the total darkness, due to shower of dust and arrows, such that neither sky was visible nor direction comprehensible to the extent warriors could not recognize each other and could fight only after announcing their names to each other [105].

I conjecture that rising of dust was the cause of disappearance of full moon during the night's fight on the 14th day. In addition, the warriors and their horses and elephants were exhausted. Against this background, Arjuna suggested that both sides should stop the fight and take some rest until the moonrise or reappearance of the Moon, before resuming the fight [92]. This is when both parties accepted the offer and slept for some time [94].

Error Elimination – Experiment 62

Why did the fight continued into the night?

I was under the impression that both parties agreed to end the fight each day at sunset. I do not know why I made such an erroneous assumption! No wonder I was surprised to read that the fight continued into the night on the 14th day. In addition, no leaders of either side objected to the continuation of fight past sunset. This episode made me re-read portions of the Mahabharata text where ground rules for the War were set. This is when I realized my mistake. The rules emphasized maintaining respectful relationship after the battle of the day was over, but never stated that the fighting should be stopped at sunset[107].

I conjecture that while no strict rules were in place to end the fight, the fight continued each day as long as there was sufficient light to carry it out. Notwithstanding the rules laid down for the war etiquettes, it appears that both parties engaged in a fight on any given day either until they were severely exhausted or until severe darkness forced them to stop the fight.

I reproduce relevant observations from chapter 8:

> The fight stopped on the first day with the sunset and the darkness was such that it was impossible to decipher anything[37]. The fight continued for some time after the sunset on the 6th day of war[40].

The fight continued into the night on the 8th day of war until fighters on both sides were utterly exhausted[42] and until leaders of
both sides ordered to stop the fight. Many fighters had run away
from the battlefield while many others were feeling sleepy and
could not see each other [42]. The fierce fight began when the Sun
was ready to set on the western horizon, on the 9th day of War[44].
The Sun set while Bhishma was fiercely killing the Pandava army
and the entire army, utterly exhausted, was hoping for the fight to
cease[45]. It is not clear if fight indeed stopped at this time, for all
Sanjay tells Dhritarashtra is that he did not <u>observe</u> the fight after
this time[46]. The Mahabharata text is not explicit on the duration of
the fight for each day of the War however it is clear that the fight
continued throughout the night at the end of 14th day of War. The
fight also continued into the night on the 18th (and the last) day of
War.

The Mahabharata text has no descriptions of the moon for the first 8
days of War and abundance of 'full moon' descriptions for the last 7
days of War. These observations when combined with many more
described in this chapter, point to 14th day of the War as being close
to the full moon day.

Error Elimination – Experiment 63

Reappearance of the Full Moon vs. Late Moonrise

The soldiers, eyewitnesses and key warriors were exhausted,
sleepy and delirious while fighting late into the night. The Mahabharata text provides graphic descriptions of this situation. Loss of
visibility due to rising dust was becoming a common occurrence leading to loss of directions and such instances were occurring even
during the day [105]. Cessation of fight would have allowed the dust to
settle which in turn would have made the full moon, already in the
sky, visible to all.

I conjecture that once one of the ancient commentators of
Mahabharata translated this observation of the reappearance of the
Moon[93] as 'late moonrise', the entire episode (and subsequent com-
mentaries) took a life of its own. I interpret that *'punah:'*[93] refers to
'reappearance of the Moon' (*Chandramas udite punah*) and not referring to *'resumption'* (punah = resume or again) of the fight. My

130

interpretation not only solves the problem of the late moonrise but also provides consistent explanation for all Mahabharata observations related to the fight, including full moonlike descriptions, on the night of 14th day of War.

On the other hand what we do know is that if one insists on 'late moonrise' interpretation, such an assumption contradicts practically all observations discussed in the context of 'late moonrise' of the 14th day as well as all Mahabharata observations discussed in Chapter 8 and one observation of seven planets attacking moon of Chapter 7.

3. *Bhishma Nirvana*

Bhishma, the first general of the Kaurava army, fell down in the battlefield on the 10th day of War. Bhishma could control the timing of his death by employing the siddhi awarded to him. Bhishma realized that the Sun was still in *Dakshinayan* (southward motion), which also meant improper time for one's death (per the understanding of Mahabharata times). He decided to postpone his death until the Sun turned northward. He chose to delay his death, while lying on the bed of arrows, until the first day of *Uttarayan* (beginning of northward journey of the Sun along the ecliptic), i.e., either the day of winter solstice or one day after the day of winter solstice.

The Problem

Bhishma passed away when the Sun turned northward, i.e. on the day of winter solstice or one day after the winter solstice[108]. Bhishma says that he was lying on the bed of arrows for 58 nights and that the lunar month appeared to be month of *Magha* and 3/4th of, either month or *Paksha*, remained[109]. Another Mahabharata observation states specific lunar date of *Bhishma Nirvana* as *Magha Shuddha Ashtami* and when the Moon was near *Rohini*[110].

The day of *Bhishma Nirvana*, based on 2 (or 3) specific Mahabharata observations[108-110] has to satisfy the following,

(1) The day has to be not more than +/- 1 day from the day of winter solstice

(2) Lunar Month of *Magha*

(3) *Shuddha Ashtami* (i.e. 8th day of the bright half of lunar month *Magha*) considering 3/4th referred to the lunar month, or *Magha* Shuddha 4 or *Magha* Krishna 4 considering 3/4th referred to the lunar *Paksha*.

(4) The Moon near *Rohini*

(5) Time interval of 58 nights between fall of Bhishma (in the battlefield) and the day of *Bhishma Nirvana*.

Many researchers claim above observations as critical in building their timelines however, not a single researcher (at least among 20 works I analyzed) corroborates all five attributes for his proposed timeline!

Error Elimination – Experiment 64

Review: Vartak & other Researchers

I begin with the solution proposed by Vartak, since I have accepted his timeline for the 18 days of Mahabharata War. Vartak proposes 22nd December 5561 B.C. as the day of *Bhishma Nirvana*. The day is indeed 58 days after Bhishma fell down in the battlefield and month is lunar month of *Magha*, day of *Shuddha Ashtami* and the Moon near *Rohini*. Thus Vartak's proposed day for *Bhishma Nirvana* corroborates 4 out of 5 conditions recognized by current and past Mahabharata researchers. The only problem for this timing is that the day of winter solstice was still some 40 days away, in the future, i.e. on 30th January 5560 B.C. This is indeed a significant problem.

The point of winter solstice is a movable point. This motion is extremely slow and thus I was willing to accept a difference of +/- 1 day from the actual point (day) of winter solstice. My reading of the Mahabharata text reinforced this view further. The Mahabharata text has references, which corroborate my conjecture that Mahabharata astronomers were capable of predicting the day of winter solstice with precision. I had to look for either entirely different year or entirely different explanation. I felt as if I had reached a dead end. The difference of more than 1-2 days was unacceptable; never mind the difference of 40 days! I decided to accept the conclusion that year 5561 B.C., although superior to any other attempt and in spite of

132

being the best approximation to the truth, was at least not corroborated by the Mahabharata observations related to *Bhishma Nirvana*.

Naturally I was curious to verify corroboration claimed by other researchers for the day of *Bhishma Nirvana*. Other researchers have proposed multiple years separated by millenniums. These researchers were not only convinced that they could explain the Mahabharata observations of *Bhishma Nirvana* but also considered these Mahabharata observations as critical in building their timeline. What is more interesting is the fact that these researchers were blissfully unaware of the contradictions their proposed day of *Bhishma Nirvana* posed for these observations.

For example, the day proposed by Raghavan/Achar results in time interval of only 43 days (and not 58 days) between fall of Bhishma and the day of winter solstice. In addition, their proposed day of *Bhishma Nirvana* keeps Bhishma waiting for 4 additional days beyond winter solstice, which also results in time interval of 46-47 days (and not 58 days) between fall of Bhishma and *Bhishma Nirvana*.

The Day proposed by Holay does provide interval of 58 days between Bhishma falling in the battle and the day of winter solstice, position of the Moon near *Rohini* and the lunar month of Magha (with the additional assumption of *Adhika Masa*). Moreover he does not keep Bhishma waiting beyond the day of winter solstice, however, all of this comes at the cost of an ad hoc hypothesis Holay had to introduce, i.e. the hypothesis of the break in the War for 12 days after the fall of Bhishma. No corroborative evidence exists within the Mahabharata text for such an ad hoc hypothesis; on the other hand, it could be shown that numerous Mahabharata observations (Chapters 6, 7, 8 & 9) contradict Holay's modified war timeline.

Day of *Bhishma Nirvana* proposed by Mohan Gupta is removed by 13 days from the day of winter solstice. Raghavan/Achar, Holay & Gupta consider Mahabharata observations of *Bhishma Nirvana* critical in building their timeline but fail to corroborate the very observations for their proposed timeline. I may mention that lack of corroboration for the timeline proposed by these researchers is not limited to observations of *Bhishma Nirvana*, but extends to numerous other planetary and astral observations.

P.C Sengupta proposes 10 January 2448 B.C. as the day of *Bhishma Nirvana*. The Moon is near *Anuradha* (nowhere close to *Rohini*), 3/4th of the month has expired (as opposed to 3/4th of the month or *Paksha* remaining) and the proposal keeps Bhishma waiting for 2-3 days beyond the day of winter solstice.

Numerous other Mahabharata researchers have provided lip service to the importance of *Bhishma Nirvana* observations, but have not bothered either to explain its relevance for their proposed timeline or to corroborate relevant Mahabharata observations with their proposed timeline.

Error Elimination – Experiment 65

Time Interval: Fall of Bhishma & *Bhishma Nirvana*

I speculated, purely from the idea of truth, i.e. if my theory, and its predictions were independently testable, was also true, my theory would then provide me with successful predictions, and I should able to find observations corroborating my proposed timeline. The reader should understand that even a successful prediction is not a guarantee of reaching 'the truth', but such an occurrence is definitely an indication of a better theory, i.e. better than existing theories.

I decided to re-read the Mahabharata text, this time, with emphasis on post-war incidents. I re-read the Mahabharata text, by now a familiar and useful exercise, specifically Bhishma and Shalya and then Sauptic, Stri, Shanti and Anushasan *Parvas*, looking for any and all observations that would allow me to build the timeline between 'Fall of Bhishma' and '*Bhishma Nirvana*'. I was, by luck, immensely rewarded for my efforts.

Bhishma fell in the battle on the 10th day of War and the War continued for 8 more days. Ashwatthama killed Dhristadyumna, Shikhandi and sons of Draupadi during the night of 18th day of the War. The Pandavas subdued Ashwatthama the next day and the Kuru women visited the battlefield in search of the bodies of their beloved. Yudhishthir asked Sudharma, Dhaumya and others to perform final fire rights for those fallen in the War. Vidura, Sudharma, Dhaumya, Indrasen and others arranged fire rights and made huge funeral pyres[111]. After these events, Yudhishthir went, with his brothers and Dhritarashtra, to the bank of Ganga[112] and spent up to a month on the bank of Ganga [113].

The Pandavas returned to Hastinapur amid a great celebration, after spending a month on the bank of Ganga, and the timing appears to be near full moon day [114-117]. Yudhishthir was crowned as the King and he assigned his brothers and other surviving members of the Kuru family to various posts. Yudhishthir assigned various palaces to his brothers, paid compensation to the relatives of deceased warriors, and honored Krishna. The Mahabharata text is not explicit on the length of time interval when these incidents took place.

After the crowning of Yudhishthir and assignment of offices, Krishna asked Yudhishthir to visit Bhishma and seek guidance from Bhishma. Yudhishthir left Hastinapur, per Krishna's suggestion, along with his brothers, Krishna, Satyaki, Kripacharya, Yuyutsu, and Sanjay to meet Bhishma[118]. Yudhishthir and his entourage arrived at Kurukshetra. The place was filled with hair, flesh and bones, and was covered with piles of elephant and horse bones, and with human skulls that appeared like conch shells[119]. They also saw places where thousands of funeral pyres had burnt[119].

The party met Bhishma, and Krishna told Bhishma that the latter had 56 more days to live, i.e. there were 56 more days before the sun turned northward[120]. Yudhishthir spent a few days in conversations with Bhishma. I could estimate this time period to be equal to 6 days. The incidents of these 6 days, when Yudhishthir sought guidance from Bhishma, can be traced with remarkable accuracy using Mahabharata observations from Shanti and Anushasan *Parva*s.

Yudhishthir and his party spent the first day in conversation with Bhishma. When the Sun was ready to set, they took leave of Bhishma and left for Hastinapur. It appears that Yudhishthir had carried a good-sized army along with him, for the army on foot could be seen for a great distance ahead of and also behind the chariots. As they were traveling towards Hastinapur, the moon rose in the sky and pleased the army with its rays. They reached Hastinapur, late at night, utterly exhausted[121]. This was the end of the 56th day before *Bhishma Nirvana*.

Next morning, (55 days before *Bhishma Nirvana*) Yudhishthir decided not to take the army and rest of the entourage with him as he proceeded to meet Bhishma. Yudhishthir thought it unwise to take all common men with him since it would disturb Bhishma and he also thought it wise to seek counseling in private as Bhishma would be consulting him in ways of **Rajaniti** and other critical matters, and proceeded to Kurukshetra only with his brothers, Krishna and Satyaki [122]. Yudhishthir and party took leave of Bhishma (55 days before *Bhishma Nirvana*) and performed their *'Sandhya'* at *'Drishtavati'* on their return journey to Hastinapur [123].

Next day, Yudhishthir along with his brothers, Krishna and Satyaki left for Kurukshetra in the morning to meet Bhishma. This was 54th day before *Bhishma Nirvana*[124]. The Mahabharata text does not explicitly refers to return of Yudhishthir to Hastinapur, at the end of 54th day before *Bhishma Nirvana*, however, absence of such reference does not pose any difficulty in establishing chronology of events.

The Mahabharata text preserves an interesting reference where Yudhishthir spent a day discussing various subject matters with Bhishma, and at the end of the day returned to Hastinapur to discuss it further with his brothers[125]. I have interpreted this observation as follows. The description of Yudhishthir returning to Hastinapur to 'discuss it with his brothers' suggest that he had gone to see Bhishma alone, i.e. without the company of his brothers. Since we have a reference of his brothers accompanying him to see Bhishma on 54th day before Bhishma Nirvana[124], I interpreted the day, when Yudhishthir returned to Hastinapur, after discussing various subjects with Bhishma, and do discuss them further with his brothers[125], as 53rd day before *Bhishma Nirvana*.

Next day (52nd day before Bhishma Nirvana) Yudhishthir returned to Bhishma, after consulting with his brothers, for additional discussion and to seek guidance[126]. The Mahabharata text does not explicitly record the return of Yudhishthir at the end of 52nd day before *Bhishma Nirvana* however again this lack of records does not pose any problem. The lack of descriptions for Yudhishthir and/or his brothers returning to Hastinapur for two nights is compensated by clear reference to Yudhishthir spending 50 nights in Hastinapur, after meeting Bhishma last but one time [130].

The Mahabharata text preserves one stray reference, which appears in the text after a long discussion between Bhishma and Yudhishthir[127] where Yudhishthir says that only few days are now remaining for the day of winter solstice (and thus for Bhishma Nirvana). This is then the reference made on 52nd day before Bhishma Nirvana.

Yudhishthir visited Bhishma for last but one time, on the 51st day before *Bhishma Nirvana*, along with extended entourage that included Dhritarashtra, Gandhari, royal priests and ministers [128, 129].

Bhishma asked them to come back when the sun would turn north [129]. In this way, Yudhishthir spent six days (51-56th days before *Bhishma Nirvana*) in the company of Bhishma, seeking guidance from the latter. Yudhishthir took leave of Bhishma at the end of the 6th day (51st day before *Bhishma Nirvana*), promising to return as soon as the sun turned north, went to Hastinapur and remained engaged in the affairs of the state for next 50 nights [130].

Yudhishthir returned to Bhishma, after spending 50 nights in Hastinapur, when the sun turned northward [130]. I conjecture this day to be either the day of winter solstice or one day after the day of winter solstice. The point I want to emphasize is that the day of winter solstice could be predicted with a precision and that is how it was predicted during the time of Mahabharata [120, 129, 130].

I could draw following conclusions,

(1) Bhishma was lying on the bed of arrows for 9 nights out of 18 days (or nights) of the War.

(2) He was also lying on bed of arrows when the Pandavas spent approximately one month on the bank of Ganga. I estimated 27 (sidereal month) days, as a conservative estimate, for this month long period[113]. The actual time period could be anywhere from 27 to 30 days.

(3) The Mahabharata text is not explicit on number of days between return of the Pandavas to Hastinapur and their first visit to Bhishma. Let's assume that the number of days for this time interval was equal to 'X'.

(4) Bhishma spent additional 56 days leading to the day of *Bhishma Nirvana*[120].

I estimated total number of nights spent by Bhishma, on the bed of arrows as follows,

Total Number of nights spent by Bhishma, on bed of arrows

10 through 18 days of the War	09
The Pandavas on the bank of Ganga	27
Time Interval: Return to Hastinapur & meet Bhishma	X
Time Interval: First meeting & *Bhishma Nirvana*	56
=	**92 + X (days)**

My proposal for post war events, beginning with the end of the War and ending with *Bhishma Nirvana*, is as follows. The War ended on 2nd November 5561 B.C. The Pandavas spent approximately a month on the bank of Ganga. Estimating this duration to be equal to a sidereal month, the Pandavas returned to Hastinapur around 30 November 5561 B.C. Crowning of Yudhishthir, making arrangements for the relatives of the diseased, assignment of offices and palaces, and finally honoring of Krishna took place during the time interval; 30 November through 6 December 5561 B.C. Yudhishthir went to see Bhishma, along with his brothers, Krishna, Satyaki, Yuyutsu, Kripacharya, Sanjay and the army, either on the 5th or the 6th of December. The day after winter solstice (31st January 5560 B.C.) is the day when the Sun truly turns north and thus my preference for the 6th December as the first day of Yudhishthir visiting Bhishma. I assert that Bhishma was lying on the bed of arrows, based on above timeline, for 98, and not 58 nights.

Is it possible that original 'Ashta-*navatee*' was modified to 'Ashta-*pancha*-shatam' in later times [109]?

Error Elimination – Experiment 66

Implications: Winter Solstice = *Magha Shuddha* 8: [109, 110]

I would like to state implications of the observation that directly contradicts my timeline. Lunar day (*Tithi*) moves by 10-11 days each year while the day of winter solstice, dated per western calendar, would not move (i.e. not more than 1-2 days) over a short span of time. This means time period predicted for the Mahabharata War based on the day of winter solstice coinciding with '*Magha Shuddha Ashtami*' would be a range and not a single specific year.

I ran Voyager simulation to identify this time interval and found out that median time interval for such a scenario would have existed during 1700-1900 B.C. (e.g. 1852 B.C.). The calculations are based on median values. The actual time interval would stretch for at least 2000 years, and if one adds the spice of '*Adhika masa*' (extra lunar month inserted periodically to align lunar and solar calendars), the time interval would stretch up to 3000-4000 years.

I realized that even the author of this alleged interpolation, whoever he may be, had assumed *Kartika Amawasya* as the first day

138

of Mahabharata War. This is because the reference assumes the day of winter solstice, 58 days removed from the fall of Bhishma which also means 68 days removed from the first day of Mahabharata War, and since the day of winter solstice is described as *Magha Shuddha Ashtami*, it follows that *Kartika Amawasya* was the first day of Mahabharata War, 68 days before the day of winter solstice.

The immediate problem I faced was the rationale for this reference and its inclusion in the Mahabharata text, the reference being that of the day of *Bhishma Nirvana* being the 58th day from the fall of Bhishma and also the day of winter solstice with *Magha Shuddha Ashtami* & *Rohini nakshatra*. Specific references to *Magha Shuddha Ashtami* and *Rohini nakshatra* are understood to be later interpolations. I do not know the criteria used to categorize this reference as interpolation.

In any case, I would add that reference to 58 days also points to the day of *Magha Shuddha Ashtami* and *Rohini nakshatra*. And these references individually or together also point to Kartika *Amawasya* as the first day of War, i.e. (20-21 days of *Margashirsha* + 29-30 days of *Pausha* + 7-8 days of *Magha*), an obvious fact lost on those researchers who have proposed a day other than *Kartika Amawasya* as the first day of War (Raghavan/Achar, Karandikar, Sengupta) while still claiming observations surrounding *Bhishma Nirvana* as critical in building their timeline.

Do we have evidence of interpolation? I would like to make a case for it. The Critical edition does not treat references to 'month of *Magha* and 3/4th of the month (or *Paksha*)' as interpolations. Assuming '3/4th' refers to the 'month', one can easily infer this day to be *Magha Shuddha Ashtami*. This interpolation, if at all one can make a convincing case for it, would have referred to median time interval of 1700-1900 B.C. The period (1700-1900 B.C.) referred to is only an estimate since instances where *Magha Shuddha Ashtami* coinciding with the day of Winter solstice can be identified over an extended period of up to 3000-4000 years.

Critical edition provides another version where '**Magho yam samanu prapto masa punyo Yudhishthir**' is replaced with '**Maso yam samanu prapto Masa Pushya Yudhishthir**' and I speculate that this change would have been inserted in later times when winter solstice was indeed in *Pushya* (*Purnima*). Transcribers of this specific manuscript of Mahabharata might have reconciled what they saw in the sky (or when they thought Mahabharata happened) with what they read in Mahabharata. Thus we have transcription journey of the day of winter solstice beginning with full moon days of *Hasta* (5561 B.C.) through (*Phalguni*) through *Magha* and ending in *Pushya*. Winter solstice occurred in the month of *Phalguna* during 5561 B.C. Today winter solstice occurs near '*Margashirsha Purnima*', which means some 2000 years ago it was near '*Pausha Purnima*' and some 4000 years ago it was near '*Magha Purnima*'. It is then interesting to note that alternate readings within the Mahabharata text does refer to winter solstice (and thus *Bhishma Nirvana*) occurring near *Pausha Purnima*'. I want to highlight this reference as possible evidence of Mahabharata interpolation as late as 2000 years ago. The median time when winter solstice occurred near *Pausha Purnima* is around 550 B.C.

On the other hand assuming '3/4th' refers to the '*Paksha*', one can infer this day to be either *Magha Shuddha Chaturthi* or *Magha Krishna Chaturthi*.

Error Elimination – Experiment 67

Month of *Magha* and ¾ of *Paksha*

I read something curious and unintelligible, i.e. unintelligible to me, in the writings of P V Kane, and my brief note is for the benefit of Indian calendar experts who might able to make some sense out of what Kane wrote and thus accept or reject my explanation. Other-wise, this attempt of mine, to rationalize month of *Magha* and 3/4th of *Paksha* is unnecessary. This is because I wholeheartedly accept my inability to corroborate two Mahabharata observations and their cor-responding inferences for the day of *Bhishma Nirvana*,

(1) 58 days time interval between 'Fall of Bhishma' and 'Bhishma *Nirvana*'
(2) The day of *Bhishma Nirvana* to be *Magha Shuddha Ashtami*
(3) *The Moon in Rohini*
(4) 58th day is the day of winter solstice

With one exception of P V Holay, no other Mahabharata researcher has corroborated these 4 inferences due to Mahabharata observa-

140

tions [109, 110] related to *Bhishma Nirvana*. P V Holay made an ad hoc conjecture of the War stopping for 12 days after the fall of Bhishma, before it resumed. There is not a single Mahabharata observation that supports such a conjecture. On the other hand, modified war timeline of Holay, especially for last 8 days of the War is falsified by all Mahabharata observations discussed in Chapter 8. Holay had to make an additional conjecture of *Adhika Masa* (extra lunar month) in order to show that the lunar month was *Magha*.

Day proposed by Vartak (22nd December 5561 B.C.) corroborates 3 of the 4 conditions (it was not the day of winter solstice), while day proposed by Raghavan/Achar (17 January 3066 B.C.) corroborates only 2 of the 4 conditions, and that too only after keeping Bhishma in waiting for 4 more days beyond the day of winter solstice.

Returning to the discussion of Mahabharata observations of *Bhishma Nirvana*, it is important to realize that first 3 outcomes are not 3 independent Mahabharata observations but rather one Mahabharata observation (or interpolation) of *Magha Shuddha Ashtami* as the day of *Bhishma Nirvana*.

Moreover, I have shown that 21 distinct observations corroborate my timeline while 2 observations (*Magha* and *Magha Shuddha Ashtami*) contradict my timeline. It goes without saying that 21 distinct observations, identified by me, directly contradict claim(s) for 58 nights and therefore all claims for the timing of Mahabharata War based on it. These 21 distinct observations also contradict *Magha Shuddha Ashtami* and the Moon in *Rohini* as the day of Winter solstice at the time of Mahabharata War.

Once I established post-war timeline leading to 31st January 5560 B.C. - the day of *Bhishma Nirvana*, I was curious to know the identification of lunar month and lunar day (*Tithi*) for the day of *Bhishma Nirvana*. Assuming *Amanta* reckoning for a lunar month, I matched lunar months with dates of western calendar. Per *Amanta* reckoning, the month is determined by proximity of the position of full moon with respect to key *nakshatras*. The outcome is summarized in Table 12.

Add to this fun one *Adhika* masa. For example if one interprets *Magha* (the full moon of 28-29 December 5561 B.C.) as *Adhik Magha* (intercalary month) and next month (the full moon of 27 January 5560 B.C.) as *Magha*, in that case, Bhishma died on *Magha Krishna 4*.

P V Kane writes in interpreting observation[159] of *Bhishma Nirvana*,

> The difficulty is how to connect '*Tribhagashesh*', whether as an adjective of '*masa*' or of '*Paksha*'. If we take it the first way, these words were uttered on 8th of *Magha Shukla*. If we take it as an adjective of '*Paksha*', then they will have to be taken as uttered on the 4th of the bright half or on the 4th of the dark half, which may be regarded in its astrological effects as equal to *Shukla Paksha* (though the *Tithi* itself is in the dark half).

I do not claim to understand the meaning of 'astrological effects'. All I want to point out is; with one 'assumption' of *Adhika Magha*, interpretation and explanation of Kane, unintelligible to me, does apply successfully to my proposed date of *Bhishma Nirvana*.

Let me repeat. This is highly speculative and my timeline does not require such patchworks. My preference would be to mention these observations [109, 110] as not corroborated by my timeline (my timeline corroborated 21 distinct Mahabharata observations, in turn, identified by me) and leave it at that.

While many researchers are content with presenting only two observations [109, 110] in the context of *Bhishma Nirvana*, I have presented twenty three [108-130] observations and have shown that 21 out of 23 observations not only corroborate my proposed timeline but also falsify proposals of <u>all</u> previous researchers. I have shown that one of the two remaining observations can be corroborated with my timeline by making an assumption of '*Adhika Masa* (insertion of extra lunar month)' and employing 'astrological effects' explanation of P V Kane[109]. I have made a case, with corroborative support, for interpolated nature of the remaining Mahabharata observation[110].

4. The Mahabharata War & *KaliYuga*

Numerous researchers have proposed years for the Mahabharata War that fall within the time interval of 3102 B.C. +/- 500 Years. Most of these researchers, if not all, were driven by two specific 'traditional' beliefs,

(1) *KaliYuga* begins with the year 3102 B.C.
(2) The Mahabharata War took place either 36 or some years before the beginning of *KaliYuga*.

142

Both of these beliefs are external to the Mahabharata text however the second belief does borrow the time interval of 36 years from the Mahabharata text. Krishna passed away 36 years after the Mahabharata War [81-83]. Many researchers combined Mahabharata references of 'Krishna passing away 36 years after the Mahabharata War' with Purana references of 'KaliYuga beginning with the 'passing away of Krishna' to arrive at the second traditional belief. These Mahabharata researchers looked at time interval surrounding 3102 B.C. as the starting point for their search of the Mahabharata War. This starting point is reasonable and useful as long as these researchers also understood conjectural nature of their assumptions that led to this time interval. Some of these researchers, when their proposed year for the Mahabharata War occurred after 3102 B.C., felt the need to justify how Mahabharata War occurred during KaliYuga. They were equally compelled to 'prove' how the Mahabharata text supported their justification.

My limited objective in this section is to discuss Mahabharata observations that refer to 'theory of Yugas' and timing of the Mahabharata War in the context of Yugas. I assert that there are no explicit references within the Mahabharata text that allude to the Mahabharata War occurring 36 years before the beginning of KaliYuga. I also assert that the Mahabharata text provides numerous observations to conclude that the Mahabharata War took place during 'Dwapara' Yuga, whatever the definition of Dwapara might be, or during the transition period between KaliYuga and Dwapara Yuga. Let me emphasize that I am not commenting or questioning the assumption or assertion of 3102 B.C. as the beginning of Kali Yuga. Rather what I am asserting is that the Mahabharata text contains varied definitions of Yuga and none of them would convincingly lead us to year 3102 B.C.

The words 'Dwapara' and 'Krita' are employed as referring to something other than Yuga as well. For example, Virata Parva refers to 'Dwapara' and 'Krita' in the sense of throw of dice in the game of 'Dyuta' [132]. Mahabharata text also refers to 'Yuga' in the sense of five solar and lunar years together. Krishna refers to Yuga in the sense of outcome of an activity, i.e. creation of a Yuga by human activity. Krishna tells Karna that when the Pandavas will begin the War, Karna and the Kauravas will face horrendous bloodshed, and thus perceive

143

the time as if it is *KaliYuga*, as opposed to that of *Treta, Krita* or *Dwapara Yugas*[131].

The impact of 3102 B.C. as the beginning of *Kali Yuga* and its connection with the Mahabharata War appears to be strong among many Mahabharata researchers, to the extent 50% of all proposed dates for the Mahabharata War fall around 3000 B.C.

Error Elimination – Experiment 68

I present theories of *Yuga* as described in the Mahabharata text. I have named them after the person advocating it.

Yuga theory of Hanuman [133-135]

Hanuman describes (to Bhima) four *Yuga*s in terms of the characteristics of each *Yuga*, symbolic color, and the nature of actions and morality prevailing during specific *Yuga*[133].

Hanuman alludes to the passing away of *Krita* and *Treta* and thus the time of his conversation with Bhima is that of *Dwapara Yuga*[134]. This inference is also confirmed by Hanuman's comment that soon the *KaliYuga* would begin and this means at the time of conversation, *Dwapara* was still in vogue[135].

Yuga theory of Sage Markandeya[136]

Sage Markandeya describes the four *Yuga*s as referring to 'a long period of time'. He assigns specific years for each *Yuga*. Many researchers have translated these years as referring to *Divya* (divine) years. While I consider this as a possibility, I have translated them as ordinary years since I did not find the word '*Divya*' mentioned anywhere. Markandeya defines *Krita, Treta, Dwapara* and *Kali* as made up of 4000, 3000, 2000 and 1000 years (or *Divya* years), respectively. He defines the transition periods, '*Sandhya* or '*Sandhyamshash*', of 400 years each for *Krita*. The transition periods are of 300, 200 and 100 years long for *Treta, Dwapara* and *Kali Yuga*s, respectively. Markandeya explains that this time interval of 12000 years (4800 + 3600 + 2400 + 1200) makes one *ChaturYuga* and that a day of Brahma consists of 1000 *ChaturYugas*. Markandeya also explains characteristics of each *Yuga*.

Yuga theory of Sanjay[137]

Sanjay describes his version of *Yuga* theory to Dhritarashtra. He describes four *Yuga*s in terms of the life span of human beings. It is not clear how he defines 'life span', i.e. whether in terms of quality, piety or purely in terms of number of years lived. He states that 'life span' is equivalent to 4000 years in *Krita* and 3000 in *Treta*. Sanjay does not specify 'life span' for *KaliYuga*, however mentions that infant mortality is a common occurrence[137]. Sanjay states that the land of Himavat surpasses BharatVarsha in virtues, and HariVarsha as superior, even to Himavat[139].

Sanjay states that during the present time of *Dwapara Yuga*, i.e. at the time of conversation between him and Dhritarashtra, people live for 2000 years[138]. He goes on to explain the characteristics of human beings in each *Yuga* and reiterates the time of his conversation with Dhritarashtra as that of *Dwapara Yuga*[139].

Yuga theory of Bhishma[140]

Bhishma defines the theory of *ChaturYuga* in terms of qualities, actions and characteristics of the ruling King. Bhishma describes the actions, of the king, responsible for bringing 'Krita', "Treta', 'Dwapara' or 'Kali' Yuga and describes rewards king receives depending on the *Yuga* King creates with his actions, and states that the King is wholly responsible for the precipitation of a specific *Yuga*.

Yuga theory of Vyasa

(As told to Shuka, quoted by Bhishma) [141]

The theory of Vyasa, as recalled by Bhishma, is a combination of above theories, has similarities with that of Markendaya, while with few twists of its own. Bhishma describes a day of Gods as equivalent to one year of human beings. Bhishma does not explicitly state if the years mentioned are '*Divya*', i.e. 'years of gods' or years of human beings. Markandeya describes 1000 *ChaturYugas* equal to one day of Brahma, without specifying the definition of the day, i.e. day constituting '*Aha*' + '*Ratra*' or only '*Aha*'. Vyasa also refers to 1000 *ChaturYugas* being equal to one day of Brahma, however specifies the

145

day in the sense of 'Aha'. Vyasa holds that all creation remains in the state of 'Yoganidra' during the night of Brahma. While Sanjay describes 'life span' of human beings as 4000, 3000, 2000 years and unspecified time interval for Krita, Treta, Dwapara and Kali respectively, Vyasa describes these 'life spans' as 400, 300, 200 and 100 years, respectively for these Yugas. Vyasa also describes the characteristics of each Yuga, which are similar to those described by others.

This concludes summary of five theories of Yuga proposed by Hanuman, Markendaya, Sanjay, Bhishma and Vyasa from the Mahabharata text. Internal evidence of Mahabharata does not produce a consistent view for the concept of Yuga. Mahabharata text explains 'Yuga' in various ways including, as a period of 5 years, a long period of time, throws of dice or an outcome of King's performance and activities.

Error Elimination – Experiment 69

The Mahabharata War happened in Dwapara Yuga

Hanuman[134, 135] and Sanjay[138, 139] explicitly refer to 'Dwapara' Yuga as the time of their conversation. Adi Parva states that the Mahabharata War took place during the transition period of Dwapara and Kali Yuga[142]. Duryodhana refers to Dwapara (Nadhwam) as the time of his conversation[143]. Krishna, in order to pacify angry Balarama on the last day of War, asks Balarama to consider (pretend/assume) the time as if it was KaliYuga and thus forgive Bhima[144]. This means that even when the War was over, the KaliYuga had not begun.

I want to re-emphasize that I am not objecting to 3102 B.C. as the beginning of Kali Yuga. When exactly KaliYuga began is a separate subject and worthy of investigation, however, I consider it outside the scope of this book. All I want to emphasize is that the Mahabharata text emphasizes in no uncertain terms that the time of Mahabharata War was that of Dwapara Yuga or the transition period between Kali and Dwapara Yugas. Mahabharata references and my proposed timeline neither contradict nor support year of 3102 B.C. as the beginning of KaliYuga.

Researchers who made a big deal about the traditional date for the beginning of KaliYuga were right in their conjecture to begin with 3102 B.C. but were wrong in justifying their conjecture.

5. Bhishma appearing similar to the full moon[145]

I presented numerous 'full moon' Mahabharata observations describing incidents of 10 through 18 days of the War. I corroborated these observations with my 18-day war timeline, specifically the phases and the positions of the moon. Naturally, I was looking for any observations that would conflict with my theory and predictions of the phases and the positions of the moon. At least I found one observation. Sanjay describes Bhishma as shining like the full moon, before the War began and on the first day of War[145].

Error Elimination – Experiment 70

Bhishma compared with the Full Moon

The reader should understand the context of this comparison of Bhishma with the full moon, comparison made on *Amawasya* day. Sanjay tells Dhritarashtra that he saw Bhishma on his white horse, wearing a white turban and white armor resembling the risen (or new) Moon[146] and both armies beheld Bhishma standing in his silver chariot with a golden palm tree on his standard. Sanjay compares this latter arrangement with the Moon (or the Sun) surrounded by white clouds[147, 148].

I have interpreted this comparison of Bhishma with the full moon, as pure analogy, based on decorations of Bhishma (white turban and white armor) and his paraphernalia (silver chariot with golden palm tree as his standard).

6. Analogy of the Solar Eclipse

The War lasted for 18 days, until the day of *Pushya nakshatra* and 3 days after the full moon day. The Mahabharata text employs analogy of '*Rahu* grasping the Sun (or solar eclipse) on non-*Amawasya* day' in describing the evil portents at the time of Bhima-Duryodhana fight[149]. The analogy of the solar eclipse on the last day of War would appear to contradict my timeline, the last day being close to the full moon day.

The Mahabharata observation[149] that appears to contradict my timeline clearly states that the day is NOT *Amawasya*. This would

147

suffice as explanation for so called contradiction between this observation and my timeline. This explanation would also falsify any timeline that would claim the last day of the War as *Amawasya* (e.g. Raghavan/Achar, Holay). I could identify additional Mahabharata references and these references not only corroborate my timeline but also provide consistent and meaningful explanation for '*Rahu* grasping the Sun' on non-*Amawasya* day.

Error Elimination – Experiment 71

Last day of the War = Day near the full moon day

The club dual between Bhima and Duryodhana began, as the Sun was ready to set[150]. The cousin warriors, fighting opposite of each other, appeared similar to both the Sun and the Moon [151]. When angry Balarama proceeded to attack Bhima, after Bhima defeated Duryodhana, Krishna held hands of Balarama and these two Yadava brothers appeared similar to the Moon and the Sun at the end of the day (sunset) [152]. Only three days before this final fight between Bhima and Duryodhana, the Moon and the Sun would have been seen as described[151, 152]. Balarama approached the site of the dual and all who were present welcomed him. Balarama, surrounded by kings, appeared like the full moon surrounded by *nakshatras* [89, 153].

I will not repeat Mahabharata observations already presented in Chapter 8 that describe 'full moon' during last few days of the War. These 'full moon' descriptions exists for the last day of the War and also continue for next one or two days after the War.

Error Elimination – Experiment 72

Rahu grasping the Sun on non-*Amawasya* day

The Mahabharata text describes omens in the context of club dual between Bhima and Duryodhana. The descriptions of omens, before the club dual began, are as follows,

Strong winds started blowing and thunderstorms ensued. All directions were covered with darkness and meteors started falling from the sky. *Rahu* grasped the Sun (situation appeared similar to the

148

solar eclipse) even though the day was not *Amawasya*. The earth began trembling and dry air started blowing with showers of dust and stones while tops of the mountains began falling to the ground. Mriga of various shapes began running in all directions while goblins with horrible faces and bodies, with fire coming out of their mouths, began uttering bad omens. Water levels in the wells began rising without any cause and loud roars of goblins could be heard[154].

Or consider the descriptions of these two warriors and their comparison with the descriptions of the end of the world,

The two warriors, Bhima and Duryodhana, were unstoppable, similar to the turbulent oceans at the end of the world. They were torturing each other similar to two Mars. Both of them were shining similar to the two Suns at the end of the world[156].

The Mahabharata text also describes omens after the fall of Duryodhana in the battle,

Thunderstorms ensued along with strong wind, while the earth began trembling. Large sized meteor fell to the ground, making a loud noise and rain of dust and blood ensued. Yakshas, Rakshasas and Goblins filled the sky with roaring sounds. Birds and Mriga began running in all directions by hearing these sounds while horses, elephants and surviving warriors made tumultuous sound. Goblins could be seen dancing all over and sounds of various instruments could be heard. Water reservoirs and wells over flooded with the blood and prominent rivers began flowing in opposite direction, feminine characteristics appeared among men and vice versa[155].

I want the reader to compare these descriptions with those of *Yuganta*, end of the world, as described in the Mahabharata text. Sage Markandeya describes conditions of *Yuganta*. I present partial descriptions from his list, relevant to our problem, i.e. problem of *Rahu* grasping the Sun on non-*Amawasya* day,

When the time for the end of the world arrives, living entities will begin to become extinct, all directions will turn red and star field will lose its luster. Planets will start moving in undesirable directions, strong wind will start blowing and frequent meteor showers will commence. The Sun would appear as if afflicted by *Rahu* both

149

during the sunrise and the sunset. Women would kill their hus-
bands with the assistance of their sons. **Rahu would grasp the Sun
even on non-*Amawasya* day.** When the end of the world arrives,
crows, elephants, other birds and animals will make harsh sounds
and people would renounce their friends, relatives and servants
without any reason[157].

I conjecture that the reference to '*Rahu* grasps the Sun on non-
Amawasya day' is used in this context of comparing the intensity of
club dual between Bhima and Duryodhana with that of the end of the
world.

7. Problem of Seasons

(Krishna leaves from Upaplavya at the end of *Sharad*)

The problem of the seasons during the Mahabharata war is a
minor one. I decided to include it, at the risk of much digression, for
the sake of completeness. The timing of Krishna's departure from
Upaplavya on peace mission to Hastinapur is described as 'at the end
of *Sharad*' (*sharadante*) and 'before the arrival of winter' (*himagame*)
[158]. This Mahabharata reference contradicts practically all proposals
for the year of Mahabharata War. This Mahabharata reference also
contradicts my proposed timeline. The timing of Krishna's departure
from Upaplavya, per my timeline, is during the '*Varsha*' season. This
is based on the assumption that Mahabharata astronomers defined
the seasons in the same fashion, as we understand them today.

The Problem

The assumptions for the season with respect to the points of
solstices and equinoxes are as follows. Mahabharata calendar has six
seasons with time interval of two months each. Time interval of two
months beginning with the winter solstice is *Shishir* (winter), with the
vernal equinox as the center point is *Vasant* (spring), two months
leading to the day of the summer solstice is *Grishma* (summer), two
months following the summer solstice is *Varsha* (rain), two months
with the fall equinox as the center point is *Sharad* (Pre-Autumn) and

150

two months leading to the day of the winter solstice is *Hemanta* (Autumn).

The seasons, equinoxes, solstices and corresponding western calendar days, at the time of my proposed timeline (5561 B.C.), are shown in Table 2. Krishna left from Upaplavya on 31st August 5561 B.C. and during the time of the rainy season, per my timeline. This statement directly contradicts Mahabharata reference from Udyoga *Parva*[158].

Error Elimination – Experiment 73

The Mahabharata War during *Margashirsha* & *Sharad* season

Vartak interpreted '*Sharadante*' to mean 'during the *Sharad* season' instead of 'at the end of *Sharad* season'. While his interpretation, assuming acceptable, may allow him to get over the difficulty for his proposed timeline, it does not help explain my timeline.

The reader should keep in mind that I have conjectured time interval of one additional month and 7 days between Krishna-Karna dialogue and the first day of War while Vartak assumed time interval of only 7-8 days. I am happy to borrow '*Kaumudi*' interpretation of Vartak. Vartak interpreted '*Kaumude mase*' to mean 'during the month of lotuses' rather than 'during the month of *Kartika*' and this interpretation corroborates well with the timing of Krishna's departure from Upaplavya on 31 August, in the middle or at the end of the rainy season. The timing is also definitely before the cold season and therefore the observation of '*himagame*' also corroborates my timeline. I could confirm, using Voyager simulation, the timing of *Hemanta* (pre-autumn) from 2nd December through 30th January, i.e. until the day of the winter solstice, and the timing of *Sharad* season from 3rd October through 2nd December. I could say with certainty that the Mahabharata War itself took place during the *Sharad* season. I began re-reading the Mahabharata text, this time looking for references of '*Sharad*' season during the Mahabharata War and during the events following the Mahabharata War. The Mahabharata War, per my timeline, took place in the month of *Margashirsha*.

Bhishma says that months of *Chaitra* or *Margashirsha* (or full moon days during these months) are most suitable for mobilizing army or carrying out war due to the fact that harvest is ready, water is

151

readily available and the weather is neither too hot nor too cold[159]. This Mahabharata observation suggests months of *Margashirsha* or *Chaitra* as suitable for conducting war during Mahabharata times and the time suggested does corroborate my conjecture of the War taking place during the month of *Margashirsha*.

The time of Varsha season, when Krishna left for Hastinapur on a peace mission, is further corroborated by showers in Hastinapur brought by southwest winds (Monsoon) [217].

Error Elimination – Experiment 74

Time (and analogies) of the *Sharad* season

Descriptions of the Mahabharata War are full of analogies of the *Sharad* season. The battalion headed by Kripa, on the first day of War, appeared similar to the clouds of *Sharad* season[160] while the battlefield at the end of first day appeared similar to the sky filled with stars of the *Sharad* season[161]. The Kaurava army attacking Ghatotkacha, from all sides, were compared to the clouds of *Sharad* season pouring rain on mountaintop[162] while the response of Ghatotkacha, to this assault, was compared to the steady clouds of *Sharad* season[163]. Ghatotkacha responded to the assault, with showers of arrows, which in turn were compared to heavy rain poured by clouds of the *Sharad* season[164]. Ghatotkacha was walking like a lion in the battlefield and his towering personality appeared like the Sun of *Sharad* season[165].

The battlefield, at the end of day, appeared drenched with blood of elephants, horses and warriors, similar to the evening red clouds (red due to reflecting light of the setting sun) of *Sharad* season[166]. Some elephants were lifting warriors and throwing them on the battlefield, while some others were shouting loudly (in pain and anger) and still others were falling dead on the ground. The battlefield, covered with the bodies of elephants, looked like sky covered with the clouds of early *Sharad* season[167].

Abhimanyu was fighting mildly in the beginning, but in the end, he turned fierce against the enemy and the Mahabharata author compares this transformation of Abhimanyu with the (mild) sun of *Varsha* season, mild due to being covered by dark clouds of *Varsha*, transforming into fierce sun of the *Sharad* season[168]. Satyaki was fighting fiercely on the battlefield, while holding a circular bow, and was shining similar to the rising Sun of *Sharad* season[169]. Series of arrows shot by both warriors, appeared beautiful and similar to the pack of *Saras* birds flying in the sky of *Sharad* season[170].

Angry Karna appeared similar to bright midday Sun of *Sharad* season[171]. A warrior is criticized for lack of action and is compared with clouds of the *Sharad* season, which produce thunder but no water[172]. Karna was engaged in a fierce fight, and appeared similar to bright midday Sun, while his arrows appeared similar to Sun spreading its rays in clear sky of the *Sharad* season[173]. The warriors, riding on chariots, appeared similar to lightening clouds of the *Sharad* season[174]. The iron armor of a warrior, decorated with precious stones, was shining similar to star studded sky of the *Sharad* season[175].

The reference to *Sharad* season, as clear as it can be, is presented when the battlefield is compared with the sky above and the sky is described as filled with stars of *Sharad* season[176]. The battlefield, covered with broken chariots, appeared similar to sky covered with clouds of the *Sharad* season[177]. Arjuna dispersed the Kaurava army similar to the wind that disperses clouds of *Sharad* season[178]. Duryodhana says to Bhima, "Son of Kunti, don't exhibit empty boast like the thunder of waterless clouds of *Sharad* season"[179].

The battalion of Nairukhtas, making loud noises with bells, conches, drums, their banners floating high up in the air, appeared similar to the sky of *Sharad* season[180]. The warriors, proud of their own strength, were fighting head on, similar to the male elephants in rut during the *Sharad* season[181]. Vikarna, lying at the center of elephant army, after being killed by Bhima, looked similar to the Moon surrounded by dark clouds of *Sharad* season[182]. Canopy on the chariot of Panchal Raj looked beautiful and similar to the Moon of *Sharad* season[183]. There are additional references to *Sharad* season [40, 56, 65] during the 18 days of War, already mentioned, in Chapter 8.

Error Elimination – Experiment 75

Bhishma Nirvana & *Sharad* Season

Bhishma fell in the War on the 10th day and ~98 days before the day of winter solstice. This means the Mahabharata war began ~108 days before the day of winter solstice, and thus *Sharad* season had just begun (~12 days into the season) when the Mahabharata war started. This chronological account leading to the day of *Bhishma Nirvana* also provides corroborative support for my assertion that the Mahabharata War took place during *Sharad* season.

I have presented 27 Mahabharata observations in support of the Mahabharata War during the *Sharad* season. The lone observation[158] conflicts with these 27 observations of *Sharad*. This lone observation[158] also conflicts with 21 out of 23 observations related to *Bhishma Nirvana*.

Conclusions

While I want to leave it to others to provide criticism of my theory, its predictions and its corroboration with Mahabharata observations, I want to emphasize the importance of identifying observations/predictions that contradict a given theory. I have shown how these apparently contradictory observations, when understood in the context of additional Mahabharata observations, corroborate my proposed timeline.

Problem of Balarama *Tirthayatra* as well as that of late moonrise led me to additional descriptions of full moon at the end of War. No researcher of the past has solved the problem of Balarama *Tirthayatra*. Researchers who tried to match the *nakshatras* of Balarama's departure (on *Pushya*) and arrival (on *Shravana*) faced more serious difficulties, whether they realized (or acknowledged) it or not.

For example, even if I give benefit of doubt to Raghavan and Achar and pretend that the nakshatra on the last day of War was *Shravana* (it was *PurvaAshadha*, per timeline of Raghavan/Achar), assuming an error of +/- 2 *nakshatras*, still Balarama of Raghavan/Achar does not show up at Kurukshetra, 3 days after the War is over!

And I only wonder what would be their (Raghavan/Achar) explanation for the observation of seven planets attacking the moon on the 14th day of War. After Arjuna killed Jayadratha, fight resumed. The timing was that of the evening of 14th day of War. Bhima fighting seven Kaurava brothers is compared with seven planets attacking the Moon[23]. I have corroborated this observation using Voyager 4.5™. Presence of moon in the evening sky can corroborate timing of *Shukla*

154

Paksha or 1-2 days after the full moon day (and thus early part of *Krishna Paksha*), however, it will never corroborate the time of *Krishna Paksha* and close to *Amawasya day*, as required by proposal of Raghavan/Achar or Karandikar.

Problem of the timing of *Bhishma Nirvana* led me to 21 additional observations which not only solved the problem posed for my proposed timeline but also further narrowed down the time interval for the plausible year of Mahabharata War, the time interval already defined by the Epoch of *Arundhati*. In the process, these additional observations, related to *Bhishma Nirvana,* falsified all previous proposals for the timing of Mahabharata War.

The problem of *KaliYuga* and Mahabharata led me to five disparate theories of *Yuga* within the Mahabharata Text and to additional Mahabharata references, which emphatically corroborate the timing of Mahabharata War as that of before *KaliYuga*.

The problem of '*Rahu* grasps the Sun on Non-*Amawasya* day' provides, by itself, a falsification of any proposal that claims last day of the Mahabharata War as either *Amawasya* or close to *Amawasya* day. I stumbled on additional insights, while investigating this Mahabharata observation, on the sources and rationale for numerous non-empirical analogies, employed by Mahabharata author, e.g., *Rahu* grasping the Sun on Non-*Amawasya* day, but also the rain of flesh and blood, statues of Gods trembling and vomiting blood, animals moving in wrong direction, etc.

I identified 23+ Mahabharata observations of Sharad season that corroborate my timeline against one Mahabharata observation that contradicts it. In addition, I came across one Mahabharata observation that stated in no uncertain terms that the timing of Krishna's visit to Hastinapur was during the *Varsha* season.

155

10

Theory of P V Vartak

In the field of thought, you have more often to refute the theories of those nearer to you than those more remote. Shankaracharya did not refute the atheists so much as he refuted Samkhyavada, which is closer to his theory. That is because what is close to us differs from us only in some small detail. Thus there is a greater probability of being misled. So the closest ideas have to be formulated and defended first. Later, it does become quite clear as to where the real point of difference is.

- Vinoba Bhave

I tested all known, i.e. known to me, proposals for the year of Mahabharata War, even when the proposed timing fell outside the Epoch of *Arundhati*. The only timeline (year and 18 days of War) that withstood my falsification tests was that of Vartak. I have proposed modified timeline, different from that of Vartak's, for the pre-war events and for the day of *Bhishma Nirvana*.

The reader who is not familiar with the process of scientific methodology may question my rationale of writing a book that essentially repeats the timeline proposed by Vartak. The reader may think that after all the pre-war and the post-war incidents, where I have

156

proposed alternate timeline, are but minor details. I answer such objections in this chapter.

Since I am going to be critical of the theory of Vartak in rest of this chapter, let me at the outset make it clear that I owe my debt to Vartak and his work. 'Swayambhu' by Vartak was the first work I read on the dating of Mahabharata War, and after 12 years it still remains the best work I ever read on this subject, in any language. The only other work, on the same subject, that came close (in clarity, content and depth) is 'History of Dharmashastra – Vol III' by P V Kane. Work of P V Kane certainly matched the knowledge content and the intent of Vartak's work. I was impressed and fascinated to see a discussion of high caliber on the dating of Mahabharata War, in a book I would have hardly imagined to contain, i.e. a book dedicated to the history of *Dharmashastra*.

I am going to criticize the work of Vartak because it is worth criticizing and also because his work enables criticism. My opinion of his work, as the best on the subject, is neither because his proposed date fell within the Epoch of *Arundhati* nor because I borrowed his 18-day war timeline and the year of Mahabharata War.

When I read 'Swayambhu' for the first time, his proposed year of 5561 B.C. shocked me. Thus it was not his specific year that impressed me as much as his methodology, his ardent desire to include and test all observations/references – both corroborating and conflicting with his theory, his willingness to take risks, i.e. make his research vulnerable, his innate understanding of scientific method and his understanding of the tentative nature of any theory. The knowledge content Vartak tried to corroborate using his theory makes his effort the best. I will conclude this preamble by stating that Vartak distinguished himself from all other Mahabharata researchers by not beginning with 'a priori' assumptions, by not being selective in choice of observations and by not being inductive in his methodology.

My objective in critically discussing the theory of Vartak is to point out mistakes, to identify superfluous assumptions and, if possible, to eliminate errors. I demonstrate that some of his conjectures were unnecessary. I demonstrate how his theory has unacceptable consequences and how it did not solve the problem it set out to solve. I also show how in some instances, his conjectures merely shifted the problem, raising difficulties worse than it surmounted. In spite of these limitations, his proposal for 5561 B.C. as the year of Mahabharata War and how he arrived at this date is astonishing, and remains mystery to me. I can hardly imagine the amount of work and astronomical calculations he would have gone through, most of them done manually, unlike my use of Voyager 4.5^{TM}!

My task in criticizing the theory of Vartak can be best summarized in the words of Karl Popper,

> It is possible to show the inferior aspect of a theory by its knowledge content or by the contradiction it generates or by its complexity. I want to emphasize that scientific criticism does not try to show that the theory in question has not been proved or demonstrated. It does not try to show that theory in question has not been established or justified. It does not try to show that theory in question has a high probability. No theory has high probability! Scientific criticism does not attack the arguments, which might be used to establish, or even to support, the theory under examination. Criticism attacks the theory itself, namely solution of the problem it tries to solve. Scientific criticism examines and challenges consequences of the theory, its explanatory power, its consistency, and its compatibility with other theories.

Scientific objectivity is nothing but the fact that no scientific theory is accepted as a dogma, and that all theories are tentative and are open, all the time, to severe criticism – to a rational critical discussion aiming at the elimination of errors.

All past Mahabharata researchers have done a great service to the field of Mahabharata research, by proposing multiple theories (and proposals) for the year (and the first day) of Mahabharata War. Their works offered multiple proposed dates of the Mahabharata War for me to test. It will be an inductivist error to equate falsification of their theories (and proposed dates) with their failure.

It goes without saying that my theory, including its background assumptions, is open to criticism. I look forward to a day when my theory will be overthrown. I am confident the day (and a new and better theory that would replace my theory) would mark another quantum jump in our knowledge of Mahabharata in particular, and antiquity (or lack of antiquity) of human civilizations in general. In words of Karl Popper, "Good tests kill bad theories, we survive to guess again!"

Fall of *Abhijit*[4]

Vartak is the only researcher who understood the crux of this observation, namely the corroborative evidence for the vibrant ancient Indian tradition of astronomy observations and documentation, the crux being *Abhijit* (Vega) becoming a Pole star. All I have done is made an attempt for more consistent explanation. While I insist that my interpretation is more consistent, I consider this difference rather trivial.

The Epoch of *Arundhati*[1]

Vartak is the only researcher, as far as I am aware, who believed in the factual occurrence of this Mahabharata observation. He attempted to test the observation, proposed multiple possibilities, and recognized the limitations of his proposals. He was not happy with his conjectures, and thus, in the spirit of a true researcher, appealed to astronomy community to research it further. I could sense his conviction while reading '*Swayambhu*', even though he failed to develop experiments to test the observation. I marvel at his efforts and also at his ability to scan the Mahabharata text, looking for any and all observations, irrespective of whether these observations corroborated his conjectures or contradicted them. Vartak built his broad timeline based on numerous references outside of the Mahabharata text and then employed astronomical observations within Mahabharata to narrow down his search for a specific year.

On the other hand, I began with *Arundhati* observation, corroborated it with independent tests and have restricted myself to astronomical observations internal to Mahabharata in determining the timeline of Mahabharata War.

Sayan-Nirayan Theory

I illustrate Sayan-Nirayan theory in brief since Vartak has employed it in explaining planetary positions as well as *nakshatras* of specific events, as described in the Mahabharata text. The position of celestial objects, specifically planets, comets and the Sun, are described using the nearest *nakshatra*. This is the Nirayan method. The first place, in counting of *nakshatra*, is assigned to a *nakshatra* that is

159

at or close to the point of specific cardinal point. While some may argue over which cardinal point should be taken as the place for the first *nakshatra*, I will only state assumptions made by Vartak in determining position for the first *nakshatra*. All four researchers (Vartak, Lele, Dikshit and Modak) treated the *nakshatra* at the point of Vernal equinox as the first *nakshatra*.

Vartak proposed 5561 B.C. as the year of Mahabharata War. Vernal equinox was near *Punarvasu* in 5561 B.C., however since Vartak has assigned the first position to *Pushya nakshatra*, I presume that he assumes the convention for his 'Nirayan assignment of *nakshatra*' continued from 7440 B.C. He employs *Ashwini* as the first *nakshatra* for the Sayan method (Sayan being the original reference of first *nakshatra*, to which Nirayan is considered a deviation, due to the precession of equinoxes). This assumption of his alludes to the time of original reference, i.e. vernal equinox near *Ashwini*, to 26000 B.C. Vernal equinox also coincided with *Ashwini* in 400 B.C. and may be taken as the reference, i.e. Sayan reference – for Sayan-Nirayan theory, however, one should realize that this event (400 B.C.) occurred long after the proposed year (5561 B.C.) of Vartak for the Mahabharata War, and such posterior reference for Sayan counting is inconsistent with Sayan – Nirayan theory.

There is also some confusion related to the number assigned (zero or one) to first *nakshatra*, i.e. whether the first *nakshatra* (*nakshatra* at vernal equinox) is counted as zero or one. If one assumes that the first *nakshatra* was counted as zero, then the timing for the beginning of Sayan system would change by approximately 1000 years to ~400 A.D. (or 26000 B.C. +/- 1000 years) for *Ashwini* as the first *nakshatra* for Vartak's Sayan system. By same logic the timing for Nirayan system of Vartak should then be interpreted as belonging to ~6440 B.C. with *Punarvasu* as the first *nakshatra*.

Dikshit and Modak predicted 7300 B.C. and 5000 B.C. as approximate periods for the Mahabharata War, employing Sayan-Nirayan theory. Lele employed the same theory and proposed 5228 B.C. First two predictions proposed only approximate time intervals. I tested and falsified proposal for the year 5228 B.C.

I discuss Vartak's attempt to explain planetary positions and nakshatras during the Mahabharata War, using Sayan-Nirayan, with Ashwini as first Sayan *nakshatra* (ranked #1) and Pushya as first Nirayan *nakshatra* (ranked #1) in the context of 5561 B.C.

160

Jupiter & Saturn

Vartak employed positions of Jupiter, Saturn, and *Rahu* (node of the Moon) as described in the Mahabharata text, along with their orbital periods to predict plausible year of the Mahabharata War. Vartak interpreted Saturn near *Purva Phalguni*[10] and Jupiter near *Shravana*[11] on the first day of Mahabharata War. He assumed, correctly I think, that both Saturn and Jupiter were occupying equidistant *nakshatra* space on two sides of *Vishakha*[6] for over a year. These are visual descriptions of the sky in 5561 B.C.

I began testing Vartak's proposal for 5561 B.C. with observations of Jupiter and Saturn. Voyager simulation showed position of Saturn near *Uttara Phalguni*. The reader should note that reference to *Bhaga nakshatra* applies to both *Uttara Phalguni* and/or *Purva Phalguni*. This location immediately corroborated two Mahabharata observations of Saturn; Saturn near *Bhaga*[10], but also near *Vishakha*[6] along with Jupiter, for a year. This latter description of the position of Saturn (i.e. near *Vishakha*) makes sense only when interpreted in the context of relative position of Jupiter.

Vartak must have felt frustrated in explaining remaining observations related to Jupiter and Saturn. He invokes theory of Sayan-Nirayan to explain Jupiter near *Shravana*[11] (Nirayan) and Jupiter near (*Swati*) *Vishakha*[6] (Sayan). I think this was unnecessary, especially after a fine job he had done explaining them as visual observations. He also invokes theory of Sayan-Nirayan to explain Saturn in *Bhaga*[10] (Nirayan) and *Rohini*[8, 9] (Sayan), but then goes on to explain 'Saturn afflicting *Rohini*'[8, 9] by invoking the phenomenon of '*Rohini Shakat Bheda*'. I would ask the reader to ignore what '*Rohini Shakat Bheda*' is, however the point I want to emphasize is that Vartak himself did not seem to have been pleased with his explanation, for he provided at least two incompatible solutions while explaining positions of Jupiter as well as those of Saturn. He also introduced inconsistency in his theory, when he explained 'Jupiter near *Vishakha*'[6] using Sayan-Nirayan theory, but did not invoke the same theory to explain 'Saturn near *Vishakha*'[6].

Mahabharata has one additional observation of Jupiter[12]. Jupiter was seen afflicting *Rohini*, similar to the Sun and the Moon and becoming bright like them, after the sunset, on the 17th day of War. Vartak anticipated, I opine, straightforward explanation for Jupiter-

Rohini[12] and Saturn-*Rohini* [8, 9] observations, when he explained the timing of observation - 'the Sun and the Moon together, afflicting *Rohini*'[26], as the observation on the first day of War. It is then unfortunate, that he came so close to explaining three observations related to *Rohini*, but missed them altogether. He went on to explain 'Jupiter afflicting *Rohini*'[12] as 'poetic exaggeration' by Mahabharata author to describe the battlefield after the death of Karna.

He also proposed three distinct explanations for 'Saturn afflicting *Rohini*' [8, 9], first employing Sayan-Nirayan theory, then employing *Rohini-Shakat Bheda* and finally employing astrological *drishti*. He even alluded to the 4th conjecture where he refers to the broad timeline where Saturn was afflicting *Rohini* every ~30 years for many centuries before the War.

Vartak claims the phenomenon of *Rohini Shakat Bheda* occurring some 7 years before the War, when Saturn was in *Rohini*. Voyager simulation shows this period, i.e. when Saturn was near *Rohini*, to be rather 10 years before the War. I failed to understand the rationale of invoking a phenomenon, assuming '*Rohini Shakat Bheda*' did take place, 7 or 10 years before the War. I think he also noticed the difficulty and states that Saturn was afflicting (*Shakat-Bheda*) *Rohini* during each orbital visit for many centuries. In addition, he also invoked theory of astrological '*Drishti*' for 'Saturn afflicting *Rohini*' from wherever it (Saturn) was at the time of War.

Vakri motion: Mars & Jupiter

While Vartak translated, erroneously I think, 'Mars went retrograde near *Magha* and <u>Jupiter was near *Shravana*</u>[11]', I translate this observation as 'Mars traveled *vakri* near *Magha* and <u>so did Jupiter (traveled *vakri*) near *Shravana*</u>[11]'. It is true that Jupiter was near *Shravana* on 16 October, but then Mars was nowhere close to *Magha*. Voyager simulation confirmed that Jupiter was near *Shravana* however not retrograde on the first day of War. I could not ignore the clear reference to '*vakri*'. The Mahabharata text also refers to Mars traveling *vakri* near *Anuradha/Jyeshtha*[13] and again refers to '*vakra-anuvakri*' motion of Mars before reaching *Shravana/Abhijit*[14].

Vartak ignored '*vakri*' aspect of these planets (Mars & Jupiter) and used Sayan-Nirayan theory to explain Mars in *Anuradha*[13] (Nirayan) & *Magha*[11] (Sayan). Vartak does talk of retrograde motion of

162

Mars near *Anuradha* & *Jyeshtha*[13] however Voyager simulation shows no retrograde motion of Mars near *Anuradha/Jyeshtha*. He employs some esoteric explanation for Mars in *Shravana* and infers that *'Brhamarashi'*[14] refers to *Rohini* and to explain his inference, invokes his theory of 'astrological *Drishti'*.

Many Mahabharata researchers, including Vartak, have interpreted two observations [13, 14] as referring to some unknown planets, which should have been understood to be referring to Mars. I have shown that the observation referring to 'planet afflicting *Chitra*'[13] (interpreted by others as referring to 'some' planet), refers to Mars. Another observation of Mars, becoming steady, appearing fearsome and shining brightly while moving in *'apasavya'* direction between *Chitra* and *Swati*[14], is interpreted by many as referring to *Rahu* or other planets.

While I did not agree with explanations (Mars *vakri* near *Magha* and Jupiter *Vakri* near *Shravana*[11]) of Vartak, I struggled to come up with satisfactory explanations of my own for a long time. I could not observe *'vakri'* motions (translated by numerous researchers, including Vartak, as 'retrograde') of Mars near *Magha*[11] or near *Jyeshtha/Anuradha*[13] and that of Jupiter near *Shravana*[11]. Breakthrough occurred when I realized that the Mahabharata text was referring to two instances of *'vakri'* motions of Mars separated by only 6-7 *nakshatra* spaces (*nakshatras* between *Magha* and *Anuradha* or *Jyeshtha*). Mars completes a round through the ecliptic over a period of ~2 (1.88) years and goes retrograde only once in two years and thus the impossibility of retrograde motion occurring twice within a span of 6-7 *nakshatras*.

I ran simulations of Mars traveling through the ecliptic beginning with the current millennium (2000 A.D.). My goal was to understand the types of motions exhibited by Mars. I ran these simulations using DVA[TM], stretching over a period of 10 years by selecting 'one day' as a step change. Once familiar with movements of Mars through the ecliptic, I ran simulation beginning with 5563 B.C., two years before 5561 B.C. Mars began approaching the ecliptic, it traveled past *Rohini* (March 5562 B.C.), touched the ecliptic near *Punarvasu* (June 5562 B.C.) and had obliquely crossed the ecliptic by the time it reached *Magha*[11] (August 5562 B.C.). Mars traveled east, approached *Chitra*[13] (November 5562 B.C.), reached *Swati* (January 5561 B.C.) and then turned retrograde traveling west and approached

Chitra for the second time (March 5561 B.C.) and finally left the region of *Chitra/Swati*[14] (May 5561 B.C.). In effect, Mars had settled between *Chitra* and *Swati* for some 6 months[14]. Mars touched the ecliptic, this time traveling from the north to the south (June 5561 B.C.), approached *Anuradha* (27 June 5561 B.C.), then *Jyeshtha*[13] (9 July 5561 B.C.) and proceeded straight to the region of *Shravana/Abhijit*[14]. Mars was between *Shravana* and *Dhanishtha* and right along *Brahmarashi* (*Abhijit*) [14] on the first day of War.

I was excited that I solved the problem of Mars, and realized that Mahabharata observation 'Jupiter traveling *vakri* near *Shravana*'[11] provided an excellent opportunity to falsify my theory of *vakri* motion! Naturally I tested observation of Jupiter[11]. Jupiter was north of the ecliptic and near *Shravana* on the first day of War, touched the ecliptic (March 5560 B.C.) and traveled to the south of the ecliptic, still in the vicinity of *Shravana*. My conjecture for the *vakri* motions of Mars survived the falsification test offered by *vakri* motion of Jupiter! The movement of Jupiter is lot slower in comparison to Mars and thus oblique crossing of Jupiter is not as dramatic as that of Mars.

Venus

Vartak conjectured that Mahabharata author had made a mistake of 3 *nakshatras*. He specifically made such hypothesis in order to explain position of Venus, as assumed by him, for the first day of War. Later on he found that such conjecture was also required to justify time interval of only 58 days between 'Fall of Bhishma' and 'Bhishma Nirvana'.

Vartak assumed, wrongly I think, the timing for positions of planets, as referring to the first day of War. This assumption led Vartak to the conjecture of Mahabharata author making an error of 3 *nakshatras*. I do not see a need for such conjecture to explain either the position of Venus or time interval between 'Fall of Bhishma' and 'Bhishma Nirvana'. Once I put forward the theory of 'visual observations of the sky', I saw the futility of assuming multiple positions of planets as referring to their positions on a single specific day (e.g. the first day of War).

Vartak did a great job in recognizing the planet, in the company of Venus, near *Purva Bhadrapada*[18] to be Neptune. Venus was near *Shravana/Dhanishtha* on the first day of war, it turned north as

164

if to make *parikrama* around Neptune beginning with 17 November 5561 B.C., near *Purva Bhadrapada*, traveled west, as far as *Shatabhi-saj* (21 January 5560 B.C.) and left the region of *Purva Bhadrapada* sometime in March 5560 B.C.[18].

Although I do not agree with Vartak's conjecture of Mahabharata author making a mistake of three *nakshatras*, I want to point out that in making such an assumption, Vartak anticipated my 'correction' to his timeline, for the pre-war events. Vartak held fast to the notion that the War indeed began only 7 days after Krishna-Karna meeting. Later on Vartak hypothesized Vyasa making an error of 3 *nakshatras* (i.e. *UttaraAshadha* as being correct position of the Sun, instead of *Jyeshtha* as assumed by Vyasa) to explain position of Venus, which Vartak thought, erroneously I may add, in *Purva Bhadrapada* on the first day of War.

I have conjectured that the time interval between Krishna–Karna dialogue and the first day of Mahabharata War was rather 7 days plus one lunar month. I made this conjecture in order to corroborate Mahabharata observations of the events before the War. The events include Krishna leaving for Hastinapur[74], Duryodhana asking his fellow kings to leave for Kurukshetra on the day of *Pushya*[77], Krishna-Karna meeting 7 days before *Jyeshtha* (*Shakra*) *Amawasya*[73], Balarama visiting the Pandava camp and then leaving the camp on *Maitri* (*Anuradha*) *nakshatra*[75], Yudhishthir holding secret meeting around the full moon day[76], Uluka visiting the Pandavas, Armies leaving for Kurukshetra on *Pushya*[77-79] and arriving on *Magha*[80] and Vyasa meeting Dhritarashtra after *Krishna Chaturdashi* but one day before the War[30].

Vartak's insistence on corroboration of all Mahabharata observations led him to anticipate many of the discoveries made in this book. I speculate that random coincidence of 22 December corroborating with *Magha Shuddha* 8, moon in *Rohini* and interval of 58 nights between 25 October (fall of Bhishma) and 22 December deceived him and sent him on a tangential path. I was immensely impressed with the corroboration of Mahabharata observations with proposed date of Vartak, to the extent I spent more than six months exploring alternate explanations (*Adhika masa, Kshaya masa*, colure of the Sun around the point of winter solstice and what not) to justify 22 December as the day of *Bhishma Nirvana*.

Sun, Moon, Saturn & Jupiter afflicting *Rohini*

Vartak interpreted 'the Sun and the Moon, together, afflicting *Rohini*'[26] as the observation on the first day of War. He explained this observation not as visual observation, but rather via his theory of astrological *drishti*. I explained this observation as visual observation on the first day of War however credit goes to Vartak for suggesting the timing of this observation. The day was *Amawasya* and thus at the time of sunset, when the Sun and the Moon were together on the western horizon, *Rohini* was rising on the eastern horizon. When I re-read the Mahabharata text, I realized that Vyasa was observing the sky both before sunrise and after sunset (and of course at night), before and during the war[31].

Once I explained this observation, I predicted similar phenomenon for the remaining two observations of *Rohini*. I simulated the sky for the 17th day of War, after the sunset, and realized how appropriate the description of 'Jupiter afflicting *Rohini*, similar to the Sun and the Moon'[12] was. These three observations not only corroborate 5561 B.C. as the year of Mahabharata War, but also corroborate Amawasya day as the first day of Mahabharata War.

Although now obvious, it took me a while to visualize 'Saturn afflicting *Rohini*' [8-9] as visual observation of the morning sky before sunrise. Saturn was the only visible planet in the eastern part of the sky 'afflicting' setting *Rohini* on the western horizon, before the dawn, on the first day of War. This was also the case when Vyasa met Dhritarashtra 1-2 days before the first day of War[9]. Karna describes similar phenomenon - '*nakshatra* of Prajapati - *Rohini*, being afflicted by Saturn'[8] when he met Krishna on 9-10 September 5561 B.C. Voyager simulation shows Saturn as the only visible planet, besides the Moon (*Krishna Ashtami*), before dawn, afflicting *Rohini*.

Vartak attempted to corroborate all 3 observations related to *Rohini*. And while he failed, no other Mahabharata researcher has attempted to corroborate all 3 and some have simply ignored them especially because they could not corroborate them.

Mercury and Jupiter (17th day of the War)

An astute observer would have noticed, immediately after sunset, eastward movement of Mercury through 18 days of the War,

166

assuming Mercury could be seen, beginning with the first day of War. During the 18 days of War, apparent distance between Mercury and the Sun was increasing with each passing day. Jupiter was east of Mercury (and the Sun) on the first day of War, however by the end of the 17th day of War, it was between Mercury and the Sun. I interpreted this rising up of Mercury against the western horizon, as 'Tiryak' rising of Mercury[16]. As a result, both Mercury[16] and Jupiter[12] were visible and on the western horizon after the sunset on the 17th day of War and their positions corroborate well with Mahabharata observations.

Vartak might have been misled by Mahabharata reference to Mercury[15], which he translated as Mercury revolving in the region of 3 nakshatras (before Jyeshtha) and thus interpreted it to mean near Vishakha/Swati. No wonder he could not envision the possibility of Mercury being on the western horizon after the sunset. Subsequently he conjectured these observations as referring to Mahabharata author poetically describing 'impossible things' after the death of Karna.

I agree with Vartak when he re-interpreted observation of Mercury traveling through all nakshatras[15]. The observation is trivial however it does corroborate my conjecture that Mahabharata author included observations made over a period of up to a year before the War.

Mars, Venus & Mercury (18th day of the War) [17]

Mars, Venus and Mercury were seen in the western part of sky after the sunset on the 18th day of War[17]. Voyager simulation confirmed this to be the case after the sunset on the 2nd November 5561 B.C.

Vartak invoked astrological explanation for this observation. I conjecture that this was due to his erroneous assumption about the positions of these planets, i.e., Mars in Anuradha, Venus in Purva Bhadrapada and Mercury near Jyeshtha on the first day of War. No wonder he could not visualize seeing these 3 planets in western part of the sky, after the sunset, on the 18th day of War and consequently tried to explain them in the language of astrological jargon. Vartak's proposal thus has an interesting aspect of correct determination of the timing of Mahabharata War but wrong interpretation.

167

WHEN DID THE MAHABHARATA WAR HAPPEN?

Mark on the face of Moon [9, 27]

The Mahabharata text refers, twice, to the disappearance of the mark on the face of Moon [9, 27]. I conjectured that these observations referred to the time of lunar month close to *Amawasya*. I conjectured that in both instances, visual observer could envision the moon with its mark covered. The Lunar eclipse had not occurred, per my proposed timeline, at the time of Krishna-Karna meeting, and thus I conjectured that the observations 'the Moon with its mark covered' [9, 27] refer to the time and phase of the moon close to *Amawasya* day. This was indeed the situation when both observations were made, first observation 7 days before *Jyeshtha Amawasya*[27] (9-10 September) and second observation[9] one day before the beginning of War (15th October). Vartak has interpreted both observations as referring to the lunar eclipse.

Shweta, Shyama & Tivra/Tikshna Planets [19, 20, 21]

Mahabharata researchers have had field day with these observations since planets are described with their adjectives – *Shweta*[19] (white or bluish white), *Shyama*[20] (dark or bluish dark) or *Tivra/Tikshna*[21] (intense/rough/sharp). The Mahabharata text mentions '*Shweta*' planet near *Chitra*[19], '*Shyama*' planet near *Jyeshtha*[20] and *Tivra/Tikshna* planet or *nakshatra* near *Krittika*[21].

Vartak conjectured that '*Tivra*' planet (or *nakshatra*) was Pluto. I agree with his conjecture and have borrowed his explanation. Vartak employed Sayan-Nirayan theory to explain '*Shyama*' and '*Shweta*' planets as Neptune and Uranus. His is ingenious explanation and deserves much praise however I disagree with him because of the strong 'subjective' element employed in his interpretations.

I do agree with Vartak's conjecture that Mahabharata author knew planets Uranus, Neptune and Pluto. Vartak's research convinced me of this conjecture, however based on different set of observations. Vartak has cited these observations as evidence for Mahabharata astronomers being aware of Uranus, Neptune and Pluto. Consequently Vartak assumed telescopic abilities in Mahabharata times. Holay has also assumed telescopic abilities in making a case for Uranus. The Mahabharata text does not specifically refer to telescopes, however, does mention 'mirrors'.

168

Seven planets near the Moon and/or the Sun [23, 24, 25]

I conjectured that Mahabharata author knew Uranus, Neptune and Pluto. My conjecture is based on three observations within the Mahabharata text where,

(1) Seven planets are described as seen along with sun/moon on the first day of War[24]

(2) Seven planets are described as attacking the Moon, after sunset on the 14th day of War[23]

(3) Seven planets are described as moving away from the Sun on the 17th day of War[25]

The first observation is referring to seven planets, exclusive of the Sun and the Moon. There was a solar eclipse on the first day of War and the planets could have been seen during the eclipse. These seven planets, from east, were Neptune, Uranus, Mars, Venus, Jupiter, Mercury and Saturn. Saturn is the only planet west of the Sun.

The timing of the second observation is after sunset, on the 14th day of War and seven planets are described as attacking the Moon. Again the seven planets did not include either the Sun or the Moon. Voyager simulation shows that Saturn was below the horizon and this observation thus makes a strong case for the knowledge of Uranus, Neptune and Pluto! Rising moon on eastern horizon can be visualized as attacked by seven planets. These seven planets, from east, were Pluto, Neptune, Mars, Venus, Uranus, Mercury and Jupiter.

The third observation of seven planets appears on the 17th day of War[25]. Seven planets are described as moving away from the Sun. I have conjectured this to be an observation after the sunset, when 7 planets could be seen in the sky, all of them east of the setting sun and also moving away from the Sun. All planets have eastward motion unless they are in retrograde. Voyager simulation confirms that, beginning in the east, Pluto, Neptune, Mars, Venus, Uranus, Mercury & Jupiter, were moving eastward, only with the exception of Pluto, which was in retrograde motion. The reader should keep in mind that Pluto has extremely slow motion and would appear steady when observed over an extended period of time, to the extent Mahabharata author has referred to it as both 'Graha' and 'naksha-

169

tra'! No other Mahabharata researcher (besides Vartak) has corroborated presence of 7 planets for 3 instances, during the Mahabharata War.

Comet near *Pushya* [21, 22]

Vartak interpreted 'Haley's comet' as the *Dhumaketu* (comet) referred to in the Mahabharata text, and performed crude calculations using orbital period of 77 years, and conjectured that Haley's comet was visible during the Mahabharata War. Voyager simulation confirms location of Haley's comet near *Pushya* however the comet was not at all visible during 5561 B.C. Voyager simulation confirmed Haley's comet appearing in 5622 B.C. and again in 5547 B.C. I have already provided alternate explanation for '*Dhumaketu* near *Pushya*' in Chapter 7.

Rahu approaching the Sun [19, 27]

The Mahabharata text refers to *Rahu* approaching the Sun couple of times and Vartak has interpreted it all right as referring to the solar eclipse that occurred on the first day of War. Vartak interprets specific observation[14] as referring to Sayan position of *Rahu* and assigns '*UttaraAshadha*' as Nirayan position. Vartak did not bother to consider the explanation demanded by his conjecture, especially of 'Sayan *Rahu*' moving in *apasavya* direction between *Chitra* and *Swati*, while also shining brightly! I have provided convincing explanation for the planet (between *Chitra* and *Swati*) [14] to be Mars and not *Rahu*.

Late Moonrise on the 14th day of War[93]

Anyone claiming *Amawasya* as the first day of Mahabharata War has an onus to explain 'late moonrise' observation. Vartak is the first and the only researcher who disagreed with literal interpretation of 'late moonrise' and only researcher (among those who also propose *Amawasya* day as the first day of War) who recognized the requirement to explain this observation. He has explored numerous observations of the 14th day of War to build his case against 'late moonrise'. Vartak conjectured that the warriors (or Sanjay) were exhausted and delirious and thus they (or Sanjay) interpreted 'reappearance of the moon', after the settling of the dust, as moon-rise!

Although I have removed the need for such an assumption, Vartak's conjecture is plausible and is corroborated by Mahabharata observations [91-106]. On the other hand I feel that Vartak has needless-ly invoked the theory of 'Vyasa creating puzzles for Ganesha' in explaining observations of 'moonrise' or 'full moon-like descriptions' of the 14th night of War. I have made a case for 'reappearance of the moon' as opposed to 'late moonrise' in Chapter 9. Vartak did quote full moon descriptions of the moon during the night of 14th day of War however he interpreted them as poetic descriptions in describing visible moon in the sky.

Number of researchers who assumed the first day of War to be *Amawasya* day (e.g. Gupta, Holay), have not bothered to explain the contradiction posed by Mahabharata observation of late moon-rise. Holay did assume *Amawasya* as the first day of War however, he had no need to explain 'late moonrise on the 14th day of War' since he conjectured a break of 12 days (during the War) after the fall of Bhishma. Of course Holay must explain the rationale for his intro-duction of 12 day gap during the War and I am not aware of an explanation if he has provided one. Holay created insurmountable difficulties for his theory (and timeline) by introducing ad-hoc hypo-thesis, however at least he removed the requirement of explaining late moonrise for his proposed timeline.

On the other hand researchers (Raghavan, Achar) who have used observation of late moonrise to build their Mahabharata time-line, have not bothered to explain numerous Mahabharata observations directly contradicting their timeline, i.e., all Mahabhara-ta observations of Chapter 8 and observations related to my explanation of the reappearance of the moon from Chapter 9. Dates proposed by Karandikar as well as Vaidya also lead to late moonrise on the 14th day of War and their proposals are falsified for the same reason those of Raghavan/Achar are falsified.

Pre-War Incidents

Vartak's interpretation of 'Duryodhana asking kings on his side to leave for Kurukshetra on *Pushya* day'[77] is consistent however his explanation of Krishna leaving Hastinapur[73] and reaching Upaplavya on the same *Pushya* day is problematic. Time interval of only 7 days between Krishna-Karna meeting and the first day of War, as proposed by Vartak, is too compressed. It is then interesting that in spite of numerous changes Vartak suggested to his original timeline, he remained committed to assumption of 7 days.

Krishna-Karna Meeting – 7 days before *Amawasya*

Vartak states that Krishna-Karna meeting took place on *Pushya* day. This statement would thus conflict with '*Shakra* (*Jyeshtha*) *Amawasya* in 7 days'[73]. To make it worse, Vartak assumes, elsewhere, that the *Amawasya* in *Jyeshtha* was actually near *PurvaAshadha*. Vartak was forced to cramp numerous instances that occurred before the War, within the 7 days between Krishna-Karna meeting and *Amawasya* day. This assumption of his has introduced numerous contradictions

Krishna returning to Upaplavya

It is impossible for Krishna to be back in Upaplavya on *Pushya* day, as assumed by Vartak and this assumption of his contradicts numerous other instances. For example, we have Mahabharata references to Krishna meeting with Kauravas, then meeting Kunti and finally Karna, after the *Pushya* day[73]. Moreover, counting from *Pushya*, even by the most conservative estimate, *Amawasya* would be 10-11 days in the future, and not 7-8 days as stated by Krishna.

Krishna asking the Pandavas to leave on *Pushya*[79]

Chronological accounts, as narrated in the Mahabharata text, makes it impossible for Krishna and the Pandavas to leave for Kurukshetra on same *Pushya* day; the same day when Duryodhana asked kings on his side to proceed for Kurukshetra on *Pushya* day [77], while Krishna was still in Hastinapur.

I have conjectured an additional period of a lunar month and 7 days between Krishna-Karna meeting and the first day of War. There is no explicit reference to such a time interval however the usefulness of this conjecture of mine can be seen from its ability to explain all events leadings to the first day of War.

172

Balarama *Tirthayatra*

Vartak provides an ingenious solution to the problem created by his compressed timeline for the *Tirthayatra* of Balarama. Vartak initially proposed that Balarama met the Pandavas on *Pushya nakshatra*, long time before the War. This proposal is untenable as the Mahabharata text is clear on chronology of events. Vartak must have noticed this absurdity and thus invokes Sayan-Nirayan method to claim 'Balarama's departure on *Pushya*' as referring to Nirayan *Swati* (and thus Sayan *Pushya*). On the other hand, Vartak interprets Mahabharata observation of Balarama leaving for *Tirthayatra* on *Maitri* (*Anuradha*) *nakshatra*[75] as straightforward observation, i.e. without the Sayan-Nirayan twist.

His conjecture led him to his next problem, i.e. problem of explaining duration of Balarama *Tirthayatra,* as stated in the Mahabharata text, of 42 days[88]. The problem is that there were only 21 days between departure of Balarama and his intended arrival on the last day of the War, per proposed sequence of events by Vartak.

Vartak provides an ingenious solution. He interprets *'Aha'*, *'Ratra'* or *'Dina'* as referring to only 15 *Muhurtas* (half day) out of 30 *Muhurtas* which constitute one full day and then goes on to interpret, 42 *Aha* as 42 x 15 = 21 x 30 = 21 *AhoRatra* (full days),

Day of 24 hours (*Aha* + *Ratra*) = 30 *Muhurtas*
Duration of *Aha* = Duration of *Ratra* = 15 *Muhurtas*
42 (*Aha*) x 15 (*Muhurtas*) = 21 Days (24 hrs) x 30 (*Muhurtas*)

He claims that, per these calculations, Balarama left on Nirayan *Swati* (Sayan *Pushya*) and returned on Nirayan *Pushya*. Again Vartak has provided an ingenious solution however I assert that his solution is decidedly false. I have dealt with inconsistency and contradictions generated by Vartak's interpretation of *'Aha'*, *'Ratra'*, *'Sharvari'* or *'Dina'* elsewhere in this chapter.

More Prewar Incidents

After Balarama left the Pandava camp [75, 85], King Rukmi came to visit the Pandava camp and offered his assistance. The Pandavas politely refused and Rukmi went to Duryodhana but met with similar response, upon which he returned to his kingdom. The War preparations resumed and both parties were frantically busy establishing roads, utilities, forts and camps on the battlefield of Kurukshetra. After Balarama and Rukmi had departed from the Pandava camp, Yudhishthir held a secret meeting to discuss war strategy[76]. I conjecture that this was around the full moon day, based on Mahabharata descriptions[76]. Duryodhana sent Uluka to the Pandavas. Uluka visited the Pandava camp and returned. Both armies left for Kurukshetra on *Pushya* [77-79] and arrived there on *Magha*[80]. Both parties held a meeting to agree on rules and etiquettes to be followed during the War[107]. Vyasa met Dhritarashtra day before the War began. I assert that the time interval of 7-8 days proposed by Vartak is too compressed either to accomplish the war preparations or to accommodate pre-war incidents described in the Mahabharata text. I assert that error of 3 *nakshatras* on the part of Mahabharata author, proposed by Vartak, is not an error but rather reflects the movement of the Sun that occurred over a time period of an additional month, i.e. from *Anuradha/Jyeshtha* to somewhere between *Mula* and *PurvaAshadha*.

Activities after the War

Bhishma Nirvana is the only postwar activity that is critical in either corroborating or falsifying proposed date of the Mahabharata War. Almost all researchers have employed the timing of *Bhishma Nirvana* and many have considered it critical in determining the year of Mahabharata War.

Vartak proposed 22 December 5561 B.C. as the day of *Bhishma Nirvana*. He did not use, correctly I think, Mahabharata observations related to *Bhishma Nirvana* in building his timeline. Therefore his responsibility was limited to corroborating Mahabharata references of *Bhishma Nirvana* with his proposed timeline. On the other hand those researchers (Gupta, Holay, and Sengupta) who claimed observations of *Bhishma Nirvana* critical had responsibility not only to show how they employed these critical observations in building their timeline but also to show how their proposed timeline corroborates these very observations. While Gupta has indeed used them in predicting his timeline, he failed to show how these observations corroborate his timeline. Sengupta does corroborate 58 days between 'Fall of Bhishma' and 'Bhishma Nirvana' but not the nakshatra or lunar month or Tithi. Raghavan/Achar claim these observations as critical however they neither employ them in predicting their timeline nor corroborate them with their prediction. Holay's effort is as good as (or as bad as) that of Vartak.

I conjecture that a random but interesting coincidence deceived Vartak. He must have been pleasantly surprised when he realized that the day, 58 days from 'Fall of Bhishma', or 68 days from the first day of War was indeed during the month of Magha, Magha Shuddha Ashtami and the Moon near Rohini, as stated in the Mahabharata text. The day happened to be 22 December, which coincides with winter solstice in our times. I conjecture that this additional coincidence deceived him further.

Vartak has provided two different explanations. Both are ingenious and proceed through many twists and turns. I would encourage the reader to read 'Swayambhu' in original for the details. I limit myself to highlighting those references, which falsify the date proposed by Vartak.

Vartak quotes Mahabharata observation from Anushasan Parva[109] where Bhishma says, "It had been 58 nights since I am lying on the bed of arrows. Today is the month of Magha and one third of it (month or Paksha) remains." Another Mahabharata observation from the same Adhyaya of Anushasan, considered interpolated by many, refers to the day being Magha Shuddha Ashtami and the Moon near Rohini[110]. Bhishma supposedly passed away on this day. This means the day was either the day of winter solstice or one day after the winter solstice. Anyone claiming these two observations as crucial for determining the year of Mahabharata War must accept that Bhishma was lying on the bed of arrows for 58 nights and that the War started on or near Kartika Amawasya day (per Amanta reckoning). I stress this point since I came across many researchers who insist on these two [109, 110] Bhishma Nirvana observations as critical, but then do not bother to show how these observations corroborate their proposals.

Vartak's proposal corroborates month of Magha, day of Magha Shuddha Ashtami, the Moon near Rohini[110], Bhishma lying on the bed of arrows for 58 nights[109] and beginning of the Mahabharata War on Kartika Amawasya. The extent of corroboration is indeed impressive, however with one severe drawback! The day, 22 December 5561 B.C. is not the day of winter solstice; rather it is removed by some 39-40 days from the actual day of winter solstice. I would like to describe two attempts, made by Vartak, to solve problems for his timeline, posed by the day of winter solstice and duration of time interval between Fall of Bhishma/*Bhishma Nirvana* along with numerous events leading to the day of *Bhishma Nirvana*.

Explanation of *Bhishma Nirvana* by Vartak: Round 1

Vartak determined approximate time period of 5480 B.C. as the time of Mahabharata War in his first edition of '*Swayambhu*', published on 25 February 1980 A.D. On 21 September 1980 A.D., Vartak determined 16 October 5561 B.C. as the first day of Mahabharata War and included the details (in appendix) in the second edition of '*Swayambhu*', published in May 1981 A.D.

Vartak deals with Mahabharata observations that contradict his proposed day of *Bhishma Nirvana* as follows. Vartak interprets Mahabharata observation that refers to Yudhishthir staying in Hastinapur for 50 days[130] as referring to the time interval between the last day of War and the day of *Bhishma Nirvana*. Initially, he accepts that the Pandavas did spend a month outside Hastinapur on the bank of Ganga[113] and considers these month long period (27-30 days) as part of the total of 50 days[130]. He borrows, incorrectly I think, the translation of Nilkanth for Mahabharata observation[120] where Krishna tells Bhishma, that Bhishma had 30 (correct and straightforward translation suggests 56 more days) more days to live.

Vartak assumes, wrongly again, that this meeting between Krishna and Bhishma occurred when the Pandavas were still staying on the bank of Ganga. He offers translation of Nilkanth as a proof against conjectures of other researchers (and against the internal evidence of Mahabharata text itself) that Krishna and the Pandavas visited Bhishma only after spending 30 days outside Hastinapur. I believe that this contradiction, especially against the internal evidence of the Mahabharata text, was not lost on Vartak. No wonder he questions the very assumption (and the Mahabharata text) of the Pandavas entering Hastinapur only after spending 30 days on the bank of Ganga.

Vartak did see the need for the Sun to be near *Revati* at the time of winter solstice, in order to match the period of 5500 B.C.,

176

which also made it necessary for the full moon to be near *Hasta*. Vartak is correct in his expectations for the positions of the Sun (near *Revati*) and the full Moon (near *Hasta*), however, is wrong in assuming that the Sun and the Moon attained these positions on 22 December 5561 B.C.

Voyager simulations show that the Sun was near *Shatabhisaj* (*Shata-taraka*) and nowhere close to *Revati*, and the full moon of 28 December (closest to 22 December) was near *Purva Phalguni* and nowhere close to *Hasta*.

The Sun is almost 40^0 (2 hr and 41 min of Right Ascension measurement) away from the point of winter solstice on 22nd December 5561 B.C, i.e. the day of winter solstice was ~40 days into the future and not on 22 December 5561 B.C.

22 December 5561 B.C.
(Day of *Bhishma Nirvana* proposed by Vartak)

	RA
Sun	15h 19m
Shatabhisaj/Shata-taraka	15h 20m
Revati	18h 53m

28 December 5561 B.C. (Full Moon day)

Moon	3h 45m
Earth Shadow	3h 45m
Purva Phalguni	3h 21m
Hasta	5h 59m

Vartak invokes his conjecture of Mahabharata author making an error of 3 *nakshatras* to describe position of the Sun on 22nd December, made previously (by him) to explain the position of Venus near *Purva Bhadrapada* on the first day of War, to explain why the Sun would be near *Revati* and the full moon would be near *Hasta*.

I have shown that Vartak's conjecture of the error of 3 *nakshatras* might have been useful (to his theory and timeline) in explaining the events before the War, however, his conjecture has no effect in explaining events after the War such as *Bhishma Nirvana*. His assumption rather contradicts post-war observations.

He conjectured that there was a need (on the part of Mahabharata author) to consider one of three months of *Kartika*, *Margashirsha* or *Pausha* as *'kshaya'* (elapsed), however he claimed that Mahabharata author failed to do so. He considers this error on the part of Mahabharata author as responsible for the confusion related to the time of *Bhishma Nirvana*.

I have shown (Chapter 9) that no such conjecture, i.e. conjecture of confusion on the part of Mahabharata author, is required to explain the timing of *Bhishma Nirvana*. Instead, I have conjectured addition of extra lunar month (*Adhika masa*) *Magha* for those who feel very strongly about Mahabharata observation of Anushasan *Parva*[109], specifically the observations - 'month of *Magha*' and that 'one third of either month or *paksha* still remaining' on the day of *Bhishma Nirvana*.

Explanation of *Bhishma Nirvana* by Vartak: Round 2

Vartak published his additional work, carried out after the publication of second edition, in the 3rd edition, published in November 1987 A.D.

In this edition, Vartak proposed modified explanation for Mahabharata observations leading to the day of *Bhishma Nirvana*. He remained firm on 22 December as the day of winter solstice. He is also firm regarding the need to take one lunar month as *'kshaya'* (elapsed). This time, he proposes that the Pandavas stayed outside Hastinapur, on the bank of the river, only for 12 days (instead of a whole month[113]) and quotes an interesting reference from Manusmruti, originally quoted by Nilkanth, in support of his '12 days' proposal. The Pandavas entered Hastinapur[114], based on this proposal of Vartak, on 16th November 5561 B.C. Vartak admits his acceptance of erroneous translation[120] of Nilkanth, mentioned previously in Round-1 and suggests another conjecture. He conjectures word *'Dina'* as referring to a time interval of 15 *Muhurtas* or half day and thus interprets 56 days as rather equal to 28 days! Vartak estimated this day, going 28 days backward from 22 December, as 25th November. Vartak conjectured that the Pandavas were in Hastinapur during 16-25th November before they went to see Bhishma. This second attempt of Vartak, in explaining *Bhishma Nirvana*, leaves as many threads open as his previous explanation.

178

Vartak mentions a query from either a reader or a researcher who asked Vartak about the effect of 'leap years' on his calculations and specifically its implications for the day of winter solstice. Vartak had assumed 365.25 days for a year and thus assumed 'leap year' every 4 years. Modern calendar (Gregorian) does not assume leap year at the interval of 100 years (even though the number is divisible by 4), unless the number is also divisible by 400. In effect Vartak had used Julian calendar, as is the standard practice, for researching anything historical before 1582 A.D. His choice of Julian calendar resulted in additional ~50 days over a period of ~ 7500 years. Vartak recognized the effect of this error of ~50 days on the day of the winter solstice and I believe he anticipated, in recognizing this error, the correct explanation for Mahabharata observations and the actual day of *Bhishma Nirvana*. The opportunity eluded him when he drew following erroneous inferences,

(1) He thought that the point of winter solstice was indeed fixed on the day of 22 December
(2) He estimated maximum deviation possible in the positions of planets over a period of 50 days. He considered movement of slow moving planets such as Saturn and Jupiter, and showed the deviation in their positions to be minimal to have significant effect on his proposed timeline
(3) He felt that ancient astronomers would have made appropriate corrections to adjust the points of winter and summer solstices.

He was right on his second inference and was wrong on the other two. The point of winter solstice is not fixed when Julian calendar is employed to track time. This movement of winter solstice in Julian calendar was the very reason Roger Bacon (Chapter 5) had suggested correction to the calendar. Julian calendar came into being in 45 B.C. and dates shown before 45 B.C. are based on hypothetical nature of calendar into antiquity, i.e. how one would have dated time before 45 B.C., using Julian calendar. As a result there was no ancient astronomer to make required corrections to the calendar to ensure that 22 December coincided with the day of winter solstice.

179

I have provided detailed solution to the problem of *Bhishma Nirvana* elsewhere (Chapter 9) and thus won't repeat, however, I must resolve one last problem. I have shown that the actual day of winter solstice (30 January 5560 B.C.) was some 39-40 days in the future from 22 December 5561 B.C. The reader should still wonder about the gap of 10 days; gap between estimation of Vartak of ~50 days (between 22 December 5561 B.C. and actual day of winter solstice) and actual gap of 39-40 days shown by Voyager. Fortunately the answer to this problem is straightforward! Pope Gregory, when he made the correction, some 300 years after Roger Bacon suggested it, eliminated 10 days (5-14 October) from the calendar in year 1582 A.D. to coincide the day of winter solstice with 22 December.

Sayan - Nirayan theory

I concede that the theory of *Sayan-Nirayan* has enormous value as 'instrument' of investigation in determining the timing of Mahabharata War. My appreciation for, and concession of, '*Sayan-Nirayan*' theory is based on realization that all proposed dates that fell within 'the Epoch of *Arundhati*' were derived using the theory of Sayan- Nirayan. Visaji Raghunath Lele assumed '*Ashwini*' as the first *nakshatra* and employed theory of Sayan- Nirayan. He estimated the timing of Mahabharata War to be around 5306 B.C. and proposed specific year of 5228 B.C. as the year of Mahabharata War. S B Dikshit objected to assumption of Lele, specifically that of *Ashwini* as the first *nakshatra*. Instead, Dikshit assumed *Krittika* as the first *nakshatra* and ended up estimating the timing of Mahabharata War to be around 7300 B.C. Modak estimated 5000 B.C. and Vartak estimated 5480 B.C., using Sayan-Nirayan theory. The reader who understands the rationale behind 'the Epoch of *Arundhati*' as the time interval of the Mahabharata War would certainly recognize the value of the theory of Sayan- Nirayan as an 'instrument', if nothing else. I have no hesitation in accepting the existence of Sayan-Nirayan methodology during the time of Mahabharata War or even in further antiquity. On the other hand, I assert that Sayan-Nirayan theory fails to corroborate Mahabharata observations it was expected to corroborate.

Sayan-Nirayan theory might have helped Vartak, at least partially, to get over the difficulties of explaining multiple positions of planets. I assert that Vartak's use of this theory introduces subjective interpretations and inconsistencies.

It is understandable that accuracy of visual observation can vary +/- 1 *nakshatras* depending on the time of observation as well as the angle of the observer. On the other hand, *Sayan nakshatra* is identified by counting number of *nakshatras* beginning with the first *nakshatra* (*Ashwini, Krittika, Pushya* or *Punarvasu*) and thus there is no room whatsoever for an error. It is surprising then that Vartak is forced to match Jupiter in '*Nirayan*' *Shravana*[11] with *Sayan Vishakha* (instead of *Swati*). Jupiter and Saturn are described as settled near *Vishakha* for up to a year before the War[6]. While Vartak employs the logic of *Sayan-Nirayan* method to explain Jupiter near *Vishakha*, he does not use the same method to explain Saturn near *Vishakha*. *Nirayan Uttara Phalguni*[10] should have matched with *Sayan Mrigashirsha*, and not *Rohini*. Mahabharata observation of Jupiter near *Shravana*[11] is rather in the context of Jupiter's *vakri* motion near *Shravana*. Vartak asserts *Rahu* near *UttaraAshadha* (*Nirayan*) and interprets observation of a planet, moving in *apasavya* direction between *Chitra* and *Swati*[14], as referring to *Sayan* position of *Rahu*. Vartak nowhere explains how an imaginary and invisible planet (*Rahu*) moves in *apasavya* direction in an imaginary (*Sayan*) position.

Mars is described as *vakri* near *Magha*[11] and again near *Jyeshtha/Anuradha*[13]. Vartak explains this as Nirayan *Anuradha* and Sayan *Magha*. Vartak refers to the objection of S B Dikshit who claimed that both *Magha* (Mars) and *Shravana* (Jupiter) [11] should be considered Sayan. I assert that interpretation demanded by Dikshit is justified if we are going to value 'consistency' of a theory! I suggest treating these descriptions as 'Nirayan' since both of these planets are described '*vakri*' and it is lot easier to describe visual '*vakri*' observation of a planet, rather than imaginary *vakri* motion near imaginary (Sayan) *nakshatra*.

Dikshit also claimed that Mars, Mercury and Venus were together on the last day of War[17]. Vartak disagrees with this claim made by Dikshit. Not only I agree with Dikshit but also have shown that these three planets were in the western part of sky and were visible after the sunset on the last day of War. Vartak interprets Mahabharata observation 'Mars afflicting *Chitra*'[13] along with '*Shweta* planet near *Chitra*'[19] as referring to 'Sayan' location of Uranus! The Nirayan location for Uranus would be *Shravana* (by counting *Abhijit* as *nakshatra*) or *UttaraAshadha* (by not counting *Abhijit* as *nakshatra*). While I find this explanation ingenious, I also find it subjective, arbitrary and inconsistent. Uranus is indeed near *Shravana/Dhanishtha* but is nowhere explicitly mentioned in the Mahabharata text. Vartak interprets Mahabharata observation of a planet in the company of Venus[18] along with '*Shyama*' planet near *Jyeshtha*'[20] as referring to the position of Neptune. Again Vartak proposes '*Shyama*' planet near *Jyeshtha*'[20] as Sayan location and *Purva Bhadrapada* as Nirayan location of Neptune! Vartak's effort is ingenious indeed but it comes at the cost of introducing subjective element in his theory. Vartak does not state anywhere an objective criteria for distinguishing Mahabharata observations as either Sayan or Nirayan.

Let's look at additional contradictions introduced by Vartak while employing theory of Sayan- Nirayan. Vartak accepts, in one place, Balarama leaving for *Tirthayatra* (per him leaving the Pandava camp) on *Pushya* [78, 88]. He interprets this observation as referring to Nirayan *Swati* (11 October 5561 B.C.) and Sayan *Pushya*! In another place, Vartak interprets Mahabharata observation of *Maitri* (*Anuradha*) [75] as Nirayan and as the day when Balarama began his Saraswati *Tirthayatra*. However he treats '*Pushya*' as the *nakshatra* of the arrival of Balarama[88] on the last day of the War as Nirayan *Pushya* and here Vartak introduces a contradiction galore in his explanations. He does not explain how his Sayan-Nirayan theory explains 'Shravana' reference related to Balarama's *Tirthayatra*.

In addition Vartak mentions both armies leaving on *Pushya* [77-79] and arriving on *Magha*[80] at Kurukshetra, however, he is not only silent about their actual dates but also does not invoke theory of Sayan-Nirayan to explain it. In spite of extensive use of this theory, Vartak could not explain numerous planetary observations, e.g. Jupiter afflicting *Rohini*[12], *vakri* motions of Mars [11, 13] and Jupiter[11], Mars near *Jyeshtha*[13], Mars near *Shravana*[14], Mars, Mercury, Venus in the western part of sky[17], and was forced to invoke other explanations such as either 'astrological *drishti*' or 'descriptions of impossible events by Mahabharata author'. The problem with the latter two approaches is that once one decides to employ them, anything anywhere can be explained! Even the theories of 'Sayan- Nirayan', 'astrological *Drishti*' and 'wild exaggerations by Mahabharata author' were not sufficient to explain all Mahabharata observations and Vartak had to invoke few additional hypotheses.

Interpretation of 'Ratra' 'Kshapa' 'Sharvari' 'Aha' & 'Dina'

Vartak has interpreted 'Ratra', 'Kshapa', 'Sharvari' as referring to 'night' and 'Aha' or 'Dina' as referring to 'day' and each of them equal to time interval of 15 Muhurtas or 12 hours. Vartak assumes, correctly I think, 'Kshapa' as time interval of 12 hours (as opposed to 24 hours) when interpreting Bhishma's calculations[186] for the duration spent by the Pandavas in forest.

Calculations of Bhishma[186]:

5 years corresponds to 2 Adhika (extra) lunar months
13 years corresponds to 5.2 Adhika (extra) lunar months

(Since 0.2 lunar months equals 6 days)

Time spent by the Pandavas beyond 13 (lunar) years
= 5 months and 6 days

Calculations of Vartak:

In each solar year, Tithi (lunar date) goes back by 10 -11 (10.88) days.

Number of Tithis going back in 13 solar years

  = Time spent by the Pandavas beyond 13 years
  = 10.88 x 13
  = 141.44 days = (141.44/29.5)
  = 4.80 Lunar months (extra Lunar months)
  = 4 lunar months and 24 days.

Vartak recognized that Bhishma's calculations (5 months and 6 days) were broadly correct, sufficient to resolve the issue and pacify Duryodhana. Vartak asserts, again correctly, that while Bhishma's calculation is reasonable, the net time interval the Pandavas spent in

Vanavas (exile) beyond 13 (lunar) years is equal to 4 months and 24 days (and not 5 months and 6 days). Vartak objects to other researchers interpreting *'Kshapa'* to mean full day as opposed to only time interval of 12 hours. While his objection is valid, I want to stress that in the final analysis Vartak agrees that Bhishma's calculations are directionally correct but approximations nevertheless, and accepting either meaning does not lead to any contradiction in estimating the duration of the Pandavas in the forest for 13 years since both methods of calculations would have shown that Pandavas spent more than 13 years in the forest.

Next two interpretations of Vartak are crucial as they are critical for his justification for the timing of pre-war and post-war events. It is also critical that the reader understands the rationale used by Vartak in interpreting these observations in order to understand the inconsistencies introduced by Vartak.

Vartak interprets *'Aha'* as time interval of 12 hours (as opposed to 24 hours) while interpreting duration of the *Tirthayatra* of Balarama and claims that Balarama was doing *Tirthayatra* of Saraswati only for 21 days and not 42 days. Vartak also translates '56 *Dina*'[129] as time interval of 28 days as opposed to 56 days. Thus Vartak translated *'Kshapa* (night)'*, *'Aha* (bright portion of the day)' and *'Dina* (day)'* to mean time interval of 12 hours (instead of 24 hours) in his interpretations. I consider his approach ingenious however both inconsistent and false. Notwithstanding the rational basis for his translation, I would have conditionally allowed his translation, if Vartak had shown than such an approach works consistently in interpreting all relevant Mahabharata observations. I assert that this is not the case. By this logic we would have to interpret all words - *'Aha'*, *'Dina'*, *'Sharvari'*, *Ratra'*, *'Kshapa'* as referring to time interval of 12 hours and restrict time interval of 24 hours only when the word *'AhoRatra'* is used.

For example, we would have to interpret, Mahabharata references to 18 days of the War[216] as equal to time interval of 9 days made up of 24 hours each. This also means Bhishma remained lying on the bed of arrows only for 29 days (58 *Ratri*) and Yudhishthir spent only 25 days (50 *Sharvari*) in Hastinapur. Vartak proposed that Yudhishthir returned to Hastinapur from the bank of Ganga on 16 November and in that case he was in Hastinapur for ~36 days (16 November – 22 December) and this assumption would directly

184

contradict his calculation of 25 days, duration of the stay of the Pandavas, in Hastinapur. These ad hoc conjectures (interpretations of words such as *Ratri, Kshapa, Sharvari, Dina* or *Aha*) create more problems than they solve and the key issue of the day of winter solstice is still not resolved, i.e. the actual day of winter solstice is still 39-40 days in the future.

Krishna tells Bhishma, during their first meeting, that Bhishma had 56 more days to live[120]. I have shown with appropriate references (Chapter 9) how Yudhishthir spent 6 days (of 24 hours, and not made of 12 hours) with Bhishma, asking questions and listening to advice of Bhishma. After spending 6 days with Bhishma, Yudhishthir spent 50 days in Hastinapur[130] before returning to Kurukshetra on the day of *Bhishma Nirvana*. Let's introduce Vartak's interpretation. 56 *Dina* will turn into 28 *AhoRatras* and 50 *Sharvari* will turn into 25 *AhoRatras*! This interpretation, per Vartak's translation, would reduce the duration of Bhishma-Yudhishthir dialogues from 6 to 3 days and there is no basis to reduce 6 *AhoRatras* spent by Yudhishthir in the company of Bhishma down to 3 *AhoRatras* required for Vartak's interpretation to be consistent.

Astrological *Drishti*

Vartak was forced to invoke 'Astrological *Drishti*' to explain 'Saturn afflicting *Rohini*' while in reality Saturn was settled near *Bhaga (Uttara Phalguni) nakshatra*[10], 'Jupiter afflicting *Rohini* while Jupiter was settled near *Shravana*'[12], 'Mars afflicting *Rohini* with 7-8th *Drishti* and 'Mars afflicting *Shravana*[14] with 4th *Drishti* while Mars was settled near *Anuradha/Vishakha*' [13], 'Mars, Mercury, Venus astrologically supporting Yudhishthir[17] from whatever position they were in' and so on. The problem with 'Astrological *Drishti*' is that once one decides to employ it, anything anywhere can be explained! As soon as this happens, although theory may still retain its empirical character, is no longer falsifiable and scientific.

Ganesha puzzled by Vyasa

Vartak's explanations of Mahabharata observations using theory of Sayan-Nirayan are ingenious and original. I discarded it because it introduced inconsistencies and subjectivity in determining planetary positions. His theory also reduced information content of Mahabharata observations (e.g. *vakri* motions, planet traveling in apasavya direction). In the end, the Sayan-Nirayan theory, notwithstanding the liberties employed by Vartak to make it functional, was incapable of explaining majority of planetary observations of the Mahabharata text. Vartak was forced to invoke 'Astrological *Drishti'* to explain remaining planetary observations. Apparently hypothesis of 'Astrological *Drishti'* was not enough to explain the whole enchilada and Vartak was forced to invoke additional hypothesis of 'Vyasa deliberately composing puzzles for the scribe of Mahabharata – Ganesha'! Vartak invokes this hypothesis in support of his subjective classification of planetary positions into Sayan and Nirayan designations. This is wonderful illustration of an effort to shift the problem. Unfortunately the problem of 'subjective interpretation' did not go away however the credibility of the theory certainly went down. The incident reminds me of *'Indraya Takshkaya Swaha:'* – Subjectivity did not go away and credibility went down too!

Exaggerations by Mahabharata Author

Vartak invoked hypothesis of 'exaggerations by Mahabharata author' to explain 'Jupiter afflicting *Rohini*'[12] and *'Tiryak* rising of Mercury'[16]. Vartak claimed these Mahabharata descriptions [12, 16] to be imaginary and conjectured that Mahabharata author included such descriptions knowing well that these things were impossible. This hypothesis results in a metaphysical (irrefutable) theory.

Concluding Remarks

I still remain in awe and reverence of Mahabharata research carried out by P V Vartak. In the absence of implications derived from the Epoch of Arundhati, I would have hardly dared to go as far back as 6th millennium.

While I have proposed alternate timeline for pre-war and post-war incidents of Mahabharata, every attempt of mine to falsify 18-day timeline of War proposed by Vartak failed. My work related to pre-war and post-war incidents reinforced his timeline further. My research of *Bhishma Nirvana* shrunk the time interval for plausible year of the Mahabharata War, already defined by the Epoch of

Arundhati, down to 2000 years (6500 B.C.-4500 B.C.). I tested 38 plausible instances for the Mahabharata War over this time interval (6500 B.C. - 4500 B.C.) and the testing corroborated Vartak's timeline, again!

My admiration for his work does not stem from his specific results. After all, his proposed date (for the Mahabharata War) could have been wrong (and may be falsified in future). In addition, I have shown inconsistency, contradictions, limitations and subjectivity of his Sayan-Nirayan theory. He was forced to employ numerous patchworks such as astrological *Drishti*, forced interpretations of *Ratra*, *Kshapa*, *Dina*, *Aha*, Vyasa creating puzzles for Ganesha, awkward interpretations and modifications of Mahabharata passages leading to the day of *Bhishma Nirvana*.

My admiration for him and his work stems from his approach to the problem. Published in 1980-1987 A.D., his work was definitely an improvement over the past Mahabharata research, in any language. His work appears to be improvement over the research conducted in last 25-30 years! Stated alternately, I am asserting that no significant improvement or growth of knowledge occurred in last 30 years. To be fair to other researchers who contributed in last 30 years, I am willing to admit that I benefitted immensely from their work. Works of these researchers provided me with alternate scenarios to test. In addition, there were inspiring snippets of new information; identification of numerous astronomy observations within and outside Mahabharata by R N Iyengar, possibility of three eclipses by Achar, two eclipses within 13 days by S Balakrishna, Saraswati research by Srinivasan Kalyanaraman or by Frankfort.

Unique aspect of Vartak is his unpretentious willingness to be wrong! No wonder he could be creative in his endeavors beyond Mahabharata research. He understood the essence of Einstein's famous quote, "No amount of experimentation can ever prove me right, a single experiment can prove me wrong" and exhaustively searched for Mahabharata observations he could test and experiment, a realization lost on many. He intuitively understood tentative nature of any theory and continued to improve upon his research. He eagerly encouraged his readers to test his proposals and also to research Mahabharata observations he could not explain.

I could provide detailed critique of the work of Vartak only because he presented his work, his assumptions and presumptions, in

187

a clear fashion. I was not so fortunate when evaluating works of other researchers (Table 1). I wrote extensive criticism of the works of other researchers but decided not to include them in this book. I encourage readers to examine works of other researchers, their theories, their ad-hoc hypotheses and their proposed years (and specific timeline) for the timing of Mahabharata War.

I have developed a method to quantify knowledge content of a given theory and measuring 'truthlikeness' of multiple theories (and proposals) for the timing of Mahabharata War. I have toyed with the idea of measuring knowledge content of a given theory using qualitative and quantitative measurements.

Qualitative measurements include consistency, testability, refutability (as opposed to irrefutability), ability to retain successes of previous theories, predictive ability of a theory (as opposed to only descriptive ability), new predictions, extent of new predictions and their corroboration, and finally things forbidden or demanded by a theory which in effect also define criteria for falsifiability of a theory.

Quantitative measurements include percentage of total observations corroborated by a theory, percentage of total observations transformed into 'irrefutable observations' by a theory, percentage of total observations not explained/corroborated by a theory and finally percentage of total observations falsifying a theory. I hope to publish this work in future.

Theory of Vartak provided me an opportunity to critically analyze numerous Mahabharata observations. The reader could use similar approach in critically analyzing my theory/proposal and those of other Mahabharata researchers.

11

A Better Theory

The scientific theorist is not to be envied. For Nature, or more precisely experiment, is an exorable and not very friendly judge of his work. It never says "yes" to a theory. In the most favorable cases it says "Maybe," and in the great majority of cases simply "No." If an experiment agrees with a theory it means for the latter "Maybe," and if it does not agree it means "No." Probably every theory will someday experience its "No" - most theories, soon after conception.

- Albert Einstein

Once I started critically discussing work of others, I feared that my book would fill only with the criticism of others and my original work would get lost. I was also disappointed by the cocksure attitude of number of researchers, especially those who made their proposal based on only those Mahabharata observations that they presumed supported their timeline. Many of them did not bother to discuss numerous Mahabharata observations, which directly contradicted their timeline. I began writing criticism, i.e. criticism of the theories and corresponding proposals for the year of Mahabharata War as propounded by 20+ researchers. They all had predicted the first day and the year of Mahabharata War. I realized that these researchers, with the exceptions of Vartak and Kane, have been selective in quoting Mahabharata astronomical observations. Many of them ignored vast number of Mahabharata astronomical observations. Still others claimed to have included certain observations in building their timeline they thought critical, and I could demonstrate how their theories were contradicted by these so called 'critical' observations. These researchers appeared to be blissfully unaware of this fact. I decided, only with great reluctance, to exclude the discussion of the works of other researchers, i.e. the criticisms of their theories and timelines for the Mahabharata War, with the exception of Vartak, from this book.

What follows is summary of my theory and my proposed timeline of the Mahabharata war and why it should be considered a better theory, i.e. better than all existing theories (and proposed timelines).

My Theory

1. All astronomy observations in Mahabharata are 'visual observations' of the sky.
2. Mahabharata astronomers were meticulous and patient empirical astronomers. They were inheritors of even farther ancient tradition of astronomy observations. Mahabharata astronomers had means to observe objects in the sky, which would not be otherwise visible to a naked eye.
3. Mahabharata author's motivation for noting down specific astronomy observations during and around the time of Mahabharata War was to create records of Mahabharata War. These observations were embedded in the Mahabharata text. Mahabharata author embedded these observations as is and also in the form of similes signifying bad omens, engagement of key warriors on the battlefield or death of principal warriors.

I had also stated that one would, very likely, find numerous additional astronomy observations within the Mahabharata Text. I found numerous astronomy (or chronological) observations and corroborated them with the predictions of my theory. My list is not complete by any means and I encourage readers to search for additional Mahabharata observations.

My Proposed Timeline

The Mahabharata War timeline begins with Krishna leaving Upaplavya to visit Hastinapur before the War and ends with the passing away of Bhishma, when the Sun turned north, after the War.

1. Krishna left Upaplavya on *Maitri* (*Anuradha*) *Muhurta*, Revati *nakshatra* and in the month of Lotuses: 31 August 5561 B.C.
2. Duryodhana ordered his royal friends to leave for Kurukshetra on the day of *Pushya*: 6-7 September 5561 B.C.
3. Krishna-Karna meeting, 7 days before *Jyeshtha Amawasya* & before Krishna left for Upaplavya: 9-10 September 5561 B.C.
4. *Shakra* (*Jyeshtha or possibly Vishakha*) *Amawasya*: 16-17 September 5561 B.C.
5. Balarama left the Pandava camp, to proceed on Saraswati *Tirthayatra*, on *Anuradha* (*Maitri*) *nakshatra*: 17 September 5561 B.C.
6. Balarama began *Tirthayatra* of Saraswati around 22 September 5561 B.C.
7. *Kartika Purnima* (Full moon): 30 September – 1 October 5561 B.C.
8. Krishna left along with the Pandavas for Kurukshetra on *Pushya*: 4-5 October 5561 B.C.
9. Both armies arrived at Kurukshetra on *Magha*: 6-7 October 5561 B.C.
10. Vyasa met Dhritarashtra: 15 October 5561 B.C.
11. The First day of Mahabharata War: 16 October 5561 B.C.
12. Bhishma fell in the battlefield on the 10th day of War: 25 October 5561 B.C.
13. Abhimanyu was killed on the 13th day of War: 28 October 5561 B.C.
14. Arjuna killed Jayadratha and the fight continued into the night at the end of the 14th day of War: 29 October 5561 B.C.
15. Drona was killed on the 15th day of War: 30th October 5561 B.C.
16. Arjuna killed Karna on the 17th day of War: 1 November 5561 B.C.
17. Shalya was killed by noon and Bhima killed Duryodhana at the end of the day on the 18th day of War: 2 November 5561 B.C.
18. The Pandavas spent a month on the bank of River Ganga: 2-3 November – 30 November 5561 B.C.

19. The Pandavas entered Hastinapur after spending a lunar month on the bank of Ganga: 30 November 5561 B.C.
20. Coronation of Yudhishthir, assignment of offices & palaces, and honoring of Krishna: 30 November-5 December 5561 B.C.
21. Yudhishthir and his brothers, Krishna, Satyaki, Yuyutsu, Kripacharya and Sanjay go to Kurukshetra to visit Bhishma, 56 days before passing away of Bhishma: 5-6 December 5561 B.C.
22. Yudhishthir along with his brothers, Dhritarashtra, Gandhari and ministers visits Bhishma for last but one time, 51 days before passing away of Bhishma: 10-11 December 5561 B.C.
23. Yudhishthir leaves for Kurukshetra, after spending 50 nights at Hastinapur, to meet Bhishma when the Sun turned north: 30-31 January 5560 B.C.
24. *Bhishma Nirvana*: 30-31 January 5560 B.C.

My Key Contributions

- My theory proceeds from a simple, almost trivial, unifying idea that all astronomy observations around the time of Mahabharata War are visual observations of the sky.
- My theory is independently testable. Anyone can access astronomy software such as Voyager 4.5™, follow through my book and test each Mahabharata observation.
- I sought explanation for *Arundhati* observation, based on my theory, an observation otherwise considered absurd by entire research community (albeit with one exception), as visual observation at the time of Mahabharata War.
- My theory corroborates not only positions of the planets but also their movements as described in the Mahabharata text, specifically unique movements of Mars, Jupiter and Venus.
- My theory corroborated descriptions of planets and rationale for them shining brightly at times, e.g. Jupiter and Saturn shining brightly or Mars turning in *'apasavya'* direction while shining brightly with fearsome appearance.
- My theory predicted 'potential observations' referring to the phases and the positions of the moon, which would corroborate or falsify a proposed timeline for the 18 days of War. I

searched for these potential observations within the Mahabharata text, and by luck, found numerous observations.

- My theory corroborated 100+ astronomical observations from the Mahabharata text. More importantly my theory passed numerous critical tests, which in turn provided consistent explanations for Mahabharata astronomical observations. Some of these critical tests are,

    1. Fall of *Abhijit*
    2. The Epoch of *Arundhati*
    3. Positions of Jupiter and Saturn in the vicinity of *Vishakha* for up to a year.
    4. *Vakri* motions of Mars near *Magha* and near *Jyeshtha/Anuradha*
    5. *Vakri* motion of Jupiter near *Shravana*
    6. Mars becoming steady between *Chitra/Swati* while moving in *apasavya* direction + Mars afflicting *Chitra*
    7. Timing and rationale for specific descriptions (e.g. shining brightly) of Jupiter, Saturn & Mars
    8. Circular motion of Venus near *Purva Bhadrapada* in the company of another planet
    9. *Tiryak* rising of Mercury after the sunset on the 17th day of War
    10. Jupiter afflicting *Rohini*, similar to the Moon and the Sun, after the sunset on the 17th day of War
    11. The Phases and the positions of the moon through 18 days of the War
    12. Time interval between Fall of Bhishma and *Bhishma Nirvana*
    13. Mars, Venus and Mercury in the western part of sky, after sunset, on the last day of War

War Diary

Krishna left for Hastinapur, from Upaplavya, on 31 August 5561 B.C. The *nakshatra* was *Revati* and the month was that of lotuses, i.e. end of rainy season. Krishna reached Hastinapur in 2-3 days and stayed at the house of Vidura. Krishna held many rounds of negotiations with the Kauravas. Angry Duryodhana urged his royal friends to leave for Kurukshetra on 6 or 7 September 5561 B.C. The *nakshatra* was Pu-

shya. Krishna met Karna on 9 or 10 September 5561 B.C., 7 days before *Shakra* (Indra) Amawasya. *Shakra* Amawasya refers to an Amawasya occurring near the *nakshatra* of Indra (*Shakra*) and that means on *Jyeshtha nakshatra* (however *Vishakha* may also qualify since deity of *Vishakha* is Indra & Agni). *Shakra* Amawasya (*Jyeshtha* or *Vishakha*) occurred on 16-17 September 5561 B.C. Krishna suggested that the war preparations begin on this day.

Krishna returned to Upaplavya and met with the Pandavas. Balarama arrived at the Pandava camp, decided not to participate in the War, and left for the *Tirthayatra* of Saraswati on 17 September 5561 B.C. The *nakshatra* was *Anuradha* (Maitri). Balarama began his *Tirthayatra* on 22 September 5561 B.C.

Kartika Purnima occurred around 30 September – 1 October 5561 B.C. Yudhishthir held secret meeting to discuss war strategies and this meeting was around the time of *Kartika Purnima*. Uluka came to the Pandava camp with message of Duryodhana and returned to the Kaurava camp with message from the Pandavas. Krishna left for Kurukshetra, along with the Pandavas on 4-5 October 5561 B.C. The *nakshatra* was *Pushya*. Both armies arrived at Kurukshetra on 6-7 October 5561 B.C. The *nakshatra* was *Magha*. Both armies held a joint meeting to decide on the rules and etiquettes of the War. Vyasa met Dhritarashtra on 15 October 5561 B.C., one day before the first day of Mahabharata War.

The War began on 16 October 5561 B.C. The day was Amawasya. Solar eclipse occurred on this day and seven planets could be seen in the sky. The fighting ended with sunset and when no one could see anything in the darkness. The fighting continued, on any given day, as long as there was light on the battlefield or until the warriors were exhausted and could fight no more. Bhishma fell in the battlefield on 25 October 5561 B.C., 10th day of the War. Bhishma requested bed of arrows and Arjuna fulfilled this wish of Bhishma.

Drona became the general of the Kaurava army and the War continued. Abhimanyu was killed on 28 October 5561 B.C., on the 13th day of War. Arjuna killed Jayadratha in the evening on 29 October 5561 B.C., the next day, i.e. 14th day of the War. The moon along with 7 planets could be seen in the sky. The fighting continued into the night, Ghatotkacha was killed around the midnight, fight resumed for another hour when Arjuna suggested that warriors of both sides take some rest. Both sides agreed and rested for a while. When the dust settled and the moon (full moon) reappeared in the sky, warriors woke up and resumed the fight. The warriors took a short break at sunrise to offer their prayers. The fight began and Drona was killed. This was the 15th day of War and the date was 30 October 5561 B.C. Lunar eclipse occurred on this day and was visible at Kurukshetra in the evening, after sunset, for 90 minutes.

Karna became the general of the Kaurava army and the War continued. Arjuna killed Karna on 1 November 5561 B.C., 17th day of the War. Seven planets could be seen in the sky after the sunset.

Shalya became the general of the Kaurava army on the 18th day of War. Shalya was killed by midday and Duryodhana ran away from the battlefield. Mars, Venus and Mercury could be seen in the western part of the sky at sunset. The Pandavas discovered hiding location of Duryodhana and Bhima killed Duryodhana at the end of the day. The *nakshatra* was *Pushya*.

Ashwatthama attacked the Pandava camp at night and killed many along with the five sons of Draupadi, Dhristadyumna and Shikhandi. The Pandavas tamed Ashwatthama the next day and the Kaurava women approached the battlefield in search of their beloved. The Pandavas arranged the funeral of dead warriors and then left for the bank of Ganga, along with Dhritarashtra, Gandhari and the rest.

The Pandavas spent a month on the bank of Ganga from 3 November until 30 November 5561 B.C. They entered Hastinapur around 30 November 5561 B.C. Coronation of Yudhishthir, assignment of offices and palaces, and honoring of Krishna took place between 30 November and 5 December 5561 B.C.

Krishna suggested Yudhishthir to visit Bhishma. The Pandavas, along with Krishna, Satyaki, Yuyutsu, Kripacharya and Sanjay visited Bhishma. Krishna told Bhishma that the latter had 56 more days to live. The day was 6 December 5561 B.C., 56 days before the day of winter solstice – 30 January 5560 B.C.

Yudhishthir visited Bhishma the next day only with his brothers, Krishna and Satyaki. This was 7 December 5561 B.C. Yudhishthir did the same on 8 December 5561 B.C. Yudhishthir went to see Bhishma alone for two days; 9 and 10 December 5561 B.C. He went to see Bhishma for last but one time on 11 December 5561 B.C., this time along with Dhritarashtra, Gandhari and his ministers. Bhishma asked Yudhishthir to return to Hastinapur and requested him to return to Bhishma when the Sun turned northward, i.e. one day after the day of winter solstice.

Yudhishthir returned to Hastinapur, stayed in Hastinapur for next 50 days and returned to see Bhishma on 31 January 5560 B.C. Bhishma passed away on this day.

Duration of time interval of greater than 92 days between fall of Bhishma and Bhishma Nirvana falsified all previous proposed timelines for the Mahabharata War. The duration of 92 days is a conservative estimate, since actual number has to be indeed higher than 92. Additionally, *Arundhati* observation falsified all but 4 proposed timelines of the Mahabharata War. *Arundhati* observation presents 'ready falsification' for any proposed date, proposed in the past or that might be proposed in the future, for the Mahabharata War, that falls after 4508 B.C. Peculiar journey of Mars through 13 *nakshatras*, oblique motion of Jupiter near *Shravana*, retrograde motion of Venus near *Purva Bhadrapada*, presence of Mars, Venus and Mercury in the western part of the sky, after sunset, on the last day of War and 20 additional planetary observations present near unique scenario that must be corroborated by any proposed year of the Mahabharata War. Mahabharata observations of chapter 8 falsify any timeline for the first day of Mahabharata War that does not begin on Amawasya day.

Information, Truth & Falsity Content

A theory that corroborates more information is a better theory where information refers to set of observations that lead to growth of knowledge, *ceteris paribus*.

Let C (a) be the content of observation 'a' and C (b) be the content of observation 'b'

$$C (a) < C (ab) > C (b)$$

A theory that corroborates both 'a' and 'b' is better than a theory that corroborates 'only a' or 'only b'. All theories under comparison should use identical set of observations in evaluating corroborative (truth) and contradictory (falsity) content, i.e., critical tests of observations. A theory with higher truth content and lower falsity content is better theory than other theories whose truth content is lower and falsity content is higher.

Measurement of information, truth and falsity content becomes more useful when comparing two or more theories, and especially for two different predictions (in this case two different years for the Mahabharata War). I have included Mahabharata observations employed by all past researchers and have added many more. Mahabharata observations employed by me become the baseline, which I plan to use in critically discussing the work of other researchers, in future. For now, I encourage readers to do their own comparison of my work with those of other researchers.

Simplicity & Corroboration of Observations

It is always possible to introduce ad hoc hypothesis in any theory in order to save the theory from introducing contradictions. For this reason alone, a simple theory is preferred over a complicated one, where simplicity refers to testability. If ad hoc hypothesis leads to explaining away observations, rather than explain them, such a theory becomes inferior, especially when an alternate theory can corroborate 'observations' without an introduction of ad hoc hypothesis. Introduction of ad hoc hypothesis is a common phenomenon and is legitimate as long as ad hoc hypothesis does not turn the theory into a metaphysical program. In addition, introduction of ad hoc hypothesis should lead to growth of knowledge and at the same time should not introduce inconsistencies.

Degree of Testability

Some theories expose themselves to possible refutations more boldly than others. A theory that is more precise and thus more easily refutable than another will also be the more interesting theory. Such theory is more daring, it is also less probable but at the same time better testable since we can make our tests more precise and more severe. If such theory stands up to severe tests it will be better corroborated by these tests. Corroboration must increase with testability and it means the criteria used for comparison will itself have degrees. There will be well-testable theories, hardly testable theories, and non-testable theories.

197

While Vartak invoked multiple theories to explain Mahabharata observations, researchers such as Achar, Gupta or Holay explained away all observations of the 3rd *Adhyaya* of Bhishma *Parva*. R N Iyengar has done fine job of documenting multiple versions of same verse from different Mahabharata manuscripts; however, he fails to corroborate these observations for his proposed year of the Mahabharata War. Theories or ad hoc hypotheses that are not testable are metaphysical. This non-testable status is not permanent and with advances in our knowledge and technology these metaphysical theories may become testable.

Observations explained by previous theories

New theory, if it claims to be a better theory, must explain observations explained by previous theories. This amounts to new theory retaining the success of previous theories. This is a necessary but not sufficient condition. I collected as many works as I could, which employed astronomical observations for predicting timeline of the Mahabharata war. I identified some 20 works, which loosely (and only loosely) fit the definition of 'work based on astronomical observations'. I have discussed theory of Vartak in detail and will not repeat the successes of his theory. I limit my discussion to few other researchers and successes of their theories.

S. Balakrishna felt curious about the Mahabharata observation[29] that refers to the lunar and solar eclipses happening within a time interval of only 13 days. He collected data on numerous historical eclipses to illustrate how two eclipses within a time interval of 13 days are feasible. I have shown this to be the case for my proposed timeline.

Raghavan, Achar and Holay conjectured additional month long period between Krishna-Karna dialogue and the first day of War. I have made similar conjecture. I also want to re-emphasize that Mahabharata text does not provide explicit corroboration for this conjecture of mine, and of Raghavan, Achar or Holay. I have explicitly stated my reason for making such a conjecture. Raghavan, Achar and Holay have not explicitly stated the rationale for insertion of an additional lunar month, however I speculate that their motivation appears to be driven by the need to reconcile 42 day long *Tirthayatra* of Baia-rama.

My interpretation of 'Saturn afflicting *Rohini*', 'Jupiter afflicting *Rohini*', and 'sun and moon, together afflicting *Rohini*' is similar to the interpretation 'Saturn afflicting *Rohini*' by Holay. In Holay's words, "Here the author of the verses describes the position of the star *Rohini* in the sky in poetic manner stating that when Saturn rises in the eastern horizon day by day, it brings pressure on *Rohini* to set in the west".

While Holay does not explicitly interpret observation of *Tiryak* rising of Mercury, he mentions this Mahabharata observation as critical observation for his proposed timeline. I speculate that his interpretation of '*Tiryak* rising of Mercury' is similar to my explanation, except Mercury might not have been visible for the date proposed by Holay, unless of course unique weather conditions have had prevailed on that day. Interestingly, Holay is silent on the observation of Jupiter.

Since this section is not about analyzing work of others, I will say no further. Holay makes a case for Mahabharata author being aware of 'Uranus'. I have gone beyond (essentially re-stating work of Vartak) and have made a case for Mahabharata author being aware of not only 'Uranus', but also Neptune and Pluto.

Observations NOT explained by previous theories

I de-mystified Mahabharata observation of '*Arundhati* walking ahead of Vasistha' and showed this to be a visual observation during the Mahabharata War. In fact, I defined the time interval for the search of the year of Mahabharata War because of my de-mystification of *Arundhati* observation. Only Vartak believed in the factual nature of this observation, even though he failed to test it. RN Iyengar mentions *Arundhati* observation but only to explain it away. Two researchers (Vaidya and Kane) mention it rather in support of their assertion of how Mahabharata text also contains absurd astronomical observations. Other researchers neither realized the importance of this observation nor bothered to acknowledge its existence.

This single observation defined higher and lower bounds for the timeline of Mahabharata War, and the observation had higher degree of improbability associated with it. The explanation of *Arundhati* observation and corresponding prediction of time interval for the plausible year of Mahabharata War falsified all existing proposals for the timing of Mahabharata War, with the exception of 4 proposals that fell within the 'Epoch of *Arundhati*'. *Arundhati* observation acts as falsifying evidence for any year proposed after 4500 B.C. I could corroborate, by luck, 100+ Mahabharata observations, identified by previous researchers as well as observations predicted by my theory and later on identified, within the Mahabharata text. Other Mahabharata observations, besides that of *Arundhati*, also falsified proposals of other researchers.

Numerous Mahabharata observations, when analyzed, infer a time interval of not less than 92 days (9+ 27 + X + 56 = 92+ X) between 'Fall of Bhishma' and '*Bhishma Nirvana*'. This requirement of minimum time interval leading to *Bhishma Nirvana* has placed a limit on the duration of time interval within which plausible year of the Mahabharata War is to be searched, not unlike the limit placed by *Arundhati* observation. This inference falsifies all known proposals for the day of Bhishma Nirvana and for the year of Mahabharata War.

All planetary observations, taken together, have also provided falsifying tests for all known proposals of the Mahabharata War. Set of observations describing the phases and the positions of Moon during the 18 days of War provide corroborative evidence for *Amawasya* as the first day of War and *Kartika* Amawasya as the first day of war, which also means month of *Margashirsha* as the month of Mahabharata War.

(Additional) Requirements of a Better theory

All my explanations of Mahabharata observations (e.g. relative motions of stars, multiple positions for individual planets, positions and phases of the moon, position of comet, eclipses) flow from simple hypothesis of visual observations of the sky. This is the simple, new and powerful unifying hypothesis, and I encourage readers to compare it against the hypotheses of all past and current researchers.

I have shown my theory to be consistent, or free from contradictions, with the exceptions of two observations. I am specifically referring to the late moonrise on the 14th day of the War and the *nakshatras* related to the *Tirthayatra* of Balarama. While many researchers have employed one or both of these observations as critical in building their timeline, I did not employ them in building my timeline and my only responsibility is to corroborate them. I have attempted such corroboration by borrowing explanation provided by Vartak and adding additional observations of my own. Contrary to the claims made by other researchers, not a single researcher has corroborated the observations related to *Tirthayatra* of Balarama for their proposed timeline. Few researchers indeed corroborated 'late moonrise' for their timeline by moving the first day of War, however many are blissfully unaware of the numerous observations contradicting such adjusted timeline. I have shown that overwhelming number of Mahabharata observations contradict any timeline that claims to have late moonrise on the 14th day of War. Many researchers have built their timeline to justify 'late moonrise' on the 14th day of War' and *'nakshatras'* related to *Tirthayatra* of Balarama. If one hypothetically assumes nonexistence of these observations, these researchers will have to begin their work afresh. Such hypothetical scenario does not affect my timeline. In fact, I consider such outcome as an illustration of criteria that allows us to define 'degree of testability' or 'Degree of falsifiability' for each Mahabharata observation.

Degree of Falsifiability

I estimated degree of falsifiability of Mahabharata observation using a technique analogous to the method of stepwise regression that uses combinations of forward selection and backward elimination. I was not looking for statistical significance but rather the significance of a given Mahabharata observation for either predicting or eliminating, certain time intervals for the plausible year of Mahabharata War. I did this by running a thought experiment where all other observations are removed except a specific observation, and then assessed the change in predictions and quality of predictions due to the testing of such lone observation.

(1) Ability of *Arundhati* observation to predict the time interval for the plausible year of Mahabharata War is not affected, when all other Mahabharata observations are eliminated.

(2) When all other references, other than those related to Fall of Bhishma and *Bhishma Nirvana*, are removed, this set of *'Bhishma Nirvana'* observations defines an approximate time

interval of 6500 B.C. through 3500 B.C. for the plausible year of Mahabharata War.

(3) When all other observations (except *Arundhati*) are removed, set of planetary positions lead to a unique timeline for the Mahabharata War. It is laborious to test this set of planetary observations for each plausible year of the Mahabharata War. As a result, while I would not claim 5561 B.C. to be a unique instance corroborating this set of planetary positions, nonetheless, this set of observations has falsified all existing (and known to me) proposals of the Mahabharata War.

Preceding three sets of observations provide falsifying evidence/explanations/tests for any proposed year of the Mahabharata War. Any proposed timeline has to corroborate following sets of observations:

(4) The positions and the phases of the Moon, together, define the first day of War as well as the lunar month(s) of Mahabharata War.

(5) Season of two eclipses (lunar and solar eclipses) must exist for a proposed time interval with solar eclipse on the first day and the lunar eclipse around the 15th day of War

Next set of observations is related to the descriptions of the sky and the seasons. Proposed timeline must corroborate these observations. Many of the proposals, but not all, for the Mahabharata War corroborate Mahabharata descriptions and observations of the season. While descriptions of the season cannot be used to predict the year of Mahabharata War, they are still capable of falsifying a proposal that would propose timing of the War, far removed from the season of *Sharad*.

(6) Descriptions of the sky and the seasons

The observation of comet could be used to falsify a proposal for the year of Mahabharata War. This observation would falsify a timeline if it could be shown that Haley's comet was in apparition and thus not near *Pushya*.

(7) Position of comet (Haley's) disallows one year in every ~77 years for the timing of Mahabharata war.

This relationship between degree of falsifiability (also testability or simplicity) and the relevance/importance of corresponding Mahabharata observation for the dating of Mahabharata War is visually illustrated in Figure 11.

Conclusion

I can think of many additional criteria in defense of my theory as a better theory however that would necessitate detailed criticism of the works of other researchers. Therefore with great reluctance, I have decided to contain my enthusiasm.

I classified all Mahabharata observations into 7 groups, categorized by their degree of falsifiability. First 3 (3 of 7) sets of observations have very high degree of falsifiability. For example observation of *Arundhati* falsifies all but 4 proposals for the year of Mahabharata War, while group of planetary observations falsifies all but one (1 out of remaining 4 proposals) proposed year (Vartak) for the Mahabharata War. While group of planetary observations did not falsify year proposed by Vartak (5561 B.C.), this group (of planetary observations) does falsify his theory. Set of observations related to *Bhishma Nirvana* falsifies proposals of all researchers and also day of *Bhishma Nirvana* proposed by Vartak.

12

Implications, Predictions
&
New Problems

It might be well for all of us to remember that, while differing widely in the various little bits we know, in our infinite ignorance we are all equal.

- Karl Popper

Superior theory explains more and is better tested. If I have convinced the reader that this is indeed the case for my theory, then I want to make the reader aware of the implications of my theory for our current understanding of antiquity of astronomy observations and human civilizations.

Every worthwhile new theory raises new problems and frankly the worth of a new theory can be measured by new problems, i.e. problems of an ever-increasing depth and an ever-increasing fertility. The most lasting contribution to the growth of scientific knowledge that a new theory can make is the new problems, which it raises.

World civilizations

Many ancient civilizations such as Sumerian, Greek, Egyptian, Sindhu-Saraswati, Babylonian, Mayan and Incas have been discovered and studied. Traditional scholarship considers Sumerian civilization as the earliest known civilization and also the cradle of civilization, and assigns 3500 B.C. as roughly the timing of this civilization. Egyptian civilization is considered as old as 3100 B.C. and Sindhu (Indus) valley civilization as old as 2600 B.C. Minoan (ancient Greek) civilization also goes as far back as 3000 B.C. It is true that first settlement (Eridu) for Sumerian civilization is claimed as far back as 5300 B.C. and timing of small tribes living in Nile Valley (Egyptian civilization) settled in established agriculture go back to 5500 B.C. Ceramic Neolithic phase (Mehrgarh II) of Sindhu civilization extends back to 5500 B.C. and early food producing era (Mehrgarh I) extends even further back to 7000 B.C.

I am asserting Mahabharata civilization as an established civilization with chariots and horses, elephants and camels, explosives and weapons. I am also asserting Mahabharata civilization with cast based social system, well established system of religious rituals, advanced visual astronomy, palaces and boats, clothing made out of cotton and silk, advances in metallurgy (gold, silver, copper, iron), all of this during and before 5561 B.C. Thus my date (or my claim) of the Mahabharata War predates all known civilizations of the world, based on social and technological development and based on traditional (scholarship) dates for these ancient civilizations.

While I do not know how traditional scholarship arrived at the timing of these civilizations, all I want to emphasize is that the Mahabharata civilization turns out to be the earliest, based on the dates proposed for all other civilizations. I hope that my work will encourage other researchers not only to analyze my work and claims but also to re-visit the observations and methods employed by traditional scholarship, in determining the timing of world civilizations. Mahabharata has stray references to faraway lands, richer in resources, and I hope that my work will lead to re-searching the traditional dates assigned to other civilizations. Archeology research at Sindhu- Saraswati (Indus- Saraswati) sites leads to a period as early as 7000 B.C., however, the state of civilization claimed from such archeological data nowhere compares with the advancements described in the Mahabharata text.

There are allusions to antiquity of other world civilizations, Incas, Maya, Aztec and also plausible connections of these civilizations with Indian civilizations. There is a need to make bold conjectures and corresponding predictions, which in turn should be subjected to rational criticism.

Dating of Ramayana & Veda

Mahabharata observations (Fall of Abhijit) allude to the events of the ancient past as far back as 14500 B.C. and 22500 B.C. The Mahabharata text contains references, which indicate Veda and Ramayana predating the Mahabharata. Although exact timing of Ramayana is uncertain, what is certain is that Ramayana occurred long before the Mahabharata war. Ramayana and Mahabharata, both contain references to Veda. The Mahabharata War, as a chronological marker, pushes the timing of Ramayana and that of Veda, in further antiquity.

Saraswati

The Mahabharata text states that rivers began flowing, only after hiding themselves under the sand, in describing the time of the destruction of Vrishni dynasty. This Mahabharata observation may refer to disappearance of rivers such as Saraswati under the Sand[187]. We do not have to depend on such indirect references though. Numerous references to Saraswati appear in Vana, Bhishma and Shalya *Parva*s.

The Mahabharata text refers to benefit of taking bath in Saraswati where it meets the sea[188], and also refers to benefit of taking bath where Sindhu meets the sea[189]. The Mahabharata text describes Vinashan as the place where Saraswati disappeared from the surface [190, 204, 212, 213] (i.e. began flowing underground) and describes 'Kurukshetra' as the land south of Saraswati and north of Drishtavati [196, 198, 203]. The Mahabharata text describes Bindu Sarovar as the place of origin for seven different rivers, one of them being Saraswati[205] and Plakshapravana as the place for the origin of Saraswati, the best of best rivers [199, 202]. Saraswati was filled with Tirthakshetras (holy places of pilgrimage) on its banks and many of them had mythologized stories associated with them, even at the time of Mahabharata [188-215]. Markandeya narrates to Yudhishthir historical events that took place on the bank of Saraswati and describes location of Kurukshetra as near Saraswati[202].

Lomash describes Saraswati[204] as magnificent and fast flowing river. Lomash also describes Saraswati meeting the sea [207, 208]. It is not clear if his description refers to the time of *Yajna* of Prajapati he is narrating or the time of his conversation with Yudhishthir. This is critical because in the same line Lomash also refers to 'Vinashan', the place where Saraswati went underground in the desert and thus disappeared. Lomash also mentions 'Chamasod', another place where Saraswati reappeared and also where all sea going rivers had come together. Lomash describes Saraswati as the river that disappears and reappears multiple times. Lomash goes on to describe river Sindhu after describing Saraswati.

Descriptions of the *Tirthayatra* of Balarama[206] mention an unnamed city on the bank of Saraswati, a big city with active international marketplace, filled with people of different types (races?)! Balarama purchased horses originating from various countries, chariots, cows, jewels, pearls, and corals, plates made out of pure gold, silver, iron and copper. Balarama purchased these to distribute to Brahmanas. Balarama visited Udapana, a place of pilgrimage, and the Mahabharata text mentions that experts recognized the existence of underground Saraswati at Udapana, based on wet soil and moisture content generated by medicinal plants and trees [209]. Saraswati turned east at one location and Balarama was awestruck at the magnificent view of the river, which shifted its direction at this location[214].

One could infer from above references that Saraswati was indeed a mighty river before Mahabharata. The existence of mythologized stories in Mahabharata times also alludes to ancient nature of Saraswati, i.e. ancient with respect to Mahabharata. One could also infer that Saraswati was still flowing in many places during the Mahabharata War, but it had also appeared and disappeared[205] in many places including disappearances at Vinashan [190, 204, 213] and at Udapana [209, 210, 212]. Sutlej and Yamuna fed Saraswati in the distant past, and by the time of Mahabharata War, Sutlej had already turned west and was no longer feeding its water to Saraswati. I conjecture that these changes occurred due to tectonic shifts. The Mahabharata text contains description of Yamuna merging with Ganga[215] and Saraswati merging with Ganga[200] and thus it is reasonable to assume that Yamuna might have stopped feeding its water to Saraswati by the time of Mahabharata. This would mean only minor rivers were feeding their waters to Saraswati and thus Saraswati was no longer a grand river during the time of Mahabharata War, however, its past glory was still afresh in the minds of Mahabharata sages. Sutlej had turned west even during the time of Ramayana and Yamuna existed as distinct river in Ramayana times. This would mean Saraswati might have ceased her status as swift flowing Grand River of Rig-Veda, long before the time of Mahabharata War and possibly long before the time of Ramayana.

Mahabharata observations of Saraswati and my proposed timing of the Mahabharata War corroborate well with inferences of Francfort who thinks that the Hakra/Ghaggar River (Saraswati) predated the entire pre and proto Harappan period. Lansat satellite images show 8 km wide course of the former river. It is interesting to note that when the protohistoric (as defined by traditional scholarship) people settled in this area, no large perennial river had flowed there for a long time. Archaeological sites were located not only on the banks of former natural waterways, but even in the middle of the supposed larger riverbeds. One such excavated site situated on a dune in the middle of ancient riverbed, is at least as old as 2000 B.C. Francfort's research team concluded that the actual large paleocourses of the river have been dry since the early Holocene period or even earlier. It is important to recognize that pre harappan settlements exist from 3700 B.C. Early Holocene refers to time interval 10000 B.C. – 7000 B.C.

Out of India (OIT) Migrations

Indo-Aryan speaking civilizations such as Mittani were established in Northern Syria and South-eastern Turkey by 1500 B.C. Many other civilizations from this region have allusions to them migrating from the east. These civilizations need to be studied in the context of my Mahabharata timeline. These could be, but not necessarily, post Mahabharata migrations to the west.

On the other hand, King Pururava had two sons from Urvashi, Ayu and Amawasu. Ayu migrated to the east and his descendants were known as Kuru-Panchala and Kashi-Videhas. Amawasu migrated to the west and his descendants were known as Gandharas, Parsu and Arrattas. King Pururava is listed as descendant of Ila and Ila is descendant of Manu.

It is true that genealogy of Kings lists only prominent kings. Still, with limited list of Kings available, the Pandavas are listed after a gap of 55+ descendants of King Pururava, from the line of Ayu (Kuru-Panchalas). As a result one has to search for Amawasu migration, long before the Mahabharata War.

Sindhu Civilization

Acceptance of my Mahabharata timeline also means Harappa Civilization should be accepted as post-Mahabharata civilization, at least based on currently accepted dating of Harappa civilization.

BISAC

BISAC stands for 'Book Industry Standards and Communications categories and only ancient civilizations listed, under BISAC classifications, were Egypt, Greece and Roman. Thankfully I did find the fourth category termed 'General'. Lack of BISAC classification for ancient civilizations such as Indian, Sindu-Sarasawati, Mayan, Aztec, Incas, Olmecs and many other civilizations is a new problem that can be fixed easily, at least in theory.

Ages: Stone-Copper- Bronze -Iron

Traditional scholarship holds that Stone Age began three million years ago and ended with the beginning of Copper age (~7700 B.C.). Bronze Age began around 3300 B.C. and continued until 1200 B.C. while Iron Age began around 1800 B.C. and continued until 400 A.D. Each new discovery in archeology extends these ages further into antiquity. Descriptions of metals used in the Mahabharata text along with my proposed timeline of the Mahabharata War, contradict time intervals of at least the Bronze and Iron Ages.

I refer to these historic periods not with the intent of changing anything about their definition and usage, but rather to make the reader aware that some Mahabharata researchers have employed

209

the concept of Bronze and Iron ages, uncritically I think, in predict-ing/proposing the timing of Mahabharata War.

Domestication of Horses

While I do not accept lack of evidence for domestication of horses as evidence against my Mahabharata timeline, I consider my theory and proposed timeline of the Mahabharata War untenable if it could be proved that domesticated horses did not exist in India dur-ing 6th millennium B.C. In fact my timeline demands presence of domesticated horses in India long before 6th millennium B.C. Since nothing can be 'proved' per say, I am rather predicting existence of domesticated horses (in India) definitely around 5561 B.C., long time before the earliest date proposed (4000 B.C.) for domestication of horses and that too only outside India by traditional scholarship. In fact I am predicting existence of domesticated horses long before 5561 B.C., based on my assertion of Ramayana before Mahabharata, and Vedas before Ramayana and the fact that Mahabharata, Ra-mayana and Vedas have descriptions of domesticated horses, ashwamedha sacrifice and horse drawn chariots.

Invention of Writing

Mahabharata preserves numerous details of empirical astro-nomical observations of Mahabharata times and of times earlier to Mahabharata. Ability of these ancient civilizations to document em-pirical data amazes me.

I conjecture that writing skills existed long before 3500 B.C., the date accepted as invention of writing by traditional scholarship. I do not know where to look for such evidence or the type of empirical evidence that will convince us of the antiquity of writing skills.

Rig-Veda, Ramayana and Mahabharata contain indirect allu-sions to existence of writing nevertheless I desire independent evidence.

Astronomy observations

While I feel as if I am stuck on the subject of antiquity of writ-ing skills, I have shown that ability to make accurate visual astronomy observations existed for a long period of time, much longer than traditional scholarship is willing to comprehend.

I predict that additional corroborative evidence will come from astronomy references within ancient literature and also from archeo-astronomy researches of pyramids or such man-made structures. My work has obvious implications for the history of astronomy. I have made a case for history of astronomy in India as far back as 22500 B.C. and beyond. Even by conservative estimate of 5561 B.C., i.e., the timeline of Mahabharata War, we must consider Babylonian, Egyptian, Greek and other schools of astronomy as only recent.

There are allusions to knowledge of astronomy in Egypt that would parallel my proposed timeline for the history of astronomy in India, however additional research is required to make a convincing case for such antiquity in Egypt.

Future Research

I suggest that genealogies of Kings, astronomy, genetics and archeology are promising areas for additional insights into antiquity of civilizations in general and Indian civilization in particular. Puranas contain references to multiple incidents of Mahabharata and it would be interesting to investigate extent of corroboration of these Purana references, keeping in mind that lot that is in the Puranas is conjectural. Harivamsha, an appendix to Mahabharata, was another source I wanted to investigate for additional observations related to Mahabharata. While I have already begun my work on Harivamsha, I encourage readers and other researchers to bring forth all astronomy observations within ancient Indian literature.

Hypothesis Non Fingo

One of my friends, conversant in astronomy but otherwise not familiar with Mahabharata, asked me, after he had read draft of this book: "What if the Mahabharata and the Mahabharata War is proved to be a myth and not a fact?" He was curious to know how I would explain, in such case, fascinating corroboration of 100+ Mahabharata observations, for the year 5561 B.C. He was equally curious to know how I would explain existence of certain astronomy

211

observations within the Mahabharata text (Epoch of Arundhati or Fall of Abhijit) which can only be understood, at least with our current understanding of ancient civilizations, as visual observations.

"Hypothesis Non Fingo," I replied.

On a second thought, I told him that if such a scenario presented itself, one would be forced to search for that unknown great astronomer and a poet in India who wrote the Mahabharata. This unknown astronomer must have had in his possession Newton's laws and his formulae, corrections suggested by La Grange, accuracy of astronomy data that would equal NASA database, documented empirical astronomy observations of multiple millenniums and advanced telescopic capability. I told my friend that the timing of this person cannot be later than 200 B.C. - 400 AD, the timing, albeit speculative, for the last recasting of the Mahabharata text.

My friend was satisfied with my response however his satisfied look lasted only for a moment. Suddenly his eyes widened, he stared at me and asked, "Why would this great Indian astronomer and poet, generate series of astronomical statements to fit 5561 B.C. as the timing of his fiction – the Mahabharata?"

"Hypothesis Non Fingo," replied I.

Notes

Introduction
1. I had direct access to works of P V Vartak, P V Holay, Srinivas Rag-havan, BNN Achar, P V Kane, Anand Sharan, Mohan Gupta, R N Iyengar, Kota Venkatachalam, S Balakrishna, C V Vaidya and Sub-hash Kak. I came to know works of other researchers (Ketkar, P C Sengupta, Karandikar, Siddarth, Velandi Ayyer, Kochhar, V R Lele, P S Shastri and R Vaidya) only through above mentioned direct sources.

2. I have quoted numerous passages from works of Karl Popper. These quotations are from his diverse works however I predomi-nantly consulted three; The Logic of Scientific Discovery, Conjectures and Refutations, The Poverty of Historicism.

3. Quotes listed at the beginning of each chapter are from multiple sources, readily available on Internet.

Chapter 3
1. The content of this chapter (Astronomy Basics) is readily available, and in extensive detail, on numerous public sites including Wikipe-dia. Brief descriptions are presented in this chapter to eliminate the need for the reader to access other sources, for basics of as-tronomy. I encourage readers to access other resources on astronomy, if they so desire. On the other hand, the basics pre-sented in this chapter are sufficient to understand and to enjoy contents of this book.

Chapter 4
1. *Nakshatra* of a given day (and thus position of the moon) can be stated either by mathematical calculations or by visual observation of the moon and corresponding *nakshatra* in the sky. As a result, variation of +/- 1 or 2 *nakshatras* is possible in stating the position of Moon, depending on the time of observation and angle of obser-vation. The reader should bear this in mind while studying positions of moon and thus *nakshatra* of the day, as stated in the Mahabha-rata text and their corroboration using Astronomy software (e.g. Voyager 4.5^{TM}). The same logic applies to positions of planets, comets and the Sun.

Chapter 9

1. I have made an ad-hoc conjecture of an additional lunar month (in addition to 7 days) between Krishna-Karna meeting and the first day of Mahabharata War. I saw the need for such a conjecture in order to make sense of multiple pre-war instances (and Mahabharata observations). This conjecture of mine certainly corroborates all pre-war observations while removal of such conjecture only affects corroboration of pre-war observations. All observations related to 18 days of the War and all post-war observations are not affected by this conjecture of mine.

2. Srinivas Raghavan, BNN Achar as well as P V Holay have also made a conjecture of additional lunar month between Krishna-Karna meeting and the first day of War. In both cases I could not ascertain their motivation for such a conjecture. I guess that they made conjecture of additional lunar month to accommodate duration of Balarama *Tirthayatra*. Holay makes additional conjecture of a gap of 12 days (i.e. war stopping for 12 days) after fall of Bhishma. Again, it appears to me that Holay made this conjecture to corroborate *nakshatras*, Pushya and Shravana, related to *Tirthayatra* of Balarama.

Chapter 11

1. Making a case for a better theory makes it necessary that I present critical analysis of other theories. This requirement would have expanded the scope and size of this book. While I have not presented detailed criticism of other theories, I have studied them and have critically analyzed them before reaching the conclusion for my attempt as a better theory.

Chapter 12

1. Mahabharata has posed numerous other problems, irrespective of the timing proposed for its occurrence. For example,
   a. Ability of Bhishma to stay alive for an extended period of time
   b. Descriptions of *Divya* weapons
   c. Size of army (including horses, elephants, etc.,)

2. My objective in stating new problems is to provide the reader with a flavor of how new (and better) theory generates problems of higher dimensions. My goal was not be exhaustive, but rather representative. Naturally I have mentioned only few problems. This is intentional.

Selected Bibliography

1. Vartak, P. V., Swayambhu, Pune (1996)
2. Vaidya, C. V. 'Epic India, or, India as described in the Mahabharata and the Ramayana' 1861-1938. (Pages 309-311)
3. Iyengar, R.N., "Internal Consistency of Eclipses and Planetary Positions in Mahabharata", IJHS, 38.2 (2003) 77-115
4. Iyengar, R. N., " Some Celestial Observations Associated with Krishna-Lore" IJHS, 41.1 (2006) 1-13
5. Holay, P. V., " The Year of Kaurava- Pandava War", Mahabharata-The End of an Era (*Yuga*nta) (2004) 64
6. Vartak, P. V, " The Fall of the Star Vega", Treasures of ancient Indian astronomy: All Indian seminar on ancient Indian astronomy (1993) Ajanta Publications
7. Vaidya, C. V., "The Mahabharata: a Criticism" Mehar Chand Lachman Das (1966) 64
8. Kane, P. V., "History of Dharmashastra Vol III" BORI (1968) 905
9. Sathe S, Deshmukh V, and Joshi, P, Bharatiya *Yuddha*: Astronomical References, Shri Baba Saheb Apte Smarak Samiti, Pune 1985
10. Raghavan, K. Srinivas, "The Date of the Maha Bharata War and Kali Yugadhi', 1969
11. Achar, BNN, "On the Identification of Vedic *nakshatras*", University of Memphis (2004)
12. Achar BNN, "Planetarium Software and the Date of the Mahabharata War", The Mahabharata: What is not here is nowhere else (edited by T. S. Rukmani) (2005) 247
13. Gupta, Mohan," The Date of Mahabharata War", Mahabharata-The End of an Era (*Yuga*nta) (2004) 41
14. Francfort, Henri-Paul, "Evidence for Harappan Irrigation system in Haryana and Rajasthan'", Eastern Anthropologist (1992) 45:87-103
15. Mahabharata with Hindi Translation, Gita Press, Gorakhpur
16. Mahabharata, Critical Edition by BORI, Pune
17. Popper, Karl, Conjectures and Refutations
18. Popper, Karl, The Logic of Scientific Discovery
19. Popper, Karl, The Poverty of Historicism
20. Vartak, P. V., 'Wastav Ramayana, Pune

Tables and Figures

Table 1
Years proposed for the Mahabharata War

Researcher	Proposed Year for the MB War	First day of the War (if proposed)
P V Vartak	5561 BC	16 October
P V Holay	3143 BC	13 November
S Raghavan	3067 BC	22 November
BNN Achar	3067 BC	22 November
Ketkar	2585 BC	8 November
P V Kane	2526 BC	Margashirsha S 1
P C Sen-Gupta	2449 BC	4 November
Anand Sharan	2156 BC	31 October
Mohan Gupta	1952 BC	17 October
Karandikar	1931 BC	Margashirsha S 11
RN Iyengar	1478 BC	26 October
Siddarth	1311 BC or 1312 BC	24 June
Velandi Aiyer	1194 BC	14 October
K. L. Daftari	1196 BC	
D. N. Khedwal	1963 BC	
Kochhar - 1st proposal	955 BC	4 October
Kochhar - 2nd proposal	847 BC	4 July
V R Lele	5228 BC	
Kota Venkatachalam	3138 BC	
P S Shastri	3142 BC	
S Balakrishna	2559 BC or 3129 BC	
Vaidya - 1st proposal	3101 BC	Kartika Amawasya
Vaidya - 2nd proposal	3101 BC	Margashirsha S 14
Vaidya - 3rd proposal	2526 BC	
VarahaMihir (Kane)	2604 BC	
Subhash Kak	1924 BC or 3137 BC	
R Vaidya	2789 BC	

Figure 1: Motions of the Earth

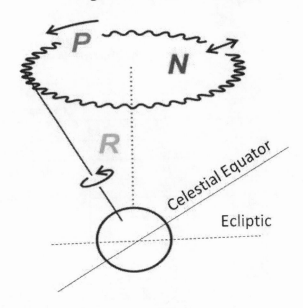

Figure 2: Right Ascension & Declination Coordinates

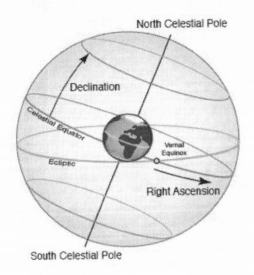

Equatorial Coordinates, the Ecliptic, and the Vernal Equinox

Table 2
Equinoxes, Solstices, Seasons & Lunar months

Lunar Months/Sampat/Ayana Bindu	Year 5561	Seasons/Equinoxes/Solstices
Jyeshtha-Ashadha- Shravan	4 April – 3 June	Vasanta
Shravana-Bhadrapada - (extra Bhadrapada)Ashwin	3 June – 4 August	Grishma
(Extra Bhadra) Ashwin- Kartika-Adhik Kartika	4 August – 3 October	Varsha
Adhik Kartika-Margashirhsa-Pausha	3 October – 2 December	Sharad
Pausha-Magha-Phalguna	2 December – 30 January	Hemanta
Phalguna-Chaitra-Vaishakha	30 January – 4 April	Shishir
Vasanta Sampat	3 May 5561 BC	Spring Equinox
Dakshinayan Bindu	4 August 5561 BC	Summer Solstice
Sharad Sampat	31 October 5561 BC	Fall Equinox
Uttarayan Bindu	30 January 5560 BC	Winter Solstice

Table 3
Nakshatra, Nakshatra Devata, Modern star, RA & Dec
(5561 B.C.)

Nakshatra	Yoga Tara	Nakshatra Devata	RA	DEC	Nirayan	Sayan
			arc-sec	arc-sec	(Vartak)	(Vartak)
Punarvasu	Pollux	Aditi	25,200	35,040	28	7
Pushya	Altarf	Brihaspati	81,900	(7,440)	1	8
Ashlesha	zeta Hydrae	Nagas/Sarpah	117,900	3,900	2	9
Magha	Regulus	Pitarah	156,600	61,800	3	10
Purva-Phalguni	Zosma	Aryaman (Bhaga)	180,000	120,480	4	11
Uttara Phalguni	Denebola	Bhaga (Aryaman)	229,500	124,980	5	12
Hasta	Algorab	Savitar (Sun?)	323,100	44,820	6	13
Chitra	Spica	Twastra (Indra)	361,800	79,380	7	14
Swati	Zeta Bootis	Vayu	381,600	213,360	8	15
Vishakha	Zubeneschamali	Indragni	469,800	102,180	9	16
Anuradha	Dschubba	Mitra	506,700	52,800	10	17
Jyeshtha	Antares	Indra (Varuna)	528,300	35,580	11	18
Moola	Shaula	Pitarah (Nirriti)	566,100	(14,160)	12	19
Purva-Ashadha	Kaus Australis	Apah	603,900	(19,140)	13	20
Uttara-Ashadha	Nunki	Visve Devah	639,000	(5,100)	14	21
Shravana	Altair	Vishnu	745,200	74,040	15	22
(Abhijit)	Vega	Brahma	784,800	193,320	16	23
Dhanishtha	Sualocin	Vasavah	802,800	67,260	17	24
Shatabhisaj (Shatataraka?)	Sadalmelik	Indra (Varuna)	828,000	(25,980)	18	25
Purva-Bhadrapada	Markab	Aja Ekapad	902,700	(10,500)	19	26
Uttara-Bhadrapada	Algenib	Ahir-Budhnya	954,900	(41,100)	20	27
Revati	Kullat Nunu	Pusan	1,019,700	(66,240)	21	28
Ashwini	Hamal	Asvinau	1,056,600	(44,040)	22	1
Bharani	41 Arietis	Yama	1,094,400	(35,820)	23	2
Krittika	Pleiades	Agni	1,143,000	(47,880)	24	3
Rohini	Aldebaran	Prajapati	1,188,000	(68,040)	25	4
Mriga- shirshya	Bellatrix	Soma	1,245,600	(92,040)	26	5
Ardra	Betelgeuse	Rudra	1,270,800	(78,480)	27	6

Figure 3
Abhijit (Vega)
(Declination measurement through 26000 years)

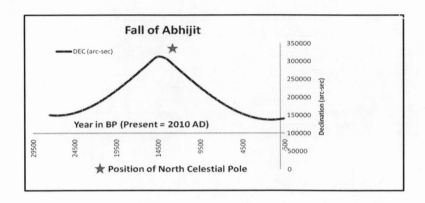

Figure 4
Right Ascension Delta - RAD (Arundhati – Vasistha)
The Epoch of Arundhati

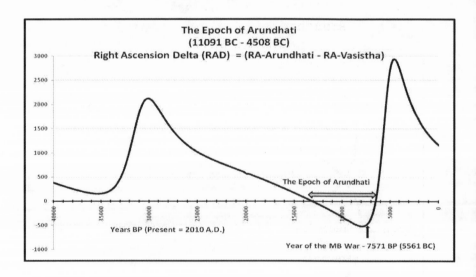

Table 4
The Epoch of Arundhati
(11091 B.C. – 4508 B.C.)

Date	Arundhati (Alcor)	Vasistha (Mizar)	RAD
(Years in A.D./B.C.)	Right Ascension (arc-sec)	Right Ascension (arc-sec)	(arc-sec)
16 October 2010 A.D.	725070.9	723903	1167.9
16 October 1000 A.D.	687250.95	685872.9	1378.05
16 October 1000 B.C.	591380.1	589246.5	2133.6
16 October 1500 B.C.	557076.15	554644.65	2431.5
16 October 2000 B.C.	514163.85	511420.95	2742.9
16 October 2500 B.C.	458861.4	455926.8	2934.6
16 October 3000 B.C.	388649.4	385940.4	2709
16 October 3500 B.C.	308065.2	306210.75	1854.45
16 October 4000 B.C.	230395.05	229624.5	770.55
16 October 4508 B.C.	165261.45	165260.4	1.05
16 October 4509 B.C.	165132.9	165133.2	-0.3
16 October 5000 B.C.	116405.1	116764.5	-359.4
16 October 5561 B.C.	73453.35	73952.7	-499.35
16 October 5700 B.C.	64294.05	64804.2	-510.15
16 October 5800 B.C.	58040.85	58554.15	-513.3
16 October 5900 B.C.	52048.95	52563.15	-514.2
16 October 6000 B.C.	46170	46683.15	-513.15
16 October 6250 B.C.	32493.9	32995.65	-501.75
16 October 6500 B.C.	19733.4	20216.85	-483.45
16 October 11088 B.C.	1148624.85	1148625	-0.15
16 Octoer 11091 B.C.	1148540.1	1148539.95	0.15
16 October 13000 B.C.	1087086.15	1086913.65	172.5

Figure 5
Arundhati walking ahead of Vasistha

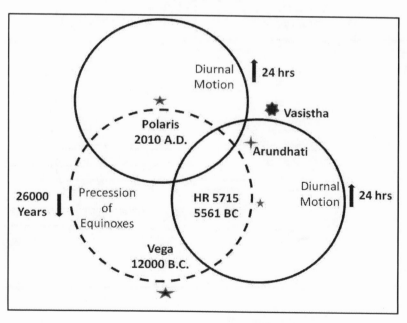

Figure 6
Jupiter & Saturn near *Vishakha* for a year
(5562 B.C. – 5561 B.C.)

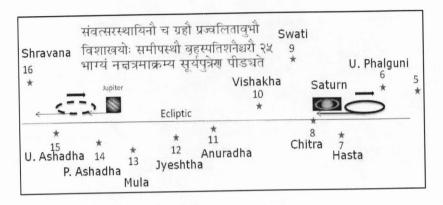

Table 5
Jupiter & Saturn near Vishakha
(Before the War)

When	Jupiter (RA)	Saturn (RA)
15 October 5563 BC	503496	261603
15 December 5563 BC	541488	257326
14 February 5562 BC	549238	240675
16 April 5562 BC	526269	238449
16 June 5562 BC	517992	256675
16 August 5562 BC	545162	284283
16 October 5562 BC	589943	305328
16 December 5562 BC	633435	305194
15 February 5561 BC	658386	288566
16 April 5561 BC	649746	282286
16 June 5561 BC	628135	297497
16 August 5561 BC	637162	324716
16 October 5561 BC	674536	348093

Figure 7
Journey of Mars during the War
(Schematic)

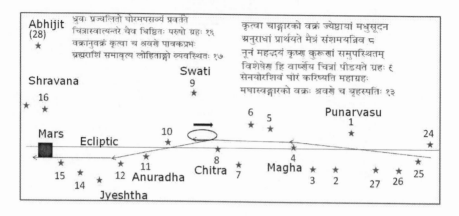

Figure 8
Journey of Mars during the War
(Voyager4.5™ simulation)

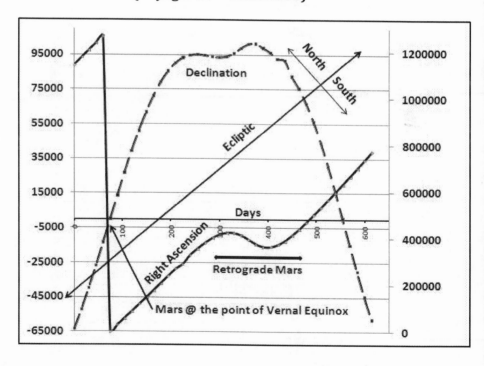

Table 6
Journey of Mars during the War

Date	Location of Mars	Days	RA	DEC	Magnitude
21 March 5562 BC	Near Krittika	0	1143000	-63480	1.6
4 April 5562 BC	South of Ecliptic	15	1175400	-52260	1.6
18 April 5562 BC	Crossing Ecliptic	30	1206900	-39960	1.7
2 May 5562 BC	North of Ecliptic	45	1237500	-26940	1.7
16 May 5562 BC	North of Ecliptic	60	1267200	-13500	1.8
30 May 5562 BC	North of Ecliptic	75	900	60	1.8
13 June 5562 BC	North of Ecliptic	90	29700	13560	1.8
27 June 5562 BC	North of Ecliptic	105	58500	26700	1.8
11 July 5562 BC	North of Ecliptic	120	87300	39240	1.7
25 July 5562 BC	North of Ecliptic	135	117000	50940	1.7
8 August 5562 BC	Near Magha	150	146700	61620	1.6
22 August 5562 BC	Near Magha	165	177300	71040	1.6
5 Sept 5562 BC	North of Ecliptic	180	207900	79020	1.4
19 Sept 5562 BC	North of Ecliptic	195	239400	85380	1.3
3 Oct 5562 BC	North of Ecliptic	210	270000	90120	1.2
17 Oct 5562 BC	North of Ecliptic	225	291600	93180	1
31 Oct 5562 BC	North of Ecliptic	240	329400	94740	0.8
14 Nov 5562 BC	Near Chitra	255	356400	95100	0.5
28 Nov 5562 BC	Near Swati	270	380700	94620	0.2
12 Dec 5562 BC	Near Swati	285	401400	93840	-0.1
26 Dec 5562 BC	Retrograde	300	416700	93420	-0.5
9 Jan 5561 BC	Retrograde	315	424800	93960	-0.9
23 Jan 5561 BC	Retrograde	330	423900	95940	-1.4
6 Feb 5561 BC	Retrograde	345	414000	98820	-1.8
20 Feb 5561 BC	Retrograde	360	396000	101220	-2.1
5 March 5561 BC	Retrograde	375	377100	101460	-2
19 March 5561 BC	Near Chitra	390	365400	98940	-1.7
2 April 5561 BC	Near Chitra	405	364500	96420	-1.4
16 April 5561 BC	Near Swati	420	373500	92640	-1.1
30 April 5561 BC	Near Swati	435	390600	91740	-0.8
14 May 5561 BC	North of Ecliptic	450	414000	82560	-0.6
28 May 5561 BC	North of Ecliptic	465	441000	75540	-0.3
11 June 5561 BC	Crossing Ecliptic	480	470700	66780	-0.2
25 June 5561 BC	Near Anuradha	495	502200	56280	0
9 July 5561 BC	Near Jyeshtha	510	533700	44100	0.2
23 July 5561 BC	South of Ecliptic	525	567000	30540	0.3
6 Aug 5561 BC	South of Ecliptic	540	600300	15840	0.4
20 Aug 5561 BC	South of Ecliptic	555	633600	480	0.6
3 Sept 5561 BC	South of Ecliptic	570	667800	-15000	0.7
17 Sept 5561 BC	South of Ecliptic	585	702000	-30240	0.8
1 Oct 5561 BC	South of Ecliptic	600	737100	-44760	0.9
15 Oct 5561 BC	Vega/Shravana	615	773100	-57960	1

Figure 9
Jupiter *vakri* near *Shravana*

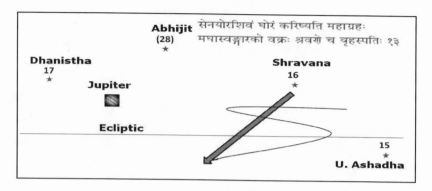

Table 7
Jupiter crossing the ecliptic (Time of Mahabharata War)

Date	Position	Magnitude	Days	RA	Dec
16 Oct 5561 BC	North of Ecliptic	-1.9	0	674100	-10560
30 Oct 5561 BC	North of Ecliptic	-1.9	14	684900	-15360
13 Nov 5561 BC	North of Ecliptic	-1.9	28	695700	-20220
27 Nov 5561 BC	North of Ecliptic	-1.9	42	706500	-25020
11 Dec 5561 BC	North of Ecliptic	-1.9	56	717300	-29640
25 Dec 5561 BC	North of Ecliptic	-2	70	728100	-34020
8 Jan 5560 BC	North of Ecliptic	-2	84	738000	-38100
22 Jan 5560 BC	North of Ecliptic	-2	98	747000	-41820
5 Feb 5560 BC	North of Ecliptic	-2.1	112	755100	-45060
19 Feb 5560 BC	North of Ecliptic	-2.2	126	762300	-47700
5 March 5560 BC	North of Ecliptic	-2.3	140	767700	-49800
19 March 5560 BC	North of Ecliptic	-2.4	154	771300	-51300
2 April 5560 BC	North of Ecliptic	-2.5	168	773100	-52020
6 April 5560 BC	Crossing Ecliptic	-2.5	172	773100	-52080
16 April 5560 BC	South of ecliptic	-2.6	182	772200	-52020
30 April 5560 BC	South of ecliptic	-2.7	196	770400	-51300
30 May 5560 BC	South of ecliptic	-2.8	226	758700	-47760
29 June 5560 BC	South of ecliptic	-2.8	256	746100	-43260
29 July 5560 BC	South of ecliptic	-2.6	286	738900	-40800
28 Aug 5560 BC	South of ecliptic	-2.4	316	741600	-42060
13 Sept 5560 BC	Crossing Ecliptic	-2.3	332	747000	-44160
13 Oct 5560 BC	North of Ecliptic	-2.1	362	763200	-50280
24 Oct 5560 BC	Crossing Ecliptic	-2.1	373	770400	-52980
23 Nov 5560 BC	South of ecliptic	-2	403	793800	-60780
23 Dec 5560 BC	South of ecliptic	-2	433	820800	-68460
30 Dec 5560 BC	Crossing Ecliptic	-2	440	825300	-70140
10 Jan 5559 BC	North of Ecliptic	-2	451	835200	-72600
15 Jan 5559 BC	Crossing Ecliptic	-2	456	838800	-73680
16 Jan 5559 BC	Crossing Ecliptic	-2	457	839700	-73920
20 Jan 5559 BC	South of ecliptic	-2	461	844200	-74940

Figure 10
Venus retrograde near *Purva Bhadrapada*

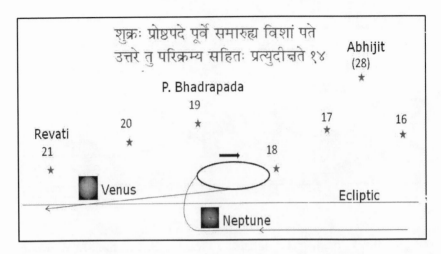

Table 8
Journey of Venus near Purva Bhadrapada

When	Days	Position	Magnitude	RA	DEC
16 Oct 5561 BC	0	Near Shravana	-4.4	747900	-55020
23 Oct 5561 BC	7	South of ecliptic	-4.5	774000	-64200
30 Oct 5561 BC	14	South of ecliptic	-4.5	798300	-71400
6 Nov 5561 BC	21	Near Shatataraka	-4.5	821700	-76860
13 Nov 5561 BC	28	South of ecliptic	-4.6	843300	-80280
20 Nov 5561 BC	35	South of ecliptic	-4.6	862200	-81600
27 Nov 5561 BC	42	Crossing Ecliptic	-4.6	877500	-80760
4 Dec 5561 BC	49	North of ecliptic	-4.6	886500	-77760
11 Dec 5561 BC	56	Near Purva Bhadrapada	-4.5	889200	-72780
18 Dec 5561 BC	63	Retrograde	-4.3	884700	-66000
25 Dec 5561 BC	70	Retrograde	-4.1	873000	-58200
1 Jan 5560 BC	77	Retrograde	-4	857700	-50820
8 Jan 5560 BC	84	Retrograde	-4.2	844200	-45660
15 Jan 5560 BC	91	Retrograde	-4.4	835200	-43680
22 Jan 5560 BC	98	Near Shatataraka	-4.5	833400	-44940
29 Jan 5560 BC	105	North of ecliptic	-4.5	837000	-48780
5 Feb 5560 BC	112	North of ecliptic	-4.5	846900	-54300
12 Feb 5560 BC	119	North of ecliptic	-4.5	860400	-60720
19 Feb 5560 BC	126	North of ecliptic	-4.4	878400	-67320
26 Feb 5560 BC	133	near Purva Bhadrapada	-4.4	899100	-73560
5 March 5560 BC	140	North of ecliptic	-4.3	922500	-79020
12 March 5560 BC	147	North of ecliptic	-4.3	945900	-82920
19 March 5560 BC	154	North of ecliptic	-4.2	972000	-85920
26 March 5560 BC	161	Crossing Ecliptic	-4.2	1000800	-87300
2 April 5560 BC	168	South of ecliptic	-4.1	1029600	-86820

Table 9
Positions of planets, comet, the Sun & the Moon
18 days of the War

9-a

When	Who	RA (arc-sec)	DEC (arc-sec)	Description	MB Reference
16 October 5561 BC	Sun	595628	23173	afflicting Rohini	26
(12:00 PM)	Moon	591373	18132	afflicting Rohini	26
First day of the MB Wa	Mercury	625806	2905	1 of 7 planets near the Sun	24
	Venus	748182	-55028	2 of 7 planets near the Sun	24
	Mars	775327	58479	near Shravana/Abhijit	14
	Jupiter	674322	-10455	near Vishakha for a year	6
	Saturn	348017	93144	Saturn afflicts Rohini	6, 8-10
	Uranus	787623	-57175	3 of 7 planets near the Sun	24
	Neptune	861120	-78024	4 of 7 planets near the Sun	24
	Pluto	1192788	-92747	Tikshna/Tivra planet near Krittika	21
	Haley's comet	69276	-35248	Comet near Pushya	21-22

9-b

When	Who	RA (arc-sec)	DEC (arc-sec)	Description	MB Reference
29 October 5561 BC	Moon	1212940	-30426	Moon near Rahu (node)	52
(7:10 PM)	Pluto	1191988	-92908	1 of 7 planets attacking the Moon	23
After sunset	Neptune	861888	-78174	2 of 7 planets attacking the Moon	23
14 day of the MB War	Mars	808028	-68625	3 of 7 planets attacking the Moon	23
	Venus	792036	-69641	4 of 7 planets attacking the Moon	23
	Uranus	790124	-57749	5 of 7 planets attacking the Moon	23
	Mercury	689919	-26323	6 of 7 planets attacking the Moon	23
	Jupiter	683562	-14657	7 of 7 planets attacking the Moon	23

9-c

When	Who	RA (arc-sec)	DEC (arc-sec)	Description	MB Reference
1 November 5561 BC	Pluto	1191806	-92936	1 of 7 planets going away from the Sun	25
(7:03 PM)	Neptune	862121	-78220	2 of 7 planets going away from the Sun	25
After sunset	Mars	816110	-70859	3 of 7 planets going away from the Sun	25
17 day of the MB War	Venus	802382	-72410	4 of 7 planets going away from the Sun	25
	Uranus	789867	-57903	5 of 7 planets going away from the Sun	25
	Mercury	704366	-31679	6 of 7 planets going away from the Sun	25
	Jupiter	685839	-15690	7 of 7 planets going away from the Sun	25
	Sun	647196	353	Sun below the horizon	25

9-d

When	Who	RA (arc-sec)	DEC (arc-sec)	Description	MB Reference
1 November 5561 BC	Rohini	1188700	-68040	Rohini in eastern party of the sky	12
(7:03 PM)	Jupiter	685839	-15690	Jupiter afflicting Rohini (similar to Sun/Moon)	12
17 day of the MB War	Sun	647196	353	Sun below the horizon	12

9-e

When	Who	RA (arc-sec)	DEC (arc-sec)	Description	MB Reference
2 November 5561 BC	Mars	821554	-72300	Mars in western part of the sky	17
(7:15 PM)	Venus	809202	-74076	Venus in western part of the sky	17
After sunset	Mercury	713225	-34507	Mercury in western part of the sky	17
18 day of the MB War	Sun	653924	-2669	Sun below the horizon	17

9-f

When (7:00 PM)	Mercury (RA)	Jupiter (RA)	Sun (RA)	Description	MB Reference
16 October 5561 BC	627330	674536	596612	Tirayk rising of Mercury	16
17 October 5561 BC	632582	675275	600013	Tirayk rising of Mercury	16
18 October 5561 BC	637841	676017	603410	Tirayk rising of Mercury	16
19 October 5561 BC	643105	676760	606801	Tirayk rising of Mercury	16
20 October 5561 BC	648371	677507	610187	Tirayk rising of Mercury	16
21 October 5561 BC	653636	678255	613568	Tirayk rising of Mercury	16
22 October 5561 BC	658895	679005	616944	Tirayk rising of Mercury	16
23 October 5561 BC	664143	679758	620317	Tirayk rising of Mercury	16
24 October 5561 BC	669373	680512	623686	Tirayk rising of Mercury	16
25 October 5561 BC	674425	681268	627051	Tirayk rising of Mercury	16
26 October 5561 BC	679737	682026	630413	Tirayk rising of Mercury	16
27 October 5561 BC	684846	682785	633773	Tirayk rising of Mercury	16
28 October 5561 BC	689885	683546	637129	Tirayk rising of Mercury	16
29 October 5561 BC	694832	684308	640484	Tirayk rising of Mercury	16
30 October 5561 BC	699665	685072	643837	Tirayk rising of Mercury	16
31 October 5561 BC	704357	685838	647189	Tirayk rising of Mercury	16
1 November 5561 BC	708874	686604	650539	Tirayk rising of Mercury	16

Table 10
Moon's Phases, Positions, RA & Percentage Illumination
18 days of the War

Date	Lunar Month	Paksha	Tithi	Nakshatra	RA of Moon	Illumination
				(7:10 AM)	(7:10 AM)	(Percentage)
16 October 5561 BC	Kartika	Krishna	Amavasya	Mula (10h 29 min)	10h 40 min	0.1
17 October 5561 BC	Margashirsha	Shukla	Pratipada	PurvaAshadha (11h 11 min)	11h 41 min	0.8
18 October 5561 BC	Margashirsha	Shukla	Dwitiya	UttaraAshadha (11h 50 min)	12h 34 min	4
19 October 5561 BC	Margashirsha	Shukla	Tritiya	Shravana (13h 48 min)	13h 28 min	9.7
20 October 5561 BC	Margashirsha	Shukla	Chaturthi	Dhanishtha (14h 52 min)	14h 22 min	17.4
21 October 5561 BC	Margashirsha	Shukla	Panchami	Shatabhishaj (15h 20 min)	15h 19 min	26.8
22 October 5561 BC	Margashirsha	Shukla	Shasthi	PurvaBhadrapada (16h 43 min)	16h 16 min	37.4
23 October 5561 BC	Margashirsha	Shukla	Saptami	UttaraBhadrapada (17h 41 min)	17h 14 min	48.6
24 October 5561 BC	Margashirsha	Shukla	Ashtami	Revati (18h 53 min)	18h 13 min	59.7
25 October 5561 BC	Margashirsha	Shukla	Navami	Ashwini (19h 34 min)	19h 11 min	70.3
26 October 5561 BC	Margashirsha	Shukla	Dashami	Bharani (20h 16 min)	20h 8 min	79.8
27 October 5561 BC	Margashirsha	Shukla	Ekadashi	Krittika (21h 10 min)	21h 2 min	87.7
28 October 5561 BC	Margashirsha	Shukla	Dwadashi	Rohini (22h 0 min)	21h 55 min	93.9
29 October 5561 BC	Margashirsha	Shukla	Trayodashi	Mrigashirsha (23h 4 min)	22h 47 min	98
30 October 5561 BC	Margashirsha	Shukla	Chaturdashi	Ardra (23h 32 min)	23h 36 min	99.9
31 October 5561 BC	Margashirsha	Shukla	Purnima	Punarvasu (0h 28 min)	0h 25 min	99.6
1 November 5561 BC	Margashirsha	Krishna	Pratipada	Pushya (1h 31 min)	1h 13 min	97.3
2 November 5561 BC	Margashirsha	Krishna	Dwitiya	Ashlesha (2h 11 min)	2h 1 min	93.1

Table 11
Lunar & Solar Eclipses

When	What	Local Time	Angle (Degree)	Visible at Kurukshetra	MB Reference
30 September 5561 BC	Lunar Eclipse?	9:58 PM	2.726	Entire Night	28
16 October 5561 BC	Solar Eclipse	12:57 PM	1.8	Entire Day	29, 34-36, 38
30 October 5561 BC	Lunar Eclipse	12:19 PM	0.127	~2 hrs after sunset	29, 64

Table 12
Plausible scenario for explanation by P V Kane

Astral location	RA	When (Full Moon day)	Lunar Month
Earth's Shadow	20h 3 min	1 September 5561 BC	Ashwin
Moon	20h 3 min	1 September 5561 BC	Ashwin
Ashwini	19h 34 min	1 September 5561 BC	Ashwin
Earth's Shadow	22h 2 min	1 October 5561 BC	Kartika
Moon	22h 2 min	1 October 5561 BC	Kartika
Krittika	21h 10 min	1 October 5561 BC	Kartika
Mrigashirsha	23h 4 min	1 October 5561 BC	Kartika
Earth's Shadow	23h 55 min	30 October 5561 BC	Margahshirsha
Moon	23h 55 min	30 October 5561 BC	Margahshirsha
Mrigashirsha	23h 4 min	30 October 5561 BC	Margahshirsha
Pushya	1h 32 min	30 October 5561 BC	Margahshirsha
Earth's Shadow	1h 45 min	29 November 5561 BC	Pausha
Moon	1h 45 min	29 November 5561 BC	Pausha
Pushya	1h 32 min	29 November 5561 BC	Pausha
Magha	2h 54 min	29 November 5561 BC	Pausha
Earth's Shadow	3h 45 min	29 December 5561 BC	~ Magha
Moon	3h 45 min	29 December 5561 BC	~ Magha
Magha	2h 54 min	29 December 5561 BC	~ Magha
Purva Phalguni	3h 21 min	29 December 5561 BC	~ Magha
Earth's Shadow	5h 50min	27 January 5560 BC	~Phalguna
Moon	5h 50min	27 January 5560 BC	~Phalguna
Hasta	5h 59 min	27 January 5560 BC	~Phalguna
Purva Phalguni	3h 21 min	27 January 5560 BC	~Phalguna
Uttara Phalguni	4h 15 min	27 January 5560 BC	~Phalguna

Figure 11
Mahabharata Observations
Degree of Falsifiability & Relevance for the War

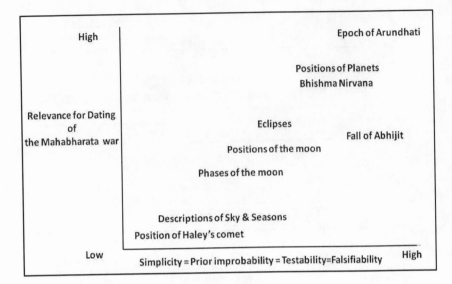

Figure 12
Time Interval of the Mahabharata War
(*Arundhati* and *Bhishma Nirvana*)

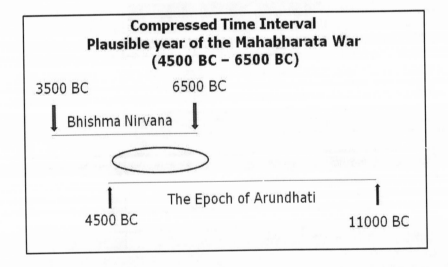

Mahabharata References

1. Bhishma (CE 2:31, GP 2:31)

yA caiSA vizrutA rAjaMs trailokye sAdhusaMmatA
arundhati tayApy eSa vasiSThaH pRSThataH kRtaH

2. Virata (CE 47:3-4, GP 52:3-4)

teSAM kAlAtirekeNa jyotiSAM ca vyatikramAt
paJcame paJcame varSe dvau mAsAv upajAyataH

teSAm abhyadhikA mAsAH paJca dvAdaza ca kSapAH
trayodazAnAM varSANAm iti me vartate matiH

3. Virata (Bombay Edition 47.3)

gate varShadvaye caiva paJcapakSe dinadvaye
divasASTame bhAge patatyekodhikamAsaH

4. Vana (CE 219:8-11, GP 230:8-11)

abhijit spardhamAnA tu rohiNyA kanyasI svasA
icchanti jyeSThatAM devI tapas taptuM vanaM gatA

tatra mUDho 'smi bhadraM te nakSatraM gaganAc cyutam
kAlaM tv imaM paraM skanda brahmaNA saha cintaya

dhaniSThAdis tadA kAlo brahmaNA parinirmitaH
rohiNyAdyo 'bhavat pUrvam evaM saMkhyA samAbhavat

evam ukte tu zakreNa tridivaM kRttikA gatAH
nakSatraM zakaTAkAraM bhAti tad vahnidaivatam

5. Adi (CE 57:72-75, GP 63:87-90)

pAdApasAriNaM dharmaM vidvAn sa tu yuge yuge
AyuH zaktiM ca martyAnAM yugAnugam avekSya ca

brahmaNo brAhmaNAnAM ca tathAnugrahakAmyayA
vivyAsa vedAn yasmAc ca tasmAd vyAsa iti smRtaH

vedAn adhyApayAm Asa mahAbhAratapaJcamAn
sumantuM jaiminiM pailaM zukaM caiva svam Atmajam

prabhur variSTho varado vaizaMpAyanam eva ca
saMhitAs taiH pRthaktvena bhAratasya prakAzitAH

6. Bhishma (CE 3.24-25, GP 3.26-27)

grahau tAmrAruNazikhau prajvalantAv iva sthitau
saptarSINAm udArANAM samavacchAdya vai prabhAm 24

saMvatsarasthAyinau ca grahau prajvalitAv ubhau
vizAkhayoH samIpasthau bRhaspatizanaizcarau 25

7. Udyoga (CE 109:12, GP 111.14)

atra te RSayaH sapta devI cArundhatI tathA
atra tiSThati vai svAtir atrAsyA udayaH smRtaH

8. Udyoga (CE 141:7, GP 143:8)

prAjApatyaM hi nakSatraM grahas tIkSNo mahAdyutiH
zanaizcaraH pIDayati pIDayan prANino 'dhikam

9. Bhishma (CE 2:32, GP 2:32)

rohiNIM pIDayann eSa sthito rAjaJ zanaizcaraH
vyAvRttaM lakSma somasya bhaviSyati mahad bhayam

10. Bhishma (CE 3:14, GP 3:14)

bhAgyaM nakSatram Akramya sUryaputreNa pIDyate

11. Bhishma (CE 3:13, GP 3:13-)

senayor azivaM ghoraM kariSyati mahAgrahaH
maghAsv aGgArako vakraH zravaNe ca bRhaspatiH

12. Karna (CE 68:49, GP 94:51)

sakAnanAH sAdricayAz cakampuH;
pravivyathur bhUtagaNAz ca mAriSa
bRhaspati rohiNIM saMprapIDya;
babhUva candrArkasamAnavarNaH

13. Udyoga (CE 141:8-9, GP 143:9-10)

kRtvA cAGgArako vakraM jyeSThAyAM madhusUdana
anurAdhAM prArthayate maitraM saMzamayann iva

nUnaM mahad bhayaM kRSNa kurUNAM samupasthitam
vizeSeNa hi vArSNeya citrAM pIDayate grahaH

14. Bhishma (CE 3:16-17, GP 17-18)

dhruvaH prajvalito ghoram apasavyaM pravartate
citrAsvAtyantare caiva dhiSThitaH paruSo grahaH

vakrAnuvakraM kRtvA ca zravaNe pAvakaprabhaH
brahmarAziM samAvRtya lohitAGgo vyavasthitaH

15. Bhishma (CE 3:27, GP 3.31)

triSu pUrveSu sarveSu nakSatreSu vizAM pate
budhaH saMpatate 'bhikSNaM janayan sumahad bhayam

16-a Karna (CE 68:47)

hate sma karNe sarito na sravanti;
jagAma cAstaM kaluSo divAkaraH
grahaz ca tiryag jvalitArkavarNo;
yamasya putro 'bhyudiyAya rAjan

16-b Karna (GP 94:49)

hate karNe sarito na prasannu
jagAm cAstam sawitA diwAkaraH
grahazca tiryag jwalanArkavarnaH
somasya putro'bhyudiyAya tiryak

17. Shalya (GP 11:17)

bhrugusUnudharAputrou zazijena samanvitou
caramaM pANDuputrANAm purastAt sarwabhubhujAm

18. Bhishma (CE 3:14, GP 3:15)

zukraH proSThapade pUrve samAruhya vizAM pate
uttare tu parikramya sahitaH pratyudIkSate

19. Bhishma (CE 3:11, GP 3:11-12)

abhikSNaM kampate bhUmir arkaM rAhus tathAgrasat
zveto grahas tathA citrAM samatikramya tiSThati

20. Bhishma (CE 3:15, GP 3:16)

zyAmo grahaH prajvalitaH sadhUmaH sahapAvakaH
aindraM tejasvi nakSatraM jyeSThAm Akramya tiSThati

21. Bhishma (CE 3: 26, GP 3:30)

kRttikAsu grahas tivro nakSatre prathame jvalan
vapUMSy apaharan bhAsA dhUmaketur iva sthitaH

22. Bhishma (CE 3:12, GP: 12-13)

abhAvaM hi vizeSeNa kurUNAM pratipazyati
dhUmaketur mahAghorAH puSyam Akramya tiSThati

23. Drona (CE 112.22, GP 137:22)

te 'pIDayan bhimasenaM kruddhAH sapta mahArathAH
prajAsaMharaNe rAjan somaM sapta grahA iva

24. Bhishma (CE 17:2, GP 17:2)

maghAviSayagaH somas tad dinaM pratyapadyata
dIpyamAnAz ca saMpetur divi sapta mahAgrahAH

25. Karna (CE 26:34, GP 37:4-5)

nizcaranto vyadRzyanta sUryAt sapta mahAgrahAH
ulkApAtaz ca saMjajJe dizAM dAhas tathaiva ca
tathAzanayaz ca saMpetur vavur vAtAz ca dAruNAH

26. Bhishma (GP 3:17)

rohiNi pIDayatyevamubhou ca zazibhAskarou

27. Udyoga (CE 141:10, GP 143:11)

somasya lakSma vyAvRttaM rAhur arkam upeSyati
divaz colkAH patanty etAH sanirghAtAH sakampanAH

28. Bhishma (CE 2:23, GP 2:23)

alakSyaH prabhayA hInaM paurNamAsIM ca kArttikIm
candro 'bhUd agnivarNaz ca samavarNe nabhastale

29. Bhishma (CE 3:28-29, GP 3:32-33)**

caturdazIM paJcadazIM bhUtapUrvAM ca SoDazIm
imAM tu nAbhijAnAmi amAvAsyAM trayodazIm

candrasUryAv ubhau grastAv ekamAse trayodazIm
aparvaNi grahAv etau prajAH saMkSapayiSyataH

**CaturdasIM paJcadazIM kadAcidapi ZoDazIm
imAM tu nAbhijAnAmi bhUtapUrvAM trayodazIm

30. Bhishma (CE 3:30-31, GP 3:33)

rajovRtA dizaH sarvAH pAMsuvarSaiH samantataH
utpAtameghA raudrAz ca rAtrau varSanti zoNitam

mAMsavarSaM punas tIvram AsIt kRSNacaturdazIm
ardharAtre mahAghoram atRpyaMs tatra rAkSasAH

31. Bhishma (CE 2:20, GP 2:20)

ubhe pUrvApare saMdhye nityaM pazyAmi bhArata
udayAstamane sUryaM kabandhaiH parivAritam

32. Bhishma (CE 1:5, GP 1:5)

abhiyAya ca durdharSAM dhArtarASTrasya vAhinIm
prAGmukhAH pazcime bhAge nyavizanta sasainikAH

33. Bhishma (CE 20:5, GP 20:5)

pazcAnmukhAH kuravo dhArtarASTrAH;
sthitAH pArthAH prAGmukhA yotsyamAnAH
daityendraseneva ca kauravANAM;
devendraseneva ca pANDavAnAm

34. Bhishma (CE 17:3, GP 17:3)

dvidhAbhUta ivAditya udaye pratyadRzyata
jvalantyA zikhayA bhUyo bhAnumAn udito divi

35. Bhishma (CE 19:36-39, GP 37-40)

saMdhyAM tiSThatsu sainyeSu sUryasyodayanaM prati
prAvAt sapRSato vAyur anabhre stanayitnumAn

viSvagvAtAz ca vAnty ugrA nIcaiH zarkarakarSiNaH
rajaz coddhUyamAnAM tu tamasAc chAdayaj jagat

papAta mahatI colkA prAGmukhI bharatarSabha
udyantaM sUryam Ahatya vyaziryata mahAsvanA

atha sajjiyamAneSu sainyeSu bharatarSabha
niSprabho 'bhyudiyAt sUryaH saghoSo bhUz cacAla ha

36. Bhishma (CE 42:28, GP 44:28)

ubhayoH senayos tIvraH sainyAnAM sa samAgamaH
antardhIyata cAdityaH sainyena rajasAvRtaH

37. Bhishma (CE 45:62, GP 49:52)

tataH sainyeSu bhagneSu mathiteSu ca sarvazaH
prApte cAstaM dinakare na prAjJAyata kiM cana

38. Bhishma (CE 54:23, GP 58:25)

zuzubhAte tadA tau tu zaineyakurupuMgavau
amAvAsyAM gatau yadvat somasUryau nabhastale

39. Bhishma (CE 55:15, GP 59:16)

vikIrNaiH kavacaiz citrair dhvajaiz chatraiz ca mAriSa
zuzubhe tad raNasthAnaM zaradIva nabhastalam

40. Bhishma (CE 75:55, GP 79:60)

anyonyAgaskRtAM rAjan yamarASTravivardhanam
muHUrtAstamite sUrye cakrur yuddhaM sudAruNam
rathinaH sAdinaz caiva vyakIryanta sahasrazaH

41. Bhishma (CE 92:73-75, GP 96:75-77)

narendracUDAmaNibhir vicitraiz ca mahAdhanaiH
chatrais tathApaviddhaiz ca cAmaravyajanair api
padmendudyutibhiz caiva vadanaiz cArukuNDalaiH
kLptazmazrubhir atyarthaM vIrANAM samalaMkRtaiH

apaviddhair mahArAja suvarNojjvalakuNDalaiH
grahanakSatrazabalA dyaur ivAsId vasuMdharA

42. Bhishma (CE 92:77-78, GP 96:78-79)

teSu zrAnteSu bhagneSu mRditeSu ca bhArata
rAtriH samabhavad ghorA nApazyAma tato raNam

tato 'vahAraM sainyAnAM pracakruH kurupANDavAH
ghore nizAmukhe raudre vartamAne sudAruNe

43. Bhishma (CE 93:30-31, GP 97:31-32)

pradIpaiH kAJcanais tatra gandhatailAvasecanaiH
parivavrur mahAtmAnaM prajvaladbhiH samantataH

sa taiH parivRto rAjA pradIpaiH kAJcanaiH zubhaiH
zuzubhe candramA yukto dIptair iva mahAgrahaiH

44. Bhishma (CE 101:33, GP 105:35)

tato yuddhaM mahAghoraM prAvartata sudAruNam
aparAM dizam AsthAya dyotamAne divAkare

45. Bhishma (CE 102:78, GP 106:85)

vimRdnatas tasya tu pANDusenAm;
astaM jagAmAtha sahasrarazmiH
tato balAnAM zramakarzitAnAM;
mano 'vahAraM prati saMbabhUva

46. Bhishma (CE 103:1, GP 107:1)

yudhyatAm eva teSAM tu bhAskare 'stam upAgate
saMdhyA samabhavad ghorA nApazyAma tato raNam

47. Bhishma (CE 106:35, GP 110:37)**

duHzAsanaM tataH kruddhaH pIDayAm Asa pANDavaH
parvaNIva susaMkruddho rAhur ugro nizAkaram

**duHzAsanaM tataH kruddhaH pIDayAmAsa pANDavaH
parvaNIva susaMkruddho rAhuH pUrNaM nizAkaram

48. Bhishma (CE 108:12, GP 112:12)

apasavyaM grahAz cakrur alakSmANaM nizAkaram
avAkzirAz ca bhagavAn udatiSThata candramAH

49. Drona (CE 15:52, GP 16:54)

masAragalvarkasuvarNarUpyair;
vajrapravAlasphaTikaiz ca mukhyaiH
citre rathe pANDusuto babhAse;
nakSatracitre viyativa candraH

50. Drona (CE 19:18, GP 20:17)

mAlyadAmavatA rAjA zvetacchatreNa dhAryatA
kRttikAyogayuktena paurNamAsyAm ivendunA

51. Drona (CE 30:26, GP 31:26)

saMpUrNacandrAbhamukhaH padmapatranibhekSaNaH
prAMzur utpalagarbhAbho nihato nyapatat kSitau

52. Drona (CE 48:16-17, GP 49:17-18)

vimRdya taruzRGgANi saMnivRttam ivAnilam
astaM gatam ivAdityaM taptvA bhAratavAhinIm

upaplutaM yathA somaM saMzuSkam iva sAgaram
pUrNacandrAbhavadanaM kAkapakSavRtAkSakam

53. Drona (CE 48:22, GP 49:23)

tasmiMs tu nihate vire bahv azobhata medinI
dyaur yathA pUrNacandreNa nakSatragaNamAlinI

54. Karna (CE 8:3, GP 12:3)

pUrNacandrArkapadmAnAM kAntitviDgandhataH samaIH
uttamAGgair nRsiMhAnAM nRsiMhAs tastarur mahIm

55. Karna (CE 14:50, GP 19:49-50)**

candranakSatrabhAsaiz ca vadanaiz cArukuNDalaiH
kLptazmazrubhir atyarthaM virANAM samalaMkRtaiH
vadanaiH pazya saMchannAM mahIM zoNitakardamAm

**candranakKSatrabhAsaiz ca vadanaiz cArukuNDalaiH
kLptazmazrubhirAkirNAM pUrNacandrnibhairmahIm
56. Karna (GP 19:50-51)**

KumudotpalapadmAnAM khaNDaiH phullaM yathA saraH
tathA mahIbhrutAM vaktraiH kumudotpalasaMnibhaiH
tArAgaNavicitrasya nirmalendudyutitviSaH
pazyemAM nabhasastulyaM zarannakSatramAlinim
57. Karna (CE 15:42, GP 20:48)

ziraz ca tat pUrNazaziprabhAnanaM;
saroSatAmrAyatanetram unnasam
kSitau vibabhrAja patat sakuNDalaM;
vizAkhayor madhyagataH zazI yathA

58. Karna (CE 32:6, GP 47:6)

pArSataM tv abhi saMtasthur draupadeyA yuyutsavaH
sAnugA bhImavapuSaz candraM tArAgaNA iva

59. Karna (CE 33:16, GP 49:28)

tAv ubhau dharmarAjasya pravirau paripArzvataH
rathAbhyAze cakAzete candrasyeva punarvasU

60. Karna (CE 35:11, GP 51:12)

vivitsos tu tataH kruddho bhallenApAharac chiraH
sakuNDalazirastrANaM pUrNacandropamaM tadA
bhImena ca mahArAja sa papAta hato bhuvi

61. Karna (CE 40:104, GP 56:111)

asyAsyato 'rdhacandrAbhyAM sa bAhU parighopamau
pUrNacandrAbhavaktraM ca kSureNAbhyahanac chiraH

62. Karna (CE 43:39-40, GP 60:41-42)

pUrNacandranikAzena mUrdhni chatreNa bhArata
dhriyamANena samare tathA zatazalAkinA

eSa tvAM prekSate karNaH sakaTAkSo vizAM pate
uttamaM yatnam AsthAya dhruvam eSyati saMyuge

63. Karna (CE 55:33-34, GP 77:33-35)**

sa taiH parivRtaH zUraiH zUro rAjan samantataH
zuzubhe bharatazreSTha nakSatrair iva candramAH

**pariveZhI yathA somaH paripUrNo virAjate

sa rarAja tathA saMkhye darzanIyo narottamaH
nirvizeSaM mahArAja yathA hi vijayas tathA

64. Karna (GP 89:71)

tathopayAtaM yudhi dhrmarAjaM
driZhtvA mudA sarvabhUtAnyanandan
rAhorvimuktaM vimalaM samagraM
candraM yathaivAbhyuditaM tathaiva

65. Karna (CE 67:24, GP 91:52)

tad udyatAdityasamAnavarcasaM;
zarannabhomadhyagabhAskaropamam
varAGgam urvyAm apatac camUpater;
divAkaro 'stAd iva raktamaNDalaH

66. Karna (GP 94:37)

cAruveSadharaM viraM cArumouliZirodharam
tanmukhaM sUtaputrasya pUrNacandrasamadyuti

67. Shalya (CE 23:4, GP 24:4)

yatraitat sumahac chatraM pUrNacandrasamaprabham
yatraite satalatrANA rathAs tiSThanti daMzitAH

68. Shalya (CE 64:6, GP 65:6-7)

mahAvAtasamutthena saMzuSkam iva sAgaram
pUrNacandram iva vyomni tuSArAvRtamaNDalam

69. Stri (CE 23:4, GP 23:4)

aho dhik pazya zalyasya pUrNacandrasudarzanam
mukhaM padmapalAzAkSaM vaDair AdaSTam avraNam

70. Stri (CE 22:6, GP 22:6)

ativa mukhavarNo 'sya nihatasyApi zobhate
somasyevAbhipUrNasya paurNamAsyAM samudyataH

71. Karna (CE 12:4, GP 16:5)

zirAMsy unmathya virANAM zitair bhallair dhanaMjayaH
pUrNacandrAbhavaktrANi svakSibhrUdazanAni ca
saMtastAra kSitiM kSipraM vinAlair nalinair iva

72. Karna (CE 19:28, GP 27:34)

sakuNDalAni svakSINi pUrNacandranibhAni ca
zirAMsy urvyAm adRzyanta tArAgaNa ivAmbare
73. Udyoga (CE 140:18, 142:18)

saptamAc cApi divasAd amAvAsyA bhaviSyati
saMgrAmaM yojayet tatra tAM hy AhuH zakradevatAm

74. Udyoga (CE 81:6-7, GP 83:6-7)

tato vyapete tamasi sUrye vimala udgate
maitre muhUrte saMprApte mRdvarciSi divAkare

kaumude mAsi revatyAM zaradante himAgame
sphitasasyasukhe kAle kalyaH sattvavatAM varaH

75. Shalya (CE 34:12, GP 35:13-14)

tato manyuparitAtmA jagAma yadunandanaH
tIrthayAtrAM haladharaH sarasvatyAM mahAyazAH
maitre nakSatrayoge sma sahitaH sarvayAdavaiH

76. Udyoga (CE 155:37-38, GP 158:39-40)

gate rAme tIrthayAtrAM bhISmakasya sute tathA
upAvizan pANDaveyA mantrAya punar eva hi

samitir dharmarAjasya sA pArthivasamAkulA
zuzubhe tArakAcitrA dyauz candreNeva bhArata

77. Udyoga (CE 148:3, GP 150:3)

ajJApayac ca rAjJas tAn pArthivAn duSTacetasaH
prayAdhvaM vai kurukSetraM puSyo 'dyeti punaH punaH

78. Shalya (CE 34:14, GP 35:15)

rauhiNeye gate zUre puSyeNa madhusUdanaH
pANDaveyAn puraskRtya yayAv abhimukhaH kurUn

79. Shalya (34.9, GP 35:10)

na kurvanti vaco mahyaM kuravaH kAlacoditAH
nirgacchadhvaM pANDaveyAH puSyeNa sahitA mayA

80. Bhishma (CE 17:1-2, GP 17:1-2)

yathA sa bhagavAn vyAsaH kRSNadvaipAyano 'bravit
tathaiva sahitAH sarve samAjagmur mahIkSitaH
maghAviSayagaH somas tad dinaM pratyapadyata
dIpyamAnAz ca saMpetur divi sapta mahAgrahAH

81. Mausal (CE 1:1, GP 1:1)

SaTtriMze tv atha saMprApte varSe kauravanandanaH
dadarza viparItAni nimittAni yudhiSThiraH

82. Mausal (CE 2:2, GP 1:13)

SaTtriMze 'tha tato varSe vRSNInAm anayo mahAn
anyonyaM musalais te tu nijaghnuH kAlacoditAH

83. Mausal (CE 3:14-18, GP 2:16-20)

parasparaM ca nakSatraM hanyamAnaM punaH punaH
grahair apazyan sarve te nAtmanas tu kathaM cana

nadantaM pAJcajanyaM ca vRSNyandhakanivezane
samantAt pratyavAzyanta rAsabhA dAruNasvarAH

evaM pazyan hRSIkezaH saMprAptaM kAlaparyayam
trayodazyAm amAvasyAM tAM dRSTvA prAbravId idam

caturdazI paJcadazI kRteyaM rAhuNA punaH
tadA ca bhArate yuddhe prAptA cAdya kSayAya naH

vimRzann eva kAlaM taM paricintya janArdanaH
mene prAptaM sa SaTtriMzaM varSaM vai kezisUdanaH

84. Udyoga (CE 154:15, GP 157:16)

tad dRSTvopasthitaM yuddhaM samAsannaM mahAtyayam
prAvizad bhavanaM rAjJaH pANDavasya halAyudhaH

85. Udyoga (CE 154:33-34, GP 157:34-35)

tasmAd yAsyAmi tIrthAni sarasvatyA niSevitum
na hi zakSyAmi kauravyAn nazyamAnAn upekSitum

evam uktvA mahAbAhur anujJAtaz ca pANDavaiH
tIrthayAtrAM yayau rAmo nivartya madhusUdanam

86. Shalya (CE 34:13, GP 35:14)

AzrayAm Asa bhojas tu duryodhanam ariMdamaH
yuyudhAnena sahito vAsudevas tu pANDavAn

87. Shalya (CE 53:36-37, GP 54:40-41)

tato muhur muhuH prItyA prekSamANAH sarasvatIm
hayair yuktaM rathaM zubhram AtiSThata paraMtapaH

sa zIghragAminA tena rathena yadupuMgavaH
dIdRkSur abhisaMprAptaH ziSyayuddham upasthitam

88. Shalya (33:5, GP 34:6)

catvAriMzad ahAny adya dve ca me niHsRtasya vai
puSyeNa saMprayAto 'smi zravaNe punaragataH
ziSyayor vai gadAyuddhaM draSTukAmo 'smi mAdhava

89. Shalya (33:16-17, GP 34:19-20)

teSAM madhye mahAbAhuH zrImAn kezavapUrvajaH
nyavizat paramaprItaH pUjyamAno mahArathaiH

sa babhau rAjamadhyastho nIlavAsAH sitaprabhaH
dIvIva nakSatragaNaiH parikIrNo nizAkaraH

90. Shalya (53:22, GP 54:24)

zrutam etan mayA pUrvaM sarvam eva tapodhana
vistarazravaNe jAtaM kautUhalam ativa me

91. Drona (CE 159:11-14, GP 184:12-16)

tataH pravavRte yuddhaM zrAntavAhanasainikam
pANDavAnAM kurUNAM ca garjatAm itaretaram

nidrAndhAs te mahArAja parizrAntAz ca saMyuge
nAbhyapadyanta samare kAM cic ceSTAM mahArathAH

triyAmA rajanI caiSA ghorarUpA bhayAnakA
sahasrayAmapratimA babhUva prANahAriNI
vadhyatAM ca tathA teSAM kSatANAM ca vizeSataH

aho rAtriH samAjajJe nidrAndhAnAM vizeSataH
sarve hy Asan nirutsAhAH kSatriyA dInacetasaH
tava caiva pareSAM ca gatAstrA vigateSavaH

92. Drona (CE 159:22-24, GP 184:25-27)

teSAM etAdRzIM ceSTAM vijJAya puruSarSabhaH
uvAca vAkyaM bibhatsur uccaiH saMnAdayan dizaH

zrAntA bhavanto nidrAndhAH sarva eva savAhanAH
tamasA cAvRte sainye rajasA bahulena ca

93. Drona (CE 159:25, GP 184:28)

te yUyaM yadi manyadhvam upAramata sainikAH
nimIlayata cAtraiva raNabhUmau muhUrtakam

93. Drona (CE 159:25, GP 184:28)

ato vinidrA vizrAntAz candramasy udite punaH
saMsAdhayiSyathAnyonyaM svargAya kurupANDavAH

94. Drona (CE 159:26-30, GP 184:29-33)

tad vacaH sarvadharmajJA dhArmikasya nizamya te
arocayanta sainyAni tathA cAnyonyam abruvan

cukruzuH karNa karNeti rAjan duryodhaneti ca
upAramata pANDUnAM viratA hi varUthinI

tathA vikrozamAnasya phalgunasya tatas tataH
upAramata pANDUnAM senA tava ca bhArata

tAm asya vAcaM devAz ca RSayaz ca mahAtmanAH
sarvasainyAni cAkSudrAH prahRSTAH pratyapUjayan

tat saMpUjya vaco 'krUraM sarvasainyAni bhArata
muhUrtam asvapan rAjaJ zrAntAni bharatarSabha

95. Drona (CE 159:42, GP 184:46)

tataH kumudanAthena kAminIgaNDapANDunA
netrAnandena candreNa mAhendrI dig alaMkRtA

96. Drona (CE 161:1-2, GP 186:1-2)

tribhAgamAtrazeSAyAM rAtryAM yuddham avartata
kurUNAM pANDavAnAM ca saMhRSTAnAM vizAM pate

atha candraprabhAM muSNann Adityasya puraHsaraH
aruNo 'bhyudayAM cakre tAmrIkurvann ivAmbaram

97. Drona (CE 159:43, GP 184:49)

tato muhUrtAd bhagavAn purastAc chazalakSaNaH
aruNaM darzayAm Asa grasaJ jyotiHprabhaM prabhuH

98. Drona (CE 159:46, GP 184:52)

tato muhUrtAd bhuvanaM jyotirbhUtam ivAbhavat
aprakhyam aprakAzaM ca jagAmAzu tamas tathA

99. Drona (GP 186:3-4)

prAcyAM dizi sahastramZorAruNenArunIkRtam
tapanIyaM yathA cakraM bhrAjate ravimaNDlam

tato rathAzvAmzca manuSyayAnA
nyutsRjya sarve kurupANDuyodhAH
divAkarasyAbhimukhaM japantaH
samdhyAgatAH prAJJalayo babhUvUH

100. Drona (GP 184:48)

haravRSottamagAtrasamdyutiH
smarazarAsanapUrNasamaprabhaH
navavadhUsmitacArumanoharaH
pravisRtaH kumudAkarabAndhavaH

101. Drona (CE 159:44-45, GP 184:50-51)

aruNasya tu tasyAnu jAtarUpasamaprabham
razmijAlaM mahac candro mandaM mandam avAsRjat

utsArayantaH prabhayA tamas te candrarazmayaH
paryagacchaJ zanaiH sarvA dizaH khaM ca kSitiM tathA

102. Drona (CE 159:47, GP 184:53)

pratiprakAzite loke divAbhUte nizAkare
vicerur na viceruz ca rAjan naktaMcarAs tataH

103. Drona (CE 159:48-50, GP 184:54-56)

bodhyamAnaM tu tat sainyaM rAjaMz candrasya razmibhiH
bubudhe zatapatrANAM vanaM mahad ivAmbhasi

yathA candrodayoddhUtaH kSubhitaH sAgaro bhavet
tathA candrodayoddhUtaH sa babhUva balArNavaH

tataH pravavRte yuddhaM punar eva vizAM pate
loke lokavinAzAya paraM lokam abhIpsatAm

104. Drona (CE 159:15-21, GP 184:17-24)

te tathA pArayantaz ca hrimantaz ca vizeSataH
svadharmam anupazyanto na jahuH svAm anIkinIm

zastrANy anye samutsRjya nidrAndhAH zerate janAH
gajeSv anye ratheSv anye hayeSv anye ca bhArata

nidrAndhA no bubudhire kAM cic ceSTAM narAdhipAH
te 'nyonyaM samare yodhAH preSayanta yamakSayam

svapnAyamAnAs tv apare parAn iti vicetasaH
AtmAnaM samare jaghnuH svAn eva ca parAn api

nAnAvAco vimuJcanto nidrAndhAs te mahAraNe
yoddhavyam iti tiSThanto nidrAsaMsaktalocanAH

saMmardyAnye raNe ke cin nidrAndhAz ca parasparam
jaghnuH zUrA raNe rAjaMs tasmiMs tamasi dAruNe

hanyamAnaM tathAtmAnaM parebhyo bahavo janAH
nAbhyajAnanta samare nidrayA mohitA bhRzam

105. Drona (CE 161:15-17, GP 186:17-19)

uddhUtA rajaso vRSTiH zaravRSTis tathaiva ca
tamaz ca ghoraM zabdaz ca tadA samabhavan mahAn

na dyaur na bhUmir na dizaH prAjJAyanta tathA gate
sainyena rajasA mUDhaM sarvam andham ivAbhavat

naiva te na vayaM rAjan prajJAsISma parasparam
uddezena hi tena sma samayudhyanta pArthivAH

106. Drona (CE 159:31-41, GP 184:34-45)

sA tu saMprApya vizrAmaM dhvajinI tava bhArata
sukham AptavatI viram arjunaM pratyapUjayat

tvayi vedAs tathAstrANi tvayi buddhiparAkramau
dharmas tvayi mahAbAho dayA bhUteSu cAnagha

yac cAzvastAs tavecchAmaH zarma pArtha tad astu te
manasaz ca priyAn arthAn vira kSipram avApnuhi

iti te taM naravyAghraM prazaMsanto mahArathAH
nidrayA samavAkSiptAs tUSNIm Asan vizAM pate

azvapRSTheSu cApy anye rathanIDeSu cApare
gajaskandhagatAz cAnye zerate cApare kSitau

sAyudhAH sagadAz caiva sakhaDgAH saparazvadhAH
saprAsakavacAz cAnye narAH suptAH pRthak pRthak

gajAs te pannagAbhogair hastair bhUreNurUSitaiH
nidrAndhA vasudhAM cakrur ghrANaniHzvAsazItalAm

gajAH zuzubhire tatra niHzvasanto mahItale
vizIrNA girayo yadvan niHzvasadbhir mahoragaiH

samAM ca viSamAM cakruH khurAgrair vikSatAM mahIm
hayAH kAJcanayoktrAz ca kesarAlambibhir yugaiH
suSupus tatra rAjendra yuktA vAheSu sarvazaH

tat tathA nidrayA bhagnam avAcam asvapad balam
kuzalair iva vinyastaM paTe citram ivAdbhutam

te kSatriyAH kuNDalino yuvAnaH;
parasparaM sAyakavikSatAGgAH
kumbheSu lInAH suSupur gajAnAM;
kuceSu lagnA iva kAminInAm

107. Bhishma (CE 1:26-33, GP 1:26-33)

tatas te samayaM cakruH kurupANDavasomakAH
dharmAMz ca sthApayAm Asur yuddhAnAM bharataRSabha

nivRtte caiva no yuddhe pritiz ca syAt parasparam
yathApuraM yathAyogaM na ca syAc chalanaM punaH

vAcA yuddhe pravRtte no vAcaiva pratiyodhanam
niSkrAntaH pRtanAmadhyAn na hantavyaH kathaM cana

rathI ca rathinA yodhyo gajena gajadhUrgataH
azvenAzvI padAtiz ca padAtenaiva bhArata

yathAyogaM yathAvIryaM yathotsAhaM yathAvayaH
samAbhASya prahartavyaM na vizvaste na vihvale

pareNa saha saMyuktaH pramatto vimukhas tathA
kSINazastro vivarmA ca na hantavyaH kathaM cana

na sUteSu na dhuryeSu na ca zastropanAyiSu
na bherizaGkhavAdeSu prahartavyaH kathaM cana

evaM te samayaM kRtvA kurupANDavasomakAH
vismayaM paramaM jagmuH prekSamANAH parasparam

108. Shanti (CE 47:1-4, GP 47:1-4)

zaratalpe zayAnas tu bharatAnAM pitAmahaH
katham utsRSTavAn dehaM kaM ca yogam adhArayat

vaizaMpAyana uvAca
zRNuSvAvahito rAjaJ zucir bhUtvA samAhitaH
bhISmasya kuruzArdUla dehotsargaM mahAtmanaH

nivRttamAtre tv ayana uttare vai divAkare
samAvezayad AtmAnam Atmany eva samAhitaH

vikIrNAMzur ivAdityo bhISmaH zarazataiz citaH
zizye paramayA lakSmyA vRto brAhmaNasattamaiH

109. Anushasan (CE 153:26-28, GP 167:26-28)

diSTyA prApto 'si kaunteya sahAmAtyo yudhiSThira
parivRtto hi bhagavAn sahasrAMzur divAkaraH

aSTapaJcAzataM rAtryaH zayAnasyAdya me gatAH
zareSu nizitAgreSu yathA varSazataM tathA

mAgho 'yaM samanuprApto mAsaH puNyo yudhiSThira
tribhAgazeSaH pakSo 'yaM zuklo bhavitum arhati

110. Shanti (GP 47:3 – additional text)

zuklapakSasya cASTmyAM mAghamAsasya pArthiva
prAjApatye ca nakSatre madhyaM prApte divAkare

111. Stri (CE 26:24-43, GP 26:24-43)

evam ukto mahAprAjJaH kuntIputro yudhiSThiraH
Adideza sudharmANAM dhaumyaM sUtaM ca saMjayam

viduraM ca mahAbuddhiM yuyutsuM caiva kauravam
indrasenamukhAMz caiva bhRtyAn sUtAMz ca sarvazaH

bhavantaH kArayantv eSAM pretakAryANi sarvazaH
yathA cAnAthavat kiM cic charIraM na vinazyati

zAsanAd dharmarAjasya kSattA sUtaz ca saMjayaH
sudharmA dhaumyasahita indrasenAdayas tathA

candanAgurukASThAni tathA kAlIyakAny uta
ghRtaM tailaM ca gandhAMz ca kSaumANi vasanAni ca

samAhRtya mahArhANi dArUNAM caiva saMcayAn
rathAMz ca mRditAMs tatra nAnApraharaNAni ca

citAH kRtvA prayatnena yathAmukhyAn narAdhipAn
dAhayAm Asur avyagrA vidhidRSTena karmaNA

duryodhanaM ca rAjAnaM bhrAtqMz cAsya zatAdhikAn
zalyaM zalaM ca rAjAnaM bhUrizravasam eva ca

jayadrathaM ca rAjAnam abhimanyuM ca bhArata
dauHzasaniM lakSmaNaM ca dhRSTaketuM ca pArthivam

bRhantaM somadattaM ca sRJjayAMz ca zatAdhikAn
rAjAnaM kSemadhanvAnaM virATadrupadau tathA

zikhaNDinaM ca pAJcAlyaM dhRSTadyumnaM ca pArSatam
yudhAmanyuM ca vikrAntam uttamaujasam eva ca

kausalyaM draupadeyAMz ca zakuniM cApi saubalam
acalaM vRSakaM caiva bhagadattaM ca pArthivam

karNaM vaikartanaM caiva sahaputram amarSaNam
kekayAMz ca maheSvAsAMs trigartAMz ca mahArathAn

ghaTotkacaM rAkSasendraM bakabhrAtaram eva ca
alambusaM ca rAjAnaM jalasaMdhaM ca pArthivam

anyAMz ca pArthivAn rAjaJ zatazo 'tha sahasrazaH
ghRtadhArAhutair dIptaiH pAvakaiH samadAhayan

pitRmedhAz ca keSAM cid avartanta mahAtmanAm
sAmabhiz cApy agAyanta te 'nvazocyanta cAparaiH

sAmnAM RcAM ca nAdena strINAM ca ruditasvanaiH
kazmalaM sarvabhUtAnAM nizAyAM samapadyata

te vidhUmAH pradIptAz ca dIpyamAnAz ca pAvakAH
nabhasivAnvadRzyanta grahAs tanvabhrasaMvRtAH

ye cApy anAthAs tatrAsan nAnAdezasamAgatAH
tAMz ca sarvAn samAnayya rAzIn kRtvA sahasrazaH

citvA dArubhir avyagraH prabhUtaiH snehatApitaiH
dAhayAm Asa viduro dharmarAjasya zAsanAt

112. Stri (CE 26:44, GP 26:44)

kArayitvA kriyAs teSAM kururAjo yudhiSThiraH
dhRtarASTraM puraskRtya gaGgAm abhimukho 'gamat

113. Shanti (CE 1:1-2, GP 1:1-2)

kRtodakAs te suhRdAM sarveSAM pANDunandanAH
viduro dhRtarASTraz ca sarvAz ca bharatastriyaH

tatra te sumahAtmAno nyavasan kurunandanAH
zaucaM nivartayiSyanto mAsam ekaM bahiH purAt

114. Shanti (CE 38:30, GP 37:30)

sa taiH parivRto rAjA nakSatrair iva candramAH
dhRtarASTraM puraskRtya svapuraM praviveza ha

115. Shanti (CE 38:35-36, GP 37:35-36)

dhriyamANaM tu tac chatraM pANDuraM tasya mUrdhani
zuzubhe tArakArAjasitam abhram ivAmbare

cAmaravyajane cAsya vIrau jagRhatus tadA
candrarazmiprabhe zubhre mAdrIputrAv alaMkRte

116. Shanti (CE 39:2, GP 38:2)

sa rAjamArgaH zuzubhe samalaMkRtacatvaraH
yathA candrodaye rAjan vardhamAno mahodadhiH

117. Shanti (CE 39:16, GP 38:16)

sa saMvRtas tadA viprair AzIrvAdavivakSubhiH
zuzubhe vimalaz candras tArAgaNavRto yathA

118. Shanti (CE 47:68-71, GP 47:105-108)

viditvA bhaktiyogaM tu bhISmasya puruSottamaH
sahasotthAya saMhRSTo yAnam evAnvapadyata

kezavaH sAtyakiz caiva rathenaikena jagmatuH
apareNa mahAtmAnau yudhiSThiradhanaMjayau

bhImaseno yamau cobhau ratham ekaM samAsthitau
kRpo yuyutsuH sUtaz ca saMjayaz cAparaM ratham

te rathair nagarAkAraiH prayAtAH puruSarSabhAH
nemighoSeNa mahatA kampayanto vasuMdharAm

119. Shanti (CE 48:1-6, GP 48:1-6)

tataH sa ca hRSIkezaH sa ca rAjA yudhiSThiraH
kRpAdayaz ca te sarve catvAraH pANDavAz ca ha
rathais te nagarAkAraiH patAkAdhvajazobhitaiH
yayur Azu kurukSetraM vAjibhiH zIghragAmibhiH

te 'vatIrya kurukSetraM kezamajjAsthisaMkulam
dehanyAsaH kRto yatra kSatriyais tair mahAtmabhiH

gajAzvadehAsthicayaiH parvatair iva saMcitam
narazIrSakapAlaiz ca zaGkhair iva samAcitam

citAsahasrair nicitaM varmazastrasamAkulam
ApAnabhUmiM kAlasya tadA bhuktojjhitAm iva

bhUtasaMghAnucaritaM rakSogaNaniSevitam
pazyantas te kurukSetraM yayur Azu mahArathAH

120. Shanti (CE 51:14, GP 51:14)

paJcAzataM SaT ca kurupravIra;
zeSaM dinAnAM tava jIvitasya
tataH zubhaiH karmaphalodayais tvaM;
sameSyase bhISma vimucya deham

121. Shanti (CE 52:26-34, GP 52:26-34)

tato muhUrtAd bhagavAn sahasrAMzur divAkaraH
dahan vanam ivaikAnte praticyAM pratyadRzyata

tato maharSayaH sarve samutthAya janArdanam
bhISmam AmantrayAM cakrU rAjAnaM ca yudhiSThiram

tataH praNAmam akarot kezavaH pANDavas tathA
sAtyakiH saMjayaz caiva sa ca zAradvataH kRpaH

tatas te dharmaniratAH samyak tair abhipUjitAH
zvaH sameSyAma ity uktvA yatheSTaM tvaritA yayuH

tathaivAmantrya gAGgeyaM kezavas te ca pANDavAH
pradakSiNam upAvRtya rathAn AruruhuH zubhAn

tato rathaiH kAJcanadantakUbarair;
mahIdharAbhaiH samadaiz ca dantibhiH
hayaiH suparNair iva cAzugAmibhiH;
padAtibhiz cAttazarAsanAdibhiH

yayau rathAnAM purato hi sA camUs;
tathaiva pazcAd atimAtrasAriNI
puraz ca pazcAc ca yathA mahAnadI;
purarkSavantaM girim etya narmadA

tataH puraM surapurasaMnibhadyuti;
praviNya te yaduvRSapANDavAs tadA
yathocitAn bhavanavarAn samAvizaJ;
zramAnvitA mRgapatayo guhA iva

122. Shanti (CE 53:1-27, GP 53:1-28)

tataH pravizya bhavanaM prasupto madhusUdanaH
yAmamAtrAvazeSAyAM yAminyAM pratyabudhyata

sa dhyAnapatham Azritya sarvajjAnAni mAdhavaH
avalokya tataH pazcAd dadhyau brahma sanAtanam

tataH zrutipurAnajjAH zikSitA raktakaNThinaH
astuvan vizvakarmANaM vAsudevaM prajApatim

paThanti pANisvanikAs tathA gAyanti gAyanAH
zaGkhAnakamRdaGgAMz ca pravAdyanta sahasrazaH
vINAnavaveNUnAM svanaz cAtimanoramaH
prahAsa iva vistIrNaH zuzruve tasya vezmanaH

tathA yudhiSThirasyApi rAjJo maGgalasaMhitAH
uccerur madhurA vAco gItavAditrasaMhitAH

tata utthAya dAzArhaH snAtaH prAJjalir acyutaH
japtvA guhyaM mahAbAhur agnin Azritya tasthivAn

tataH sahasraM viprANAM caturvedavidAM tathA
gavAM sahasreNaikaikaM vAcayAm Asa mAdhavaH

maGgalAlambhanaM kRtvA AtmAnam avalokya ca
Adarze vimale kRSNas tataH sAtyakim abravIt

gaccha zaineya jAnIhi gatvA rAjanivezanam
api sajjo mahAtejA bhISmaM draSTuM yuthiSThiraH

tataH kRSNasya vacanAt sAtyakis tvarito yayau
upagamya ca rAjAnaM yudhiSThiram uvAca ha

yukto rathavaro rAjan vAsudevasya dhImataH
samIpam Apageyasya prayAsyati janArdanaH

bhavatpratikSaH kRSNo 'sau dharmarAja mahAdyute
yad atrAnantaraM kRtyaM tad bhavAn kartum arhati

yudhiSThira uvAca
yujyatAM me rathavaraH phalgunApratimadyute
na sainikaiz ca yAtavyaM yAsyAmo vayam eva hi

na ca pIDayitavyo me bhISmo dharmabhRtAM varaH
ataH puraHsarAz cApi nivartantu dhanaMjaya

adyaprabhRti gAGgeyaH paraM guhyaM pravakSyati
tato necchAmi kaunteya pRthagjanasamAgamam

vaizaMpAyana uvAca
tad vAkyam AkarNya tathA kuntiputro dhanaMjayaH
yuktaM rathavaraM tasmA AcacakSe nararSabha

tato yudhiSThiro rAjA yamau bhImArjunAv api
bhUtAnIva samastAni yayuH kRSNanivezanam

Agacchatsv atha kRSNo 'pi pANDaveSu mahAtmasu
zaineyasahito dhImAn ratham evAnvapadyata

rathasthAH saMvidaM kRtvA sukhAM pRSTvA ca zarvarim
meghaghoSai rathavaraiH prayayus te mahArathAH

meghapuSpaM balAhaM ca sainyaM sugrivam eva ca
dArukaz codayAm Asa vAsudevasya vAjinaH

te hayA vAsudevasya dArukeNa pracoditAH
gAM khurAgrais tathA rAja&l likhantaH prayayus tadA

te grasanta ivAkAzaM vegavanto mahAbalAH
kSetraM dharmasya kRtsnasya kurukSetram avAtaran

tato yayur yatra bhISmaH zaratalpagataH prabhuH
Aste brahmarSibhiH sArdhaM brahmA devagaNair yathA

tato 'vatIrya govindo rathAt sa ca yudhiSThiraH
bhImo gANDIvadhanvA ca yamau sAtyakir eva ca

RSIn abhyarcayAm AsuH karAn udyamya dakSiNAn
sa taiH parivRto rAjA nakSatrair iva candramAH

abhyAjagAma gAGgeyaM brahmANam iva vAsavaH
zaratalpe zayAnaM tam AdityaM patitaM yathA
dadarza sa mahAbAhur bhayAd AgatasAdhvasaH

123. Shanti (CE 58:27-30, GP 58:27-30)

tato dinamanA bhISmam uvAca kurusattamaH
netrAbhyAm azrupUrNAbhyAM pAdau tasya zanaiH spRzan

zva idAnIM svasaMdehaM prakSyAmi tvaM pitAmaha
upaiti savitApy astaM rasam Apiya pArthivam

tato dvijAtIn abhivAdya kezavaH;
kRpaz ca te caiva yudhiSThirAdayaH
pradakSiNIkRtya mahAnadisutaM;
tato rathAn Aruruhur mudA yutAH

dRSadvatIM cApy avagAhya suvratAH;
kRtodakAryAH kRtajapyamaGgalAH
upAsya saMdhyAM vidhivat paraMtapAs;
tataH puraM te vivizur gajAhvayam

124. Shanti (59:1-3, GP 59:1-3)

tataH kAlyaM samutthAya kRtapaurvAhNikakriyAH
yayus te nagarAkArai rathaiH pANDavayAdavAH

prapadya ca kurukSetraM bhISmam AsAdya cAnagham
sukhAM ca rajanIM pRSTvA gAGgeyaM rathinAM varam

vyAsAdIn abhivAdyarSIn sarvais taiz cAbhinanditAH
niSedur abhito bhISmaM parivArya samantataH

125. Shanti (CE 161:1, GP 167:1)

ity uktavati bhISme tu tUSNIMbhUte yudhiSThiraH
papracchAvasaraM gatvA bhrAtQn vidurapaJcamAn

126. Shanti (CE 161:48, GP 167:50-51)

sucAruvarNAkSarazabdabhUSitAM;
manonugAM nirdhutavAkyakaNTakAm
nizamya tAM pArthiva pArthabhASitAM;
giraM narendrAH prazazaMsur eva te
punaz ca papraccha saridvarAsutaM;
tataH paraM dharmam ahinasattvaH

127. Shanti (CE 291:4, GP 302:4)

zeSam alpaM dinAnAM te dakSiNAyanabhAskare
AvRtte bhagavaty arke gantAsi paramAM gatim

128. Anushasan (CE 152:2-3, GP 166:6-7)

rAjan prakRtim ApannaH kururAjo yudhiSThiraH
sahito bhrAtRbhiH sarvaiH pArthivaiz cAnuyAyibhiH

---

upAste tvAM naravyAghra saha kRSNena dhImatA
tam imaM purayAnAya tvam anujJAtum arhasi

129. Anushasan (CE 152:10-13, GP 166:14-17)

AgantavyaM ca bhavatA samaye mama pArthiva
vinivRtte dinakare pravRtte cottarAyaNe

tathety uktvA tu kaunteyaH so 'bhivAdya pitAmaham
prayayau saparivAro nagaraM nAgasAhvayam

dhRtarASTraM puraskRtya gAndhArIM ca pativratAm
saha tair RSibhiH sarvair bhrAtRbhiH kezavena ca

paurajAnapadaiz caiva mantrivRddhaiz ca pArthivaH
praviveza kururzeSTha puraM vAraNasAhvayam

130. Anushasan (CE 153:1-6, GP 167:1-6)

tataH kuntisuto rAjA paurajAnapadaM janam
pUjayitvA yathAnyAyam anujajJe gRhAn prati

sAntvayAm Asa nArIz ca hatavIrA hatezvarAH
vipulair arthadAnaiz ca tadA pANDusuto nRpaH

so 'bhiSikto mahAprAjJaH prApya rAjyaM yudhiSThiraH
avasthApya narazreSThaH sarvAH svaprakRtIs tadA

dvijebhyo balamukhyebhyo naigamebhyaz ca sarvazaH
pratigRhyAziSo mukhyAs tadA dharmabhRtAM varaH

uSitvA zarvarIM zrimAn paJcAzan nagarottame
samayaM kauravAgryasya sasmAra puruSarSabhaH

sa niryayau gajapurAd yAjakaiH parivAritaH
dRSTvA nivRttam AdityaM pravRttaM cottarAyaNam

131. Udyoga (CE 140:6-15, GP 142:6-15)

yadA drakSyasi saMgrAme zvetAzvaM kRSNasArathim
aindram astraM vikurvANam ubhe caivAgnimArute

gANDIvasya ca nirghoSaM visphUrjitam ivAzaneH
na tadA bhavitA tretA na kRtaM dvAparaM na ca

yadA drakSyasi saMgrAme kuntiputraM yudhiSThiram
japahomasamAyuktaM svAM rakSantaM mahAcamUm

Adityam iva durdharSaM tapantaM zatruvAhinim
na tadA bhavitA tretA na kRtaM dvAparaM na ca

yadA drakSyasi saMgrAme bhImasenaM mahAbalam
duHzAsanasya rudhiraM pItvA nRtyantam Ahave

prabhinnam iva mAtaGgaM pratidviradaghAtinam
na tadA bhavitA tretA na kRtaM dvAparaM na ca

yadA drakSyasi saMgrAme mAdrIputrau mahArathau
vAhinIM dhArtarASTrANAM kSobhayantau gajAv iva

vigADhe zastrasaMpAte paravirarathArujau
na tadA bhavitA tretA na kRtaM dvAparaM na ca

yadA drakSyasi saMgrAme droNaM zAMtanavaM kRpam
suyodhanaM ca rAjAnaM saindhavaM ca jayadratham
yuddhAyApatatas tUrNaM vAritAn savyasAcinA
na tadA bhavitA tretA na kRtaM dvAparaM na ca

132. Virata (CE 45:23, GP 50:24)

nAkSAn kSipati gANDIvaM na kRtaM dvAparaM na ca
jvalato nizitAn bANAMs tikSNAn kSipati gANDIvam

133. Vana (CE 148:10-36, 38-39) GP 149:11-37, 39-40)

kRtaM nAma yugaM tAta yatra dharmaH sanAtanaH
kRtam eva na kartavyaM tasmin kAle yugottame

na tatra dharmAH sIdanti na kSIyante ca vai prajAH
tataH kRtayugaM nAma kAlena guNatAM gatam

devadAnavagandharvayakSarAkSasapannagAH
nAsan kRtayuge tAta tadA na krayavikrayAH

na sAmayajuRgvarNAH kriyA nAsIc ca mAnavi
abhidhyAya phalaM tatra dharmaH saMnyAsa eva ca

na tasmin yugasaMsarge vyAdhayo nendriyakSayaH
nAsUyA nApi ruditaM na darpo nApi paizunam

na vigrahaH kutas tandrI na dveSo nApi vaikRtam
na bhayaM na ca saMtApo na cerSyA na ca matsaraH

tataH paramakaM brahma yA gatir yoginAM parA
AtmA ca sarvabhUtAnAM zuklo nArAyaNas tadA

brAhmaNAH kSatriyA vaizyAH zUdrAz ca kRtalakSaNAH
kRte yuge samabhavan svakarmaniratAH prajAH

samAzramaM samAcAraM samajJAnamatIbalam
tadA hi samakarmANo varNA dharmAn avApnuvan

03148019a ekavedasamAyuktA ekamantravidhikriyAH
03148019c pRthagdharmAs tv ekavedA dharmam ekam anuvratAH

cAturAzramyayuktena karmaNA kAlayoginA
akAmaphalasaMyogAt prApnuvanti parAM gatim

AtmayogasamAyukto dharmo 'yaM kRtalakSaNaH
kRte yuge catuSpAdaz cAturvarNyasya zAzvataH

etat kRtayugaM nAma traiguNyaparivarjitam
tretAm api nibodha tvaM yasmin satraM pravartate

pAdena hrasate dharmo raktatAM yAti cAcyutaH
satyapravRttAz ca narAH kriyAdharmaparAyaNAH

tato yajJAH pravartante dharmAz ca vividhAH kriyAH
tretAyAM bhAvasaMkalpAH kriyAdAnaphalodayAH

pracalanti na vai dharmAt tapodAnaparAyaNAH
svadharmasthAH kriyAvanto janAs tretAyuge 'bhavan

dvApare 'pi yuge dharmo dvibhAgonaH pravartate
viSNur vai pItatAM yAti caturdhA veda eva ca

tato 'nye ca caturvedAs trivedAz ca tathApare
dvivedAz caikavedAz cApy anRcaz ca tathApare

evaM zAstreSu bhinneSu bahudhA nIyate kriyA
tapodAnapravRttA ca rAjasI bhavati prajA

ekavedasya cAjJAnAd vedAs te bahavaH kRtAH
satyasya ceha vibhraMzAt satye kaz cid avasthitaH

satyAt pracyavamAnAnAM vyAdhayo bahavo 'bhavan
kAmAz copadravAz caiva tadA daivatakAritAH

yair ardyamAnAH subhRzaM tapas tapyanti mAnavAH
kAmakAmAH svargakAmA yajJAMs tanvanti cApare

evaM dvAparam AsAdya prajAH kSIyanty adharmataH
pAdenaikena kaunteya dharmaH kaliyuge sthitaH

tAmasaM yugam AsAdya kRSNo bhavati kezavaH
vedAcArAH prazAmyanti dharmayajJakriyAs tathA

Itayo vyAdhayas tandrI doSAH krodhAdayas tathA
upadravAz ca vartante Adhayo vyAdhayas tathA

yugeSv AvartamAneSu dharmo vyAvartate punaH
dharme vyAvartamAne tu loko vyAvartate punaH

loke kSINe kSayaM yAnti bhAvA lokapravartakAH
yugakSayakRtA dharmAH prArthanAni vikurvate

yac ca te matparijJAne kautUhalam ariMdama
anarthakeSu ko bhAvaH puruSasya vijAnataH

etat te sarvam AkhyAtaM yan mAM tvaM paripRcchasi
yugasaMkhyAM mahAbAho svasti prApnuhi gamyatAm

134. Vana (CE 148:6-8, GP 149:7)

anyaH kRtayuge kAlas tretAyAM dvApare 'paraH
ayaM pradhvaMsanaH kAlo nAdya tad rUpam asti me

bhUmir nadyo nagAH zailAH siddhA devA maharSayaH
kAlaM samanuvartante yathA bhAva yuge yuge
balavarSmaprabhAvA hi prahlyanty udbhavanti ca

tad alaM tava tad rUpaM draSTuM kurukulodvaha
yugaM samanuvartAmi kAlo hi duratikramaH

135. Vana (CE 148:37, GP 149:38)

etat kaliyugaM nAma acirAd yat pravartate
yugAnuvartanaM tv etat kurvanti cirajIvinaH

136. Vana (CE 186:2-5, 8-10, 18-25) (GP 188:2-6, 12-14, 22-30)

naike yugasahasrAntAs tvayA dRSTA mahAmune
na cApIha samaIH kaz cid AyuSA tava vidyate
varjayitvA mahAtmAnaM brAhmaNaM parameSThinam

anantarikSe loke 'smin devadAnavavarjite
tvam eva pralaye vipra brahmANam upatiSThasi

pralaye cApi nirvRtte prabuddhe ca pitAmahe
tvam eva sRjyamAnAni bhUtAnIha prapayyasi

caturvidhAni viprarSe yathAvat parameSThinA
vAyubhUtA dizaH kRtvA vikSipyApas tatas tataH

yadA naiva ravir nAgnir na vAyur na ca candramAH
naivAntarikSaM naivorvI zeSaM bhavati kiM cana

tasmin ekArNave loke naSTe sthAvarajaGgame
naSTe devAsuragaNe samutsannamahorage

zayAnam amitAtmAnaM padme padmaniketanam
tvam ekaH sarvabhUtezaM brahmANam upatiSThasi

catvAry AhuH sahasrANi varSANAM tat kRtaM yugam
tasya tAvacchatI saMdhyA saMdhyAMzaz ca tataH param

trINi varSasahasrANi tretAyugam ihocyate
tasya tAvacchatI saMdhyA saMdhyAMzaz ca tataH param

tathA varSasahasre dve dvAparaM parimANataH
tasyApi dvizatI saMdhyA saMdhyAMzaz ca tataH param

sahasram ekaM varSANAM tataH kaliyugaM smRtam
tasya varSazataM saMdhyA saMdhyAMzaz ca tataH param
saMdhyAsaMdhyAMzayos tulyaM pramANam upadhAraya

kSINe kaliyuge caiva pravartati kRtaM yugam
eSA dvAdazasAhasrI yugAkhyA parikIrtitA

etat sahasraparyantam aho brAhmam udAhRtam
vizvaM hi brahmabhavane sarvazaH parivartate
lokAnAM manujavyAghra pralayaM taM vidur budhAH

alpAvaziSTe tu tadA yugAnte bharatarSabha
sahasrAnte narAH sarve prAyazo 'nRtavAdinaH

yajJapratinidhiH pArtha dAnapratinidhis tathA
vratapratinidhiz caiva tasmin kAle pravartate

137. Bhishma (CE 11:3-5, 7-13, GP 10:3-5, 7-14)

catvAri bhArate varSe yugAni bharatarSabha
kRtaM tretA dvAparaM ca puSyaM ca kuruvardhana

pUrvaM kRtayugaM nAma tatas tretAyugaM vibho
saMkSepAd dvAparasyAtha tataH puSyaM pravartate

catvAri ca sahasrANi varSANAM kurusattama
AyuHsaMkhyA kRtayuge saMkhyAtA rAjasattama

na pramANasthitir hy asti puSye 'smin bharatarSabha
garbhasthAz ca mriyante 'tra tathA jAtA mriyanti ca

mahAbalA mahAsattvAH prajAguNasamanvitAH
ajAyanta kRte rAjan munayaH sutapodhanAH

mahotsAhA mahAtmAno dhArmikAH satyavAdinaH
jAtAH kRtayuge rAjan dhaninaH priyadarzanAH

AyuSmanto mahAvIrA dhanurdharavarA yudhi
jAyante kSatriyAH zUrAs tretAyAM cakravartinaH

sarvavarNA mahArAja jAyante dvApare sati
mahotsAhA mahAvIryAH parasparavadhaiSiNaH
tejasAlpena saMyuktAH krodhanAH puruSA nRpa
lubdhAz cAnRtakAz caiva puSye jAyanti bhArata

IrSyA mAnas tathA krodho mAyAsUyA tathaiva ca
puSye bhavanti martyAnAM rAgo lobhaz ca bhArata

138. Bhishma (CE 11:6, GP 10:6)

tathA trINi sahasrANi tretAyAM manujAdhipa
dvisahasraM dvApare tu zate tiSThati saMprati

139. Bhishma (CE 11:14, GP 10:15)

saMkSepo vartate rAjan dvApare 'smin narAdhipa
guNottaraM haimavataM harivarSaM tataH param

140. Shanti (CE 70:6-28, GP 69:79-101)

kAlo vA kAraNaM rAjJo rAjA vA kAlakAraNam
iti te saMzayo mA bhUd rAjA kAlasya kAraNam

daNDanItyA yadA rAjA samyak kArtsnyena vartate
tadA kRtayugaM nAma kAlaH zreSThaH pravartate

bhavet kRtayuge dharmo nAdharmo vidyate kva cit
sarveSAm eva varNAnAM nAdharme ramate manaH

yogakSemAH pravartante prajAnAM nAtra saMzayaH
vaidikAni ca karmANi bhavanty aviguNAny uta

Rtavaz ca sukhAH sarve bhavanty uta nirAmayAH
prasIdanti narANAM ca svaravarNamanAMsi ca

vyAdhayo na bhavanty atra nAlpAyur dRzyate naraH
vidhavA na bhavanty atra nRzaMso nAbhijAyate

akRSTapacyA pRthivi bhavanty oSadhayas tathA
tvakpatraphalamUlAni vIryavanti bhavanti ca

nAdharmo vidyate tatra dharma eva tu kevalaH
iti kArtayugAn etAn guNAn viddhi yudhiSThira

12070014a daNDanItyA yadA rAjA trIn aMzAn anuvartate
12070014c caturtham aMzam utsRjya tadA tretA pravartate

azubhasya caturthAMzas trIn aMzAn anuvartate
kRSTapacyaiva pRthivi bhavanty oSadhayas tathA

ardhaM tyaktvA yadA rAjA nItyardham anuvartate
tatas tu dvAparaM nAma sa kAlaH saMpravartate

azubhasya tadA ardhaM dvAv aMzAv anuvartate
kRSTapacyaiva pRthivi bhavaty alpaphalA tathA

daNDanItiM parityajya yadA kArtsnyena bhUmipaH
prajAH kliznAty ayogena pravizyati tadA kaliH

kalAv adharmo bhUyiSThaM dharmo bhavati tu kva cit
sarveSAm eva varNAnAM svadharmAc cyavate manaH

zUdrA bhaikSeNa jIvanti brAhmaNAH paricaryayA
yogakSemasya nAzaz ca vartate varNasaMkaraH

vaidikAni ca karmANi bhavanti viguNAny uta
Rtavo nasukhAH sarve bhavanty Amayinas tathA

hrasanti ca manuSyANAM svaravarNamanAMsy uta
vyAdhayaz ca bhavanty atra mriyante cAgatAyuSaH

vidhavAz ca bhavanty atra nRzaMsA jAyate prajA
kva cid varSati parjanyaH kva cit sasyaM prarohati

rasAH sarve kSayaM yAnti yadA necchati bhUmipaH
prajAH saMrakSituM samyag daNDanItisamAhitaH

rAjA kRtayugasrSTA tretAyA dvAparasya ca
yugasya ca caturthasya rAjA bhavati kAraNam

kRtasya karaNAd rAjA svargam atyantam aznute
tretAyAH karaNAd rAjA svargaM nAtyantam aznute

pravartanAd dvAparasya yathAbhAgam upAznute
kaleH pravartanAd rAjA pApam atyantam aznute

tato vasati duSkarmA narake zAzvatIH samAH
prajAnAM kalmaSe magno 'kIrtiM pApaM ca vindati

141. Shanti (CE 224:12-31, GP 231:12-31)

kASThA nimeSA daza paJca caiva;
triMzat tu kASThA gaNayet kalAM tAm
triMzat kalAz cApi bhaven muhUrto;
bhAgaH kalAyA dazamaz ca yaH syAt

triMzan muhUrtaz ca bhaved ahaz ca;
rAtriz ca saMkhyA munibhiH praNItA
mAsaH smRto rAtryahani ca triMzat;
saMvatsaro dvAdazamAsa uktaH
saMvatsaraM dve ayane vadanti;
saMkhyAvido dakSiNam uttaraM ca

ahorAtre vibhajate sUryo mAnuSalaukike
rAtriH svapnAya bhUtAnAM ceSTAyai karmaNAm ahaH

pitrye rAtryahani mAsaH pravibhAgas tayoH punaH
kRSNo 'haH karmaceSTAyaM zuklaH svapnAya zarvarI

daive rAtryahani varSaM pravibhAgas tayoH punaH
ahas tatrodagayanaM rAtriH syAd dakSiNAyanam

ye te rAtryahani pUrve kIrtite daivalaukike
tayoH saMkhyAya varSAgraM brAhme vakSyAmy ahaHkSape

teSAM saMvatsarAgrANi pravakSyAmy anupUrvazaH
kRte tretAyuge caiva dvApare ca kalau tathA

catvAry AhuH sahasrANi varSANAM tat kRtaM yugam
tasya tAvacchatI saMdhyA saMdhyAMzaz ca tathAvidhaH

itareSu sasaMdhyeSu sasaMdhyAMzeSu ca triSu
ekApAyena saMyAnti sahasrANi zatAni ca

etAni zAzvatA&l lokAn dhArayanti sanAtanAn
etad brahmavidAM tAta viditaM brahma zAzvatam

catuSpAt sakalo dharmaH satyaM caiva kRte yuge
nAdharmeNAgamaH kaz cit paras tasya pravartate

itareSv AgamAd dharmaH pAdazas tv avaropyate
caurikAnRtamAyAbhir adharmaz copacIyate

arogAH sarvasiddhArthAz caturvarSazatAyuSaH
kRte tretAdiSv eteSAM pAdazo hrasate vayaH

vedavAdAz cAnuyugAM hrasantIti ca naH zrutam
AyUMSi cAziSaz caiva vedasyaiva ca yat phalam

anye kRtayuge dharmAs tretAyAM dvApare 'pare
anye kaliyuge dharmA yathAzaktikRtA iva

tapaH paraM kRtayuge tretAyAM jJAnam uttamam
dvApare yajJam evAhur dAnam eva kalau yuge

etAM dvAdazasAhasrIM yugAkhyAM kavayo viduH
sahasraM parivRttaM tad brAhmaM divasam ucyate

rAtris tAvattithI brAhmI tadAdau vizvam IzvaraH
pralaye 'dhyAtmam Avizya suptvA so 'nte vibudhyate

sahasrayugaparyantam ahar yad brahmaNo viduH
rAtriM yugasahasrAntAM te 'horAtravido janAH

pratibuddho vikurute brahmAkSayyaM kSapAkSaye
sRjate ca mahad bhUtaM tasmAd vyaktAtmakaM manaH

142. Adi (CE 2.9, GP 2:13)

antare caiva saMprApte kalidvAparayor abhUt
samantapaJcake yuddhaM kurupANDavasenayoH

143. Sabha (CE 49:24, GP 53:25)

andheneva yugaM naddhaM viparyastaM narAdhipa
kanIyAMso vivardhante jyeSThA hIyanti bhArata

144. Shalya (CE 59:21, GP 60:25)

prAptaM kaliyugaM viddhi pratijJAM pANDavasya ca
AnRNyaM yAtu vairasya pratijJAyAz ca pANDavaH

145. Bhishma (CE 16:26, GP 16:8)

rathAnIkAny adRzyanta nagarANIva bhUrIzaH
ativa zuzubhe tatra pitA te pUrNacandravat

146. Bhishma (CE 16:40, GP16:22)

zvetoSNISaM zvetahayaM zvetavarmANam acyutam
apazyAma mahArAja bhISmaM candram ivoditam

147. Bhishma (CE 16:41-42, GP 16:23)

hematAladhvajaM bhISmaM rAjate syandane sthitam
zvetAbhra iva tikSNAMzuM dadRzuH kurupANDavAH

dRSTvA camUmukhe bhISmaM samakampanta pANDavAH
sRJjayAz ca maheSvAsA dhRSTadyumnapurogamAH

148. Bhishma (CE 17:18, GP 17:18)

tAlena mahatA bhISmaH paJcatAreNa ketunA
vimalAdityasaMkAzas tasthau kurucamUpatiH

149. Shalya (CE 55:10, GP 56:10)

rAhuz cAgrasad Adityam aparvaNi vizAM pate
cakampe ca mahAkampaM pRthivI savanadrumA

150. Shalya (CE 56:34, GP 57:37)

evaM tad abhavad yuddhaM ghorarUpam asaMvRtam
parivRtte 'hani krUraM vRtravAsavayor iva

151. Shalya (CE54:17, GP 55:21)

raNamaNDalamadhyasthau bhrAtarau tau nararSabhau
azobhetAM mahArAja candrasUryAv ivoditau

152. Shalya (CE 59:10, GP 60:12)

sitAsitau yaduvarau zuzubhAte 'dhikaM tataH
nabhogatau yathA rAjaMz candrasUryau dinakSaye

153. Shalya (CE 54:42, GP 55:49)

zuzubhe rAjamadhyastho nIlavAsAH sitaprabhaH
nakSatrair iva saMpUrNo vRto nizi nizAkaraH

154. Shalya (CE 55:8-14, GP 56:8:14)

vavur vAtAH sanirghAtAH pAMsuvarSaM papAta ca
babhUvuz ca dizaH sarvAs timireNa samAvRtAH

mahAsvanAH sanirghAtAs tumulA romaharSaNAH
petus tatholkAH zatazaH sphoTayantyo nabhastalam

rAhuz cAgrasad Adityam aparvaNi vizAM pate
cakampe ca mahAkampaM pRthivI savanadrumA

rUkSAz ca vAtAH pravavur nIcaiH zarkaravarSiNaH
girINAM zikharANy eva nyapatanta mahItale

mRgA bahuvidhAkArAH saMpatanti dizo daza
dIptAH zivAz cApy anadan ghorarUpAH sudAruNAH

nirghAtAz ca mahAghorA babhUvU romaharSaNAH
dIptAyAM dizi rAjendra mRgAz cAzubhavAdinaH

udapAnagatAz cApo vyavardhanta samantataH
azarIrA mahAnAdAH zrUyante sma tadA nRpa

155. Shalya (57:46-56, GP 58:49-59)

vavur vAtAH sanirghAtAH pAMsuvarSaM papAta ca
cacAla pRthivI cApi savRkSakSupaparvatA

tasmin nipatite vIre patyau sarvamahIkSitAm
mahAsvanA punar dIptA sanirghAtA bhayaMkarI
papAta colkA mahatI patite pRthivIpatau

tathA zoNitavarSaM ca pAMsuvarSaM ca bhArata
vavarSa maghavAMs tatra tava putre nipAtite

yakSANAM rAkSasAnAM ca pizAcAnAM tathaiva ca
antarikSe mahAnAdAH zrUyate bharatarSabha

tena zabdena ghoreNa mRgANAm atha pakSiNAm
jajJe ghoratamaH zabdo bahUnAM sarvatodizam

ye tatra vAjinaH zeSA gajAz ca manujaiH saha
mumucus te mahAnAdaM tava putre nipAtite

bherIzaGkhamRdaGgAnAm abhavac ca svano mahAn
antarbhUmigataz caiva tava putre nipAtite

bahupAdair bahubhujaiH kabandhair ghoradarzanaiH
nRtyadbhir bhayadair vyAptA dizas tatrAbhavan nRpa

dhvajavanto 'stravantaz ca zastravantas tathaiva ca
prAkampanta tato rAjaMs tava putre nipAtite

hradAH kUpAz ca rudhiram udvemur nRpasattama
nadyaz ca sumahAvegAH pratisrotovahAbhavan

pulliGgA iva nAryas tu striIliGgAH puruSAbhavan
duryodhane tadA rAjan patite tanaye tava

156. Shalya (CE 54:30-32, GP 55:35, 37)

siMhAv iva durAdharSau gadAyuddhe paraMtapau
nakhadaMSTrAyudhau virau vyAghrAv iva durutsahau

prajAsaMharaNe kSubdhau samudrAv iva dustarau
lohitAGgAv iva kruddhau pratapantau mahArathau

razmimantau mahAtmAnau dIptimantau mahAbalau
dadRzAte kuruzreSThau kAlasUryAv ivoditau

157. Vana (CE 188:75-82, GP 190:79-85)

SaDbhir anyaiz ca sahito bhAskaraH pratapiSyati
tumulAz cApi nirhrAdA digdAhAz cApi sarvazaH
kabandhAntarhito bhAnur udayAstamaye tadA

akAlavarSI ca tadA bhaviSyati sahasradRk
sasyAni ca na rokSyanti yugAnte paryupasthite

abhIkSNaM krUravAdinyaH paruSA ruditapriyAH
bhartqNAM vacane caiva na sthAsyanti tadA striyaH

putr/.z ca mAtApitarau haniSyanti yugakSaye
sUdayiSyanti ca patIn striyaH putrAn apAzritAH

aparvaNi mahArAja sUryaM rAhur upaiSyati
yugAnte hutabhuk cApi sarvataH prajvaliSyati

pAnIyaM bhojanaM caiva yAcamAnAs tadAdhvagAH
na lapsyante nivAsaM ca nirastAH pathi zerate

nirghAtavAyasA nAgAH zakunAH saMRgadvijAH
rUkSA vAco vimokSyanti yugAnte paryupasthite

mitrasaMbandhinaz cApi saMtyakSyanti narAs tadA
janaM parijanaM cApi yugAnte paryupasthite

158. Udyoga GP 147:1-4

Agamya hAstinapurAdupaplavyamriMdamaH
pANDavAnAM yathAvRttaM kezavaH sarvamuktavAn

sambhASya suciraM kAlaM mantrayitvA punaH punaH
svameva bhavanaM zourirvizrAmArthaM jagAma ha

visRjya sarvAn nRpatIn virATapramukhAMstadA
pANDavA bhrAtaraM paJca bhAnAvastaM gate sati

saMdhyAmupAsya dhyAyantastameva gatamAnasaH
AnAyya kRSNaM dAzArha punarmantramamantrayan

Udyoga GP 151:37-38

bravItu vadataM zreSTo niza samabhivartate
tataH senApatiM kRtvA kRSNasya vazavartinH

rAtreH zeSe vyatikrAnte prayAsyAmo raNAjiram
adhivAsiazastrAzca kRtakoutukamaGalAH

159. Shanti (CE 101:9-10, GP 100:10-11)

caitryAM vA mArgazirSyAM vA senAyogaH prazasyate
pakvasasyA hi pRthivI bhavaty ambumatI tathA

naivAtizIto nAtyuSNaH kAlo bhavati bhArata
tasmAt tadA yojayeta pareSAM vyasaneSu vA
eteSu yogAH senAyAH prazastAH parabAdhane

160. Bhishma (CE 17:28, GP 17:28)

tad aGgapatinA guptaM kRpeNa ca mahAtmanA
zAradAbhracayaprakhyaM prAcyAnAm abhavad balam

161. Bhishma (CE 55:15, GP 59:16)

vikIrNaiH kavacaiz citrair dhvajaiz chatraiz ca mArISa
zuzubhe tad raNasthAnaM zaradIva nabhastalam

162. Bhishma (CE 89:4, GP 93:4)

athainaM zaravarSeNa samantAt paryavArayan
parvataM vAridhArAbhiH zaradIva balAhakAH

163. Bhishma (CE 89:6, GP 93:6)

vyanadat sumahAnAdaM jImUta iva zAradaH
dizaH khaM pradizaz caiva nAdayan bhairavasvanaH

164. Bhishma (CE 90:16, GP 94:17)

bhUyaz cainaM mahAbAhuH zaraiH zighram avAkirat
parvataM vAridhArAbhiH zaradiva balAhakaH

165. Bhishma (CE 93:22, GP 97:22)

arajombarasaMvItaH siMhakhelagatir nRpaH
zuzubhe vimalArciSmaJ zaradiva divAkaraH

166. Bhishma (CE 112:130, GP 117:56)

tad gajAzvarathaughAnAM rudhireNa samukSitam
channam AyodhanaM reje raktAbhram iva zAradam

167. Drona (CE 19:41, GP 20:40)

vikSaradbhir nadadbhiz ca nipatadbhiz ca vAraNaiH
saMbabhUva mahI kIrNA meghair dyaur iva zAradI

168. Drona (CE 37:20, GP 38:21)

mRdur bhUtvA mahArAja dAruNaH samapadyata
varSAbhyatIto bhagavAJ zaradiva divAkaraH

169. Drona (CE 96:5, GP 120:5)

sadhanurmaNDalaH saMkhye tejobhAsvararazmivAn
zaradIvoditaH sUryo nRsUryo virarAja ha

170. Drona (CE 107:35, GP 132:39)

tAbhyAM muktA vyakAzanta kaGkabarhiNavAsasaH
paGktyaH zaradi mattAnAM sArasAnAm ivAmbare

171. Drona (CE 114:20, GP 139:26)

tataH kruddhaH zarAn asyan sUtaputro vyarocata
madhyaMdinagato 'rciSmAJ zaradiva divAkaraH

172. Drona (CE 117:16, GP 142:16-17)

kiM mRSoktena bahunA karmaNA tu samAcara
zAradasyeva meghasya garjitaM niSphalaM hi te

173. Drona (CE 155:26, GP 180:26-27)

tvadIyaiH puruSavyAghra yodhamukhyair mahAtmabhiH
zarajAlasahasrAMzuH zaradiva divAkaraH

174. Drona (CE 162:37, GP 187:39)

te rathAn sUryasaMkAzAn AsthitAH puruSarSabhAH
azobhanta yathA meghAH zAradAH samupasthitAH

175. Karna (CE 8:23, GP 12:23)

tasyAyasaM varmavaraM vararatnavibhUSitam
tArodbhAsasya nabhasaH zAradasya samatviSam

176. Karna (GP 19:51)

tArAgaNavicitrasya nirmalendudyutitviSH
pazyemAM nabhasastulyaM zarannakSatramAlinim

177. Karna (CE 68:24, GP 94:15)

vimuktayantrair nihatair ayasmayair;
hatAnuSaGgair viniSaGgabandhuraiH
prabhagnanaIdair maNihemamaNDitaiH;
stRtA mahi dyaur iva zAradair ghanaiH

178. Shalya (CE 3:28, GP 4:28)

vAyuneva vidhUtAni tavAnIkAni sarvazaH
zaradambhodajAlAni vyaziryanta samantataH

179. Shalya (CE 32:49, GP 33:55)

mA vRthA garja kaunteya zAradAbhram ivAjalam
darzayasva balaM yuddhe yAvat tat te 'dya vidyate

180. Shalya (CE 45:49, GP 46:55-56)

sabherIzaGkhamurajA sAyudhA sapatAkinI
zAradI dyaur ivAbhAti jyotirbhir upazobhitA

181. Shalya (CE 54:27, GP 55:32-33)

anyonyam abhidhAvantau mattAv iva mahAdvipau
vAzitAsaMgame dRptau zaradiva madotkaTau

182. Stri (CE 19:2, GP 19:2)

gajamadhyagataH zete vikarNo madhusUdana
nIlameghaparikSiptaH zaradiva divAkaraH

183. Stri (CE 25:16, GP 25:16)

pAJcAlarAjJo vipulaM puNDarIkAkSa pANDuram
AtapatraM samAbhAti zaradiva divAkaraH

184. Udyoga (CE 140:16-17, GP 142:16-17)

brUyAH karNa ito gatvA droNaM zAMtanavaM kRpam
saumyo 'yaM vartate mAsaH suprApayavasendhanaH

pakvauSadhivanasphitaH phalavAn alpamakSikaH
niSpaGko rasavat toyo nAtyuSNazizirAH sukhaH

185. Adi (GP 1:78-83)

Zrutyaitat prAha vighnezo ydi me lekhanI kSaNam
Likhato nAvatiSTHeta tadA syaM lakhako hyaham

Vyaso'pyuvAca taM devamguddhvA mA likha kvacit
omityuttavA gaNezo'pi babhUva kila lakhakaH
grandhagrandhi tada cakre munirgUDaM kutUhalAt
yasmin pratijnayA prAha munirdvaipAyanstvidam

aSTou zlokasahastraNi aSTou zlokazatAni ca
ahaM vedyi zuko vetti saMjayo vetti vA na vA

tacChlokakUTamadyApi grathitaM sudDaM mune
bhettuM na zakyate'rTasya gUDatvAt prazritasya ca

sarvojno'pi gaNezo yatkSNamAste vicArayan
tAvzcakAra vyaso'pi zlokAnanyAn bahUnapi

186. Virata (CE 47:4, GP 52:4)

teSAm abhyadhikA mAsAH paJca dvAdaza ca kSapAH
trayodazAnAM varSANAM iti me vartate matiH

187. Mausal (CE 1:3, GP 3:3)

pratyag Uhur mahAnadyo dizo nIhArasaMvRtAH
ulkAz cAGgAravarSiNyaH prapetur gaganAd bhuvi

188. Vana (CE 80:79, GP 82:60-61)

tato gatvA sarasvatyAH sAgarasya ca saMgame
gosahasraphalaM prApya svargaloke mahIyate
dIpyamAno 'gnivan nityaM prabhayA bharatarSabha

189. Vana (CE 80:85-86, GP 82:68-69)

sAgarasya ca sindhoz ca saMgamaM prApya bhArata
tIrthe salilarAjasya snAtvA prayatamAnasaH

tarpayitvA pitqn devAn RSIMz ca bharatarSabha
prApnoti vAruNaM lokaM dIpyamAnaH svatejasA

190. Vana (CE 80:118, 120-122) (GP 82:111, 114-115)

tato vinazanaM gacchen niyato niyatAzanaH
gacchaty antarhitA yatra marupRSThe sarasvatI
camase ca zivodbhede nAgodbhede ca dRzyate

snAtvA ca camasodbhede agniSTomaphalaM labhet
zivodbhede naraH snAtvA gosahasraphalaM labhet

nAgodbhede naraH snAtvA nAgalokam avApnuyAt
zazayAnaM ca rAjendra tIrtham AsAdya durlabham
zazarUpapraticchannAH puSkarA yatra bhArata

sarasvatyAM mahArAja anu saMvatsaraM hi te
snAyante bharatazreSTha vRttAM vai kArttikIM sadA

tatra snAtvA naravyAghra dyotate zazivat sadA
gosahasraphalaM caiva prApnuyAd bharatarSabha

191. Vana (CE 80:130-131, GP 82:125-126)

tato gaccheta rAjendra saMgamaM lokavizrutam
sarasvatyA mahApuNyam upAsante janArdanam

yatra brahmAdayo devA RSayaH siddhacAraNAH
abhigacchanti rAjendra caitrazuklacaturdazIm

192. Vana (CE 81:3-4, GP 83:5-6)

tatra mAsaM vased vIra sarasvatyAM yudhiSThira
yatra brahmAdayo devA RSayaH siddhacAraNAH

gandharvApsaraso yakSAH pannagAz ca mahIpate
brahmakSetraM mahApuNyam abhigacchanti bhArata

193. Vana (CE 81:42, GP 83:52)

tato gaccheta rAjendra dvArapAlam arantukam
tasya tIrthaM sarasvatyAM yakSendrasya mahAtmanaH
tatra snAtvA naro rAjann agniSTomaphalaM labhet

194. Vana (CE 81:91, GP 83:108)

zrikuJjaM ca sarasvatyAM tIrthaM bharatasattama
tatra snAtvA naro rAjann agniSTomaphalaM labhet

195. Vana (CE 81:92-93, GP 83: 109-110)

tato naimiSakuJjaM ca samAsAdya kurUdvaha
RSayaH kila rAjendra naimiSeyAs tapodhanAH
tIrthayAtrAM puraskRtya kurukSetraM gatAH purA

tataH kuJjaH sarasvatyAM kRto bharatasattama
RSINAm avakAzaH syAd yathA tuSTikaro mahAn

196. Vana (CE 81:125, GP 83:145)

puNyam AhuH kurukSetraM kurukSetrAt sarasvatIm
sarasvatyAz ca tIrthAni tIrthebhyaz ca pRthUdakam

197. Vana (CE 81:131, GP 83:151)

tato gacchen narazreSTha tIrthaM devyA yathAkramam
sarasvatyAruNAyAz ca saMgamaM lokavizrutam

198. Vana (CE 81:175, GP 83:4)

dakSiNena sarasvatyA uttareNa dRSadvatIm
ye vasanti kurukSetre te vasanti triviSTape

199. Vana (CE 82:4-6, GP 84:6-7)

siddhacAraNagandharvAH kiMnarAH samahoragAH
tad vanaM pravizann eva sarvapApaiH pramucyate

tato hi sA saricchreSTha nadInAm uttamA nadI
plakSAd devI srutA rAjan mahApuNyA sarasvatI

tatrAbhiSekaM kurvIta valmIkAn niHsRte jale
arcayitvA pitqn devAn azvamedhaphalaM labhet

200. Vana (CE 82:34, GP 84:38)

gaGgAyAz ca narazreSTha sarasvatyAz ca saMgame
snAto 'zvamedham Apnoti svargalokaM ca gacchati

201. Vana (CE 82:59, GP 84:66)

sarasvatIM samAsAdya tarpayet pitRdevatAH
sArasvateSu lokeSu modate nAtra saMzayaH

202. Vana (CE 88:2-10, GP 90:3-11)

sarasvatI puNyavahA hradinI vanamAlinI
samudragA mahAvegA yamunA yatra pANDava

tatra puNyatamaM tIrthaM plakSAvataraNaM zivam
yatra sArasvatair iSTvA gacchanty avabhRthaM dvijAH

puNyaM cAkhyAyate divyaM zivam agniziro 'nagha
sahadevo 'yajad yatra zamyAkSepeNa bhArata

etasminn eva cArtheyam indragItA yudhiSThira
gAthA carati loke 'smin gIyamAnA dvijAtibhiH

agnayaH sahadevena ye citA yamunAm anu
zataM zatasahasrANi sahasrazatadakSiNAH

tatraiva bharato rAjA cakravartI mahAyazAH
viMzatiM sapta cASTau ca hayamedhAn upAharat

kAmakRd yo dvijAtInAM zrutas tAta mayA purA
atyantam AzramaH puNyaH sarakas tasya vizrutaH

---

sarasvatI nadI sadbhiH satataM pArtha pUjitA
vAlakhilyair mahArAja yatreSTam RSibhiH purA

203. Vana (CE 129:20-22, GP 129:20-22)

dRSadvatI puNyatamA tatra khyAtA yudhiSThira
tatra vaivarNyavarNau ca supuNyau manujAdhipa

evam etan mahAbAho pazyanti paramarSayaH
sarasvatIm imAM puNyAM pazyaikazaraNAvRtAm

yatra snAtvA narazreSTha dhUtapApmA bhaviSyati
iha sArasvatair yajJair iSTavantaH surarSayaH
RSayaz caiva kaunteya tathA rAjarSayo 'pi ca

vedI prajApater eSA samantAt paJcayojanA
kuror vai yajJazIlasya kSetram etan mahAtmanaH

204. Vana (CE 130:1-7, Vana 130:1-7)

iha martyAs tapas taptvA svargaM gacchanti bhArata
martukAmA narA rAjann ihAyAnti sahasrazaH

evam AzIH prayuktA hi dakSeNa yajatA purA
iha ye vai mariSyanti te vai svargajito narAH

eSA sarasvatI puNyA divyA coghavatI nadI
etad vinazanaM nAma sarasvatyA vizAM pate

dvArAM niSAdarASTrasya yeSAM dveSAt sarasvatI
praviSTA pRthivIM vIra mA niSAdA hi mAM viduH

eSa vai camasodbhedo yatra dRzyA sarasvatI
yatrainAm abhyavartanta divyAH puNyAH samudragAH

etat sindhor mahat tIrthaM yatrAgastyam arIMdama
lopAmudrA samAgamya bhartAram avRNIta vai

etat prabhAsate tIrthaM prabhAsaM bhAskaradyute
indrasya dayitaM puNyaM pavitraM pApanAzanam

205. Bhishma (CE 7:44-47, GP 47-50)

tatra tripathagA devI prathamaM tu pratiSThitA
brahmalokAd apakrAntA saptadhA pratipadyate

vasvokasArA nalinI pAvanA ca sarasvatI
jambUnadI ca sItA ca gaGgA sindhuz ca saptamI

acintyA divyasaMkalpA prabhor eSaiva saMvidhiH
upAsate yatra satraM sahasrayugaparyaye

dRzyAdRzyA ca bhavati tatra tatra sarasvatI
etA divyAH sapta gaGgAs triSu lokeSu vizrutAH

206. Shalya (CE 34:28, 30-31 -31, GP 35:33, 35-36)

nityapramuditopetAH svAdubhakSaH zubhAnvitAH
vipaNyApaNapaNyAnAM nAnAjanazatair vRtaH
nAnAdrumalatopeto nAnAratnavibhUSitaH

tato mahAtmA niyame sthitAtmA;
puNyeSu tIrtheSu vasUni rAjan
dadau dvijebhyaH kratudakSiNAz ca;
yadupravIro halabhRt pratItaH

dogdhriz ca dhenUz ca sahasrazo vai;
suvAsasAH kAJcanabaddhazRGgIH
hayAMz ca nAnAvidhadezajAtAn;
yAnAni dAsIz ca tathA dvijebhyaH

ratnAni muktAmaNividrumaM ca;
zRGgIsuvarNaM rajataM ca zubhram
ayasmayaM tAmramayaM ca bhANDaM;
dadau dvijAtipravareSu rAmaH

207. Shalya (GP 35:77)

samudraM pazcimaM gatvA sarasvtyabdhi saGgamam
ArAdhayatu devezaM tataH kAntimavApsyati

208. Shalya (CE 34:69, GP 35:78)

sarasvatIM tataH somo jagAma RSizAsanAt
prabhAsaM paramaM tIrthaM sarasvatyA jagAma ha

209. Shalya (CE 34:78-81, GP 35:87-90)

tatas tu camasodbhedam acyutas tv agamad bali
camasodbheda ity evaM yaM janAH kathayanty uta

tatra dattvA ca dAnAni viziSTAni halAyudhaH
uSitvA rajanim ekAM snAtvA ca vidhivat tadA

udapAnam athAgacchat tvarAvAn kezavAgrajaH
AdyaM svastyayanaM caiva tatrAvApya mahat phalam

snigdhatvAd oSadhInAM ca bhUmez ca janamejaya
jAnanti siddhA rAjendra naSTAm api sarasvatIm

210. Shalya (CE 35:1, GP 36:1)

tasmAn nadigataM cApi udapAnaM yazasvinaH
tritasya ca mahArAja jagAmAtha halAyudhaH

211. Shalya (CE 35:46, GP 36:47)

tatra cormimatI rAjann utpapAta sarasvatI
tayotkSiptas tritas tasthau pUjayaMs tridivaukasaH

212. Shalya (CE 35:53, GP 36:54-55)

udapAnaM ca taM dRSTvA prazasya ca punaH punaH
nadigatam adInAtmA prApto vinazanaM tadA

213. Shalya (CE 36:1-4, GP 37:1-3)

tato vinazanaM rAjann AjagAma halAyudhaH
zUdrAbhIrAn prati dveSAd yatra naSTA sarasvatI

yasmAt sA bharatazreSTha dveSAn naSTA sarasvatI
tasmAt tad RSayo nityaM prAhur vinazaneti ha
tac cApy upaspRzya balaH sarasvatyAM mahAbalaH
subhUmikaM tato 'gacchat sarasvatyAs taTe vare

tatra cApsarasaH zubhrA nityakAlam atandritAH
krIDAbhir vimalAbhiz ca krIDanti vimalAnanAH

214. Shalya (CE 36:33-36, GP 37:35-38)

Aplutya bahuzo hRSTas teSu tIrtheSu lAGgalI
dattvA vasu dvijAtibhyo jagAmAti tapasvinaH

tatrasthAn RSisaMghAMs tAn abhivAdya halAyudhaH
tato rAmo 'gamat tIrtham RSibhiH sevitaM mahat

yatra bhUyo nivavRte prAGmukhA vai sarasvatI
RSINAM naimiSeyANAm avekSArthaM mahAtmanAm

nivRttAM tAM saricchreSThAM tatra dRSTvA tu lAGgalI
babhUva vismito rAjan balaH zvetAnulepanaH

215. Vana (CE 82:31, GP 84:35**)

gaGgAsaMgamayoz caiva snAti yaH saMgame naraH
dazAzvamedhAn Apnoti kulaM caiva samuddharet

**gaGgAyamunayormadhye snAti yaH saMgame naraH
dasAzvamedhAnApnoti kulaM caiva samuddharet

216. Adi (CE 2:26-28, GP 2:30-32)

ahAni yuyudhe bhISmo dazaiva paramAstravit
ahAni paJca droNas tu rarakSa kuruvAhinim

ahanI yuyudhe dve tu karNaH parabalArdanaH
zalyo 'rdhadivasaM tv AsId gadAyuddham ataH param

tasyaiva tu dinasyAnte hArdikyadrauNigautamAH
prasuptaM nizi vizvastaM jaghnur yaudhiSThiraM balam

217. Udyoga (CE 82:5-10, GP 84:5-10)

anabhre 'zaninirghoSaH savidyutsamajAyata
anvag eva ca parjanyaH prAvarSad vighane bhRzam

pratyag Uhur mahAnadyaH prAGmukhAH sindhusattamAH
viparItA dizaH sarvA na prAjJAyata kiM cana

prAjvalann agnayo rAjan pRthivI samakampata
udapAnAz ca kumbhAz ca prAsiJcaJ zatazo jalam

tamaHsaMvRtam apy AsIt sarvaM jagad idaM tadA
na dizo nAdizo rAjan prajJAyante sma reNunA

prAdurAsIn mahAJ zabdaH khe zariraM na dRzyate
sarveSu rAjan dezeSu tad adbhutam ivAbhavat

prAmathnAd dhAstinapuraM vAto dakSiNapazcimAH
Arujan gaNazo vRkSAn paruSo bhImanisvanaH

Author

Nilesh Nilkanth Oak was born in India. He received his B.S. in Chemical Engineering from UDCT, Mumbai University. He immigrated to Canada, where he received his M.S. in Chemical Engineering from University of Alberta. He received his executive MBA from Emory University. He works for a Fortune 500 company.

He is interested in Astronomy, Archaeology, Anthropology, Quantum Mechanics, Economics, Mythology and Philosophy.

Nilesh Oak resides in Atlanta, Georgia.